D1674452

The Foundations of Cybernetics

The Foundations of Cybernetics

F. H. GEORGE

Brunel University and The Bureau of Information Science, U.K.

GORDON AND BREACH SCIENCE PUBLISHERS
London   Paris   New York

Contents

Preface

In this book I have tried to summarise the principal features of cybernetics as I see them. As far as detail is concerned, I have tried to concentrate on examples which seem to illustrate the points made in each branch of the subject. There has of course been, as is inevitable, a time gap between the completion of the text and of the writing of this preface and a further gap which must occur prior to publication. This matters less in a book of this kind, which is concerned with examining and describing *basic principles* which are slow-changing and illustrating them with selected detail, than it would in a description of a new theory or a detailed analysis which aims to be wholly contemporary. The reader must still though make allowance for such time delays.

My own view of cybernetics is of a discipline with its "pure" and "applied" side. This book is mainly concerned with the "pure" side, and this means it is to a great extent concerned with what is called artificial intelligence (sometimes called machine intelligence). But the overlap with psychology, physiology and education are clearcut, and we have, in the text, discussed these overlapping fields in some measure. The overlap of cybernetics with sociology, business and economics on the other hand — which is perhaps one stage further removed into the applied field — we have not discussed at all. These do seem to merit separate texts.

One report that has appeared in recent years — the so-called Lighthill report — sheds some light on our subject, and we should at least mention it. It divides the field of artificial intelligence into two main branches which are essentially neurobiological (including behavioural studies) and automation (mainly special purpose automatic control systems). It accepts progress in these fields, but views it as disappointing, and regards the bridge between the two as virtually non-existent. It is this bridge category (in the terminology of the Lighthill report) that this book is largely concerned with.

The Lighthill report contributes positively in drawing attention to:

1) The difficulties encountered in a very complicated field, and reminds us in effect that all sciences go through periods where the extent of things-still-to-be-done weighs heavily — or appears to — against what has already been achieved.

2) The viewpoint adopted to what has been written in cybernetics, comes from an outside authority — an established scientist in his own fairly closely allied field, and such a view is of value to us who are perhaps too close to the subject to see it critically enough.

But against this, the report is inevitably superficial, and in particular:

1) It fails to appreciate the importance of heuristics. They are not of course second best in any sense, but represent the best possible methods used for many high level processes such as occur in thinking, planning and problem solving.

2) It talks in terms of the "combinatorial explosion" relative to the control systems needed for artificially intelligence purposes. If this, admittedly complicated, problem were insuperable then human beings themselves would not exist.

3) It fails altogether to appreciate the breadth and depth of the subject, principally because of a lack of familiarity with the literature. Such reports however — especially coming as this did from outside the subject — are of value to us within the subject if only because they allow us to analyse and evaluate the the development of cybernetics.

I have omitted to mention in this book much work of considerable cybernetic merit", such as that published by the Edinburgh group in their series of excellent books entitled "Machine Intelligence", and many articles that have appeared in the journal "Artificial Intelligence". Other work of special interest includes that of Dr. Feigenbaum on "Heuristic Dendril", and the work of Dr. Winograd in his book "Natural Language Programming" (Edinburgh University Press, 1972), a very exciting book by Russell Ackoff and M. E. Emery "On Purposefulness Systems" (Tavistock Publications, 1961) and Stafford Beer's "Platform for Change" (Wiley, 1975), and we could list many more which are not though referred to in the text.

These references have been omitted either because the work came too late to be assimilated by me or it seemed either too advanced or insufficiently central to my theme to illustrate the basic principles of the subject as I see them. The interested reader should follow up the above clues if they are interested in the broadening and deepening of their knowledge of the subject.

Finally let it be said that I hope this book will be found to be useful to many students of cybernetics at all levels, but rather especially it should give an adequate and broad account of its development as of this time to undergraduates and post-graduates in this or allied subjects.

F. H. George

Beaconsfield, England

CHAPTER 1

The fundamentals of cybernetics

Argument

In this first chapter we discuss the fundamentals of cybernetics. We also discuss where this book fits into the cybernetic literature — especially its relation to the author's own previous books on the subject.

Cybernetics is a study of control and communication systems, both in hardware and theory. It studies its occurrence both in animals and men. In one sense, the basic question has been "could machines be made to think?" but in another sense this does not matter; what matters is that machines can be made to do many complicated things for us. The point being that we might on one hand want to know whether we can design a machine more intelligent than ourselves, or we might want merely to take advantage of whatever help is available in the field of automatic control systems.

1.1 OVERVIEW

In this first chapter, it is intended to give an overview of the whole book. To allow the reader to pick his way carefully among the points of contact of various so-called disciplines and see where they have a common overlap within cybernetics.

The choice of the word "cybernetics" as a name for the subject was Norbert Wiener's (1948), and it goes without saying that there are many different ways of regarding cybernetics. We might have thought of it as information science, or information technology or even automata theory; indeed there are a large number of possible titles which more or less suitably depict this new science.

The choice of titles still leaves doubts as to the viewpoint to be adopted. We shall be thinking primarily of mathematics, logic, automata and computing as methods, and the simulation and synthesis of organismic "mainly human" behaviour as the principal aims.

The author has previously written a number of books and papers on cybernetics and allied topics, and there is therefore some need to distinguish this book from the previous ones and also to try to give some justification for the fact that this book has been written. The first book "Automation, Cybernetics and Society" (1959) was written as a semi-popular introduction to the subject from a somewhat "applied" point of view. "The Brain as a Computer" (1961 Edition II, 1973) was intended to be a detailed research orientated approach to

1

the biological and behavioural applications of cybernetics. "Cybernetics and Biology" (1965) was an outline account of biological applications of cybernetics intended for biologists only. Finally, "Models of Thinking", which was published early in 1970, is a research monograph for postgraduates and research workers in the field of cognition. None of these books provides an introduction to cybernetics from an "all-round" viewpoint aimed primarily at the undergraduate. This book aims to provide just such an introductory text.

Cybernetics has background roots in mathematics, philosophy, psychology, physiology, philosophy of science and logic, at the very least. These subjects are themselves interrelated in a fairly complicated manner. We cannot, for example, discuss in *detail* the mathematical side of the subject; some of the subject matter of set theory, recursive functions, mathematical logic, meta-mathematics, etc. must though be mentioned. All we can hope to do is to supply an outline account of the relation of these fields to automata and automata theory, and clarify the reason for studying automata within cybernetics.

We can make up for the above omission by giving a fairly lengthy list of references for each such related set of topics. With this set of references we can and shall indicate the manner in which these closely allied topics might be followed up in depth. It is rather as if our treatise is on "ball games" and we cannot sensibly give a detailed account of baseball or cricket, but we can summarize them and their development, and provide detailed references, with notes, to allow for the follow-up for those who are interested in the detail.

With this agreement as to how we are going to treat the relation of cybernetics to its forebears, we may proceed to our main purpose. Before each chapter we shall state the theme with which the chapter is concerned, and after each chapter we shall try and summarize the actual findings. The theme is intended to be abstract and the findings are intended to be relatively concrete.

For the person to whom cybernetics is peripheral, to read the abstract of each chapter, and the summary, will give him a fair idea as to the nature of the subject. We shall also in each chapter try to bring the reader up to date, with a brief summary of current progress in that aspect of cybernetics.

1.2 THE VIEWPOINT

The word "cybernetics" itself was, as we have already mentioned, first suggested by Norbert Wiener (1948) as the name for the new science of control and communication both in animals and man and indeed, of course, machines. He felt that there was a need to separate out, and study in their own right, the problems common to control and communication, which had their original background in physics, electrical engineering, computer engineering, philosophy, mathematics, physiology, psychology, psychiatry, sociology, and other sciences.

In spite of their varied origins, these subjects were all thought by Norbert Wiener to have some common features and it is these which we refer to collectively as cybernetics, and therefore the associated problems we shall call cybernetic problems.

Cybernetics therefore has a subject matter of great breadth — although the subject is primarily concerned with certain specific features of control and communication, especially those that synthesise (copy in terms of ends rather than means) or simulate (copy in terms of both ends *and* means) organismic behaviour. The first and most important point about cybernetics is that for many purposes it intentionally overlooks the distinction that is usually made between "living" and "non-living" systems. It is felt that scientific methods, especially mathematics, can be applied as effectively to biological and social systems as to inanimate systems; these are mainly physical and chemical systems. Secondly, cybernetics includes the concept of *negative feedback* and also feed-forward as central themes. It is from these concepts that the notions of adaptive systems and selectively reinforced systems arise; these are systems that modify their behaviour in the light of a changing environment and it is from these features that our simulation of organismic behaviour is derived.

Behaviour which is modified as a result of experience we call "adaptive". This includes simple adaptation from negative feedback and more complete adaptation through learning. Learning itself, in the more advanced sense, depends directly on what we call "selective reinforcement". This is the process of positively reinforcing satisfying and successful acts and negatively reinforcing unsatisfying or unsuccessful acts; more simply, it is a matter of having knowledge for future use. If we are right in an action, we must know we are right, and if we are wrong, we must know we are wrong; and in each case it is preferable to know *why* we were right or wrong.

Cybernetics is, in another sense, the search for precision. Precision may be achieved in part by introducing mathematics or logic into a subject. In cybernetics this has been done, but it is not always a mathematical model that we seek; we seek sometimes to have hardware models and sometimes verbal models which may still carry the required precision. In any case, the model must be *effective* and we shall be returning frequently to this question of effectiveness since this, perhaps more than any other single feature, is the key to cybernetics and to cybernetic thinking.

The philosophical problem of artificial intelligence is something that should also be considered, since some people feel there are basic philosophical problems concerned with our search to simulate human behaviour.

The question which is sometimes asked is: "Can (or could) machines be made to think?". This question has practical importance, since there still exists a body of opinion which regards *machines* as fundamentally different from *organisms*. Initially, we must notice that our question of machines thinking is difficult to phrase in a meaningful manner, without reducing the answer to either "obviously yes" or "obviously no".

If one starts by assuming that *thinking* is something of which only human beings and organisms are capable, then, of course, it is obviously true to say that machines (artificially constructed systems) cannot think. Similarly, unless one is careful to avoid saying that organisms are the same as machines, the argument reduces to another obvious truth, because if machines are organisms and organisms think, then by simple deduction, machines must obviously think. If we wanted to carry out a careful verbal analysis we must satisfy the condition of an independent definition of both the words "machine" and "think".

Turing (1950) used a form of argument which made sense of our basic question. His argument depended on the "interrogation game". Originally, the game was for someone to ask questions of a man or woman, to see if he could tell, by virtue of the questions and answers alone, which was the man and which the woman. The voice and the handwriting might be disregarded as irrelevant, hence all questions and answers should be typed and passed from one to the other without, of course, either seeing the other person. Turing felt that this method would make the question of whether or not machines can think, meaningful. In other words, these are the sorts of conditions that would seem to be relevant to the intended meaning of the question, of whether or not machines can be made to think. If, under the circumstances of the interrogation game, the computer connot be detected as being different from an intelligent man, then the computer must be deemed intelligent.

The point about relevance here should be explained. You do not need to have machines that run about the place, or have legs, eyes, etc. It is merely necessary to show the intellectual potential of the artificial systems; the rest is simply "window dressing".

Turing did not argue that any existing machine could play the interrogation game as efficiently as a man, but he saw no reason in principle why one should not be built that could be as efficient, and this is all one is concerned with.

There is an emotional involvement likely to occur in the above question, since far-reaching implications exist as to the rivalry of man by machines. We must be careful to realise that in our appraisal and make suitable allowances for it. So, apart from the problem of giving a careful semantic interpretation to the problem question, everyone will be expected to have a "clear idea" as to what the question means and usually to have fairly emphatic answers to it. Human beings are often proud of their superiority over other organisms and jealous of even the possibility of rivals. It seems that human beings seem to feel that they have everything to lose and nothing obvious to gain from such comparisons.

The next relevant argument is to the effect that machines only do what is built into them to do. This is polemically quite a harmless truth. The reason that the argument carries little weight is that the same condition holds for human beings. Everyone does what it is built into him to do; it could hardly be otherwise. Perhaps this point should be explained in more detail. It is that we, as human beings, are given a body as a result of a biological process of inheritance and that body — or the brain controlling it — is constructed of cells and systems of cells that are modifiable as a result of experience. Experience, through education by school teachers and parents, collectively operating on what is supplied by heredity, is precisely what is built into human beings. The only point of importance here is that each successive experience may be expected to modify what has gone before, but this in any case is the same condition as can be fulfilled by suitably chosen machines.

The idea underlying the above objection is that some machines like the early game-playing machines are committed to a rigid policy or strategy before their game or other activities start. It is this lack of elasticity or flexibility (ability to adapt to changing circumstances and changing environments) that is thought to distinguish man from the machine. The answer to this learning-machine problem is that, while chess-playing machines and other game-playing machines can be made with built-in strategies, they are not examples of learning machines, but correspond more nearly to lowly organisms whose behaviour is entirely mediated by instinctive behaviour patterns which do not vary, even when they are obviously unsuitable to the situations in which the organisms find themselves.

There is a question now as to whether or not machines can be built which show this feature which has been called "learning" and the answer is a clearcut "yes". There are already in existence, for example, conditional probability machines (Uttley, 1954, 1955, 1966) which demonstrate the ability of machines to behave in terms of the latest available information. These are machines whose strategy is not wholly fixed in advance, but whose behaviour will depend upon the latest available information. They have built into them the capacity for collecting and classifying information about the external world and acting in accordance with that information, on the basis of at least the frequency and the recency of occurrence of the events. In other words, the most frequently occuring events are most likely to be remembered, and may even become an acceptable habit while the most recent events — everything else being equal — are likely to be the best remembered. Exactly the same conditions of frequency and recency have been observed by psychologists to be two of the principal conditions in determining behaviour, especially as far as memory is concerned. There are, of course, other factors such as the value (or relative importance) of events which weigh heavily in human data retrieval.

A more careful look must now be taken at so-called learning machines. Certainly, a machine can be changed, in some important sense, during the course of its operation and yet there is also a sense in which the whole program of the machine must be fixed in advance. But the main point is that with respect to learning machines such machines will behave in a contingent or conditional manner, and we may not be in a position to predict the exact behaviour of the machine at any specified time, unless we can predict the exact inputs to which it is to be exposed. In practice, complete prediction will be quite impossible under these circumstances. External interference by unforeseen stimuli, or internal interference due to component error, etc., will make it quite impossible to decide, from the blueprint alone, what the behaviour of the machine will be. This has a direct bearing on many rather pointless arguments over "free-will".

Discipline and initiative can be introduced into the organisation of initially unorganised machinery, by which we mean that one can train a machine to behave in a sensible manner relative to its surroundings. But for this to be possible the machine should be exposed to both punishment and reward (a knowledge of results is always vital to learning); it is in this sense that motivation and the results of motivated behaviour are quite basic.

The fact that complete prediction of such a learning machine's behaviour is not always possible is obvious when the matter is viewed from another point of view. Within limits, if we start from a set of assumptions and with a deductive rule of inference, we can, as with such a well-known system as Euclidean geometry, draw up a series of theorems which can be written down one after another. Now it is far from obvious that all the theorems implied by the assumptions and the rule of inference will be known in advance. In this respect mathematical research is most often concerned with showing that some statement or other is a logical consequence of some assumption.

Having built a machine which is, in effect, made up of a set of assumptions and a rule of inference, we shall not necessarily know *a priori* what the machine will produce, because we cannot ourselves foresee all the implications of the action of one on the other.

Another aspect of our question comes from those who argue that machines are incapable of emotions. They could not, it is asserted, write poetry or enjoy other human-like pleasures.

It is enough to say at this stage that this is really not relevant to the question of learning, it is only relevant to the question of whether or not machines can be built with the same emotional systems and motivational systems as those of human beings. The simple answer seems to be that probably the actual materials used are vital to the nature of the emotional responses, so until we can build a machine from the same materials as people we shall probably never get quite the same sort of emotional responses; this is a matter which is very relevant to our next chapter. In any case, a far greater breadth of experience is needed than is at the moment possible if machines are to be artificially produced and are to exhibit the same variety of responses as human beings. It should be mentioned here that some work already exists in the field of simulation of the emotions (Loehlin, 1963).

These last thoughts lead back to a consideration of the biological side of the matter. Is there some *a priori* argument from biology as to why machines cannot think? The interesting point here is that there has, for a very long time, been a conflict in biological circles on just this point. The difference of opinion over whether or not biological explanations should be mechanistic is the same argument in another form.

This argument has been largely decided in modern biology in favour of explanation in terms of machine-like activities. There has been some opposition from believers in holistic (purposeful) types of explanation. But these holistic views are generally capable of integration into a mechanistic or machine-like type of explanatory system. At the same time it should be emphasised that this is a matter which is still very much under debate.

As far as psychology is concerned, behaviourism (in its latest and most critical form) has gained almost complete sway over all other forms of explanation. In both psychology and even in more specifically biological fields much has been made in the way of concessions by the originally narrow mechanistic views, but we can now see that the explanations used are universally machine-like in character.

Those scientists and philosophers who have argued that machines are incapable of thinking have overlooked one important aspect in their argument. They have usually overlooked the fact that organisms have the same sort of drawbacks as machines. If human beings break their parts they may not be in a position to repair themselves, without outside help, perhaps in the form of medical aid. Furthermore, it is clear that a human creature without the necessary nervous tissue will be quite as incapable as a machine of carrying out the functions of thinking, imagining and the like.

It is, of course, relatively easy to point to shortcomings in machines, and the fact that they need to be manufactured is obvious. What is not so obvious is that human beings are once again subject to the same conditions. They need parents to manufacture them and the fact that the system in the case of human beings is subtle and complex and not well understood should not blind people to the essential similarities between the human and the machine.

There is, it is clear, a very considerable philosophic debate afoot which surrounds the question of the power and the possibilities inherent in machine design. The main question is not perhaps one that is capable of being answered successfully .either way, but it does remain a matter for speculation as to whether there is any reason, in principle, why a machine should not be capable of doing what a human being can do. As soon as the possibility of machines doing all, or being capable of doing all, that a human can do is granted, we are made to realise the point of contention that it is not the fact of building automatic machinery in our factories that is the crucial question, neither is it automation that is vital, although that is important enough. What is even more important is that human beings should realise the implications of machine design for all aspects of our thought. The full range of possibilities and new conceptions of the nature of reality this implies take on rather large proportions (George, 1965, 1967, 1968, 1970).

Philosophers are interested in cybernetics partly because of the question as to whether or not machines can be made to think. This question needs very careful analysis, and is difficult to make sensible (or completely answer) verbally. The cybernetic problem is thought to be closely connected with the relation of science to philosophy and the question of whether we can understand private feelings by the use of public forms of explanation.

One last point on this difficult matter. It is because of the ingenuity of human beings that "machines" can be made to think or show intelligent behaviour, and it is man's supreme ingenuity that he can (or will be able to) make an artificial system even cleverer than himself.

We shall now try and itemise what turn out to be the principal categories of cybernetic problems. We can divide these main problems of cybernetics into three classes as follows:

1) To construct an effective theory, with or without actual hardware models, such that the various aspects of human and other sorts of organismic behaviour can be simulated, or artificial intelligence manufactured. This is the problem of *synthesis* (George, 1965).

2) To produce models and theories of human and other organismic behaviour which present these functions of human beings and other systems in the same manner in which they are performed by human beings or such other systems as are considered. In other words, it is not enough merely to produce the same result, but to produce the same result by similar, or even identical, means. This is the problem of *simulation*.

3) Finally, to produce, or simulate, the whole of human or animal behaviour by models which in their construction are identical with human beings or animals. That is, they should in the end be protoplasmic systems.

To take the last class of problems first, it would certainly seem that we are very far from tackling them at present, although we shall discuss some of the implications in the next chapter. So little thought has been given to the problem of how to build "protoplasmic" models directly, that one can and must pass fairly quickly to the other, immediately more realistic, categories of models.

In the third class of problems one might include those cases of building artificial internal organs, which may ultimately be used to replace human organs which have failed for one reason or another to function properly. At this stage, most artificial organs come in the second category, since they are obviously not made of the same materials as are used in the construction of human beings. An iron lung, for example, may perform a similar function to that of a human lung, but still does not perform the function in the same way; hence, instead of placing the iron lung inside the body, the body is placed inside the iron lung. However, there are some models of internal organs which do come nearer to being constructed in the same way as actual body organs, and therefore there is here a sub-class of problems which may be included in our third class of cybernetic problems.

A few models have already been suggested and some actually built, which are basically chemical, or physico-chemical, or even colloidal in their construction, and hence therefore enter into our third class of cybernetic problems (Pask, 1959; Mackay and Ainsworth, 1964). As is often the case with cybernetic research a great many practically useful offshoots emerge. In the case of chemical models, the possible development of a chemical storage system for computers is an offshoot of considerable commercial importance. By and large, however, the third category of cybernetic problems lies very much in the future. This is not to say that this third category will not ultimately become the most important of the three; but it is one that is bound to depend on previous development and research in the first two, as well as in the various branches of chemistry and physics which are directly relevant to this third category of problems; at any rate, as we have said, the next chapter will deal with this problem amongst others.

It will be argued that there is no reason to doubt the *possibility* of constructing a human being artificially, and one must assume that the final stage in cybernetic research will be concerned with just this. However remote the solution is to such a problem, attempts to solve it produce all sorts of useful and interesting scientific information.

Let us now return to the first category of cybernetic problems, because it is from this that the main applications of cybernetics amanate in the form of automation. Here we can construct models of the following types. They may be listed as follows:

1) finite automata;
2) infinite automata;
3) information theoretic models;
4) probability theory and other mathematical and statistical models;
5) computer programs;
6) servosystems;
7) any model whatever, in any fabric (hardware) whatever, other than those which are in our third category of cybernetic problems.

These same specific methods apply, of course, to the second category of cybernetic problems, where we try to reproduce the same end results, that of simulating human behaviour by similar means as are apparently used by human beings. Here, as far as biology is concerned, we shall be especially interested in models of the special senses (eyes, ears, etc.,), in models of learning, motivation, perception, memory, thinking and language, as well as genetics, the central nervous system, and so on.

Some of these methods will be discussed further in this book. We shall describe in outline digital computers and their programming. We shall also discuss logic to some extent, since this is especially relevant to computers. Logic is also the basis of a particular class of finite automata called neural nets. These particular types of finite automata attempt to simulate directly the human nervous system and are very closely related to developments in logic; hence a certain minimum knowledge of logic is a basic essential. We shall not however go into details on what are essentially technical matters, and which do not affect the main argument. Turing machines and some part of meta-mathematics though must be briefly discussed.

In cybernetics we are primarily interested in a special class of finite automata, namely those which learn from experience. A finite automaton itself is a system constructed according to specific rules and composed of a finite number of elements, where each of the elements is capable of being in only one of a finite number of possible states àt any particular time. The model, or automaton, has an input and output and a store for information; and we are concerned to choose our models with the specific intention of simulating various biological and behavioural systems. One can think of the model as a collection of interconnected cells, or one can think of it as a tape automaton. These may be thought of as finite tape automata, potentially infinite tape automata or infinite tape automata according to whether the tape is finite, potentially infinite or infinite. By "potentially infinite" we mean that we can add as much tape onto the end whenever it is needed, so the machine never runs off the tape. The tape is strictly finite at any instant of time, but one can go on adding tape indefinitely, hence the phrase "potentially infinite".

Figure 1 shows a Turing machine which is a tape automaton, and Turing machines can fall into any one of the three above categories.

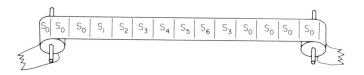

Figure 1

It is possible to show that *digital computers, tape automata and logical* or *neural* nets are, in fact, equivalent in their capability. The only reservation we must make in saying that they are equivalent is that the digital computer must, in certain circumstances, have access to all the information concerning a particular problem that has ever gone through its store. We should also add that the equivalence refers to the fact that they can all do the same things; their methods though vary considerably.

At this stage, it should be clear to the reader that he is dealing with a form of model which is *diminishing the distinction* normally made between "software" (e.g. programs) and "hardware" (e.g. computers). This is precisely what is entailed when one talks about an effective theory. What is wanted is a blueprint, and for many purposes this will be as useful as the machine that has actually to be made. Turing machines and finite automata in general are blueprints in that they are conceptual machines. By a blueprint, we mean something which is so precise that a machine could most certainly be made from it; it is, in short, effective. For example, in psychological theory there are a number of models put forward by psychologists, but virtually none of the models considered is effective in precisely the way suggested above. Even blueprints, under certain circumstances, may omit certain bits and pieces so as to make it impossible to construct a complete system, i.e. they may be high order abstractions, or may be incomplete, such as in the case of so-called "black boxes". Although in practice one should accept the fact that some cybernetic theories and models have some measure of vagueness, one does so because this is more or less essential if considerable scientific progress is to be made in the immediate future.

1.3 CURRENT RESEARCH

We cannot easily summarise current research for this our first chapter since the first chapter is itself a summary, or preview, of the whole book. However, let it be said that a certain number of important general ideas are being aired and we shall underline what seem the most important.

Automata theory is, from the mathematical point of view, going through a period of "filling in" details such as are involved in the investigation of multi-taped Turing machines, the search for algorithms (decision procedures) for independent multi-taped (both one-way and two-way) automata. Some thought is also being given to probabilistic automata and their properties.

In terms of learning machines, most of the effort has been given to trying to produce a design for a conditional probability machine of reasonable size. This means to try to design a classification system which is hierarchical, partial, partitioned and adaptive at the very least and is comparable to the human brain in both its size and abilities.

Perceptual systems continue to be the subject of much discussion (e.g. Coombs, 1969; Arbib, 1971; Morofsky and Wong, 1971) from various vantage points and we shall be describing some of the current research in more detail in later chapters; those chapters that deal with human and animal learning (Chapter 10) and pattern recognition (Chapter 16) are both especially relevant. Problem solving and thinking automata continue to be much studied (e.g. Michie, Fleming and Oldfield, 1968; Doran, 1969; Ramani, 1971) and we shall also say more about these later on.

One of the most important developments in the last few years is that of business science, especially business and management cybernetics, although this is perhaps not suitable as a major topic in an introductory book which is primarily concerned with the "pure" (as opposed to "applied") side of the subject. Readers should certainly though be aware of the considerable progress being made on the applied side (e.g. Spencer, 1970; Zannetos and Wilcox, 1970; Manescu, 1970; Beer, 1972; George, 1973).

Finally we should mention heuristic programming (Buchanan, Sutherland and Feigenbaum, 1969; George 1972). Many higher human cognitive faculties such as are involved in decision taking are carried out under conditions of incomplete information. Heuristics (cf. hypotheses) are the main methods used to try to process the relevant information. Such *ad hoc* methods of approximation can now be used on the computer.

These three fields perhaps represent some of the most important research currently being carried on in the field of cybernetics. They are, however, only meant as samples, taken from a far wider field of research.

We shall now try in this book to add detail to the general arguments and descriptions used in this chapter. We shall throughout be concerned primarily with views about artificial intelligence and simulating human behaviour which are central themes in cybernetics. In a sense the remainder of this book is a development in details and precision of the discussions that are outlined in this first chapter.

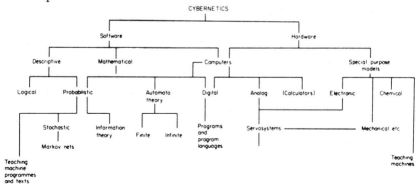

Figure 2   A schematic family tree for the principal features of cybernetics.

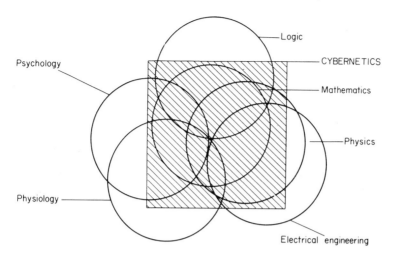

Figure 3   A diagram which shows the rough overlap of the different basic subjects which contributes towards cybernetics.

To complete this chapter we show Figure 2 and 3, which give some "rough idea" of the sub-divisions of cybernetics (Figure 2) and the relation between cybernetics and other (parent) sciences.

1.4   SUMMARY

In this first chapter we have tried to summarise some of the principal features of cybernetic development. Emphasis has been laid on the fact that there are at least three categories of cybernetic problems:

1) The problem of synthesising artificial intelligence and applying it to control system problems, regardless of any relationship it may have to human intelligence and ability.

2) The development of artificial intelligence which is a functional copy of human or animal behaviour (simulation).

3) The development of artificial intelligence and the various aspects of organic behaviour, constructed of a fabric similar to if not exactly the same as those used by actual organisms.

CHAPTER 2

The notion of feedback and closed-loop systems

Argument

Self-adapting systems are systems that are self-modifying in the sense that they change as a function of their changing environmental circumstances. They can be described and constructed in a variety of different ways, and there are many different schools of thought as to the most effective way of both constructing and describing them.

Some self-adapting systems have been described in mathematical terms, some in statistical, some in logical terms. Most of all these self-adapting systems are made with a view to simulating particular organismic processes whereas others have been constructed in a more abstract way.

A self-adapting system has certain properties of stability ("ultrastability" is the word that Ashby has used), which mark it off as different from a non-adaptive system.

Servo-systems and automatic control systems, such as appropriately programmed computers, are both examples of self-adapting systems, and these self-adapting systems can be described either in deterministic or probabilistic terms.

In general, we should say that models which are sophisticated enough and detailed enough to simulate aspects of human behaviour will be probabilistic; but approximations to the more realistic models will usually be deterministic.

2.1 IN GENERAL

Every system has an environment and the result and behaviour of the system involves an interaction between that system and its environment, except in that special case of *absolutely closed* systems where, by definition, no interaction occurs. In *relatively closed* systems we have the "in-between" case, and at the other extreme we have *open* systems where interaction is complete.

We study in cybernetics the *behaviour* and the *structure* of systems, and indeed cybernetics is the systematic study of the behaviour and structure of particular types of systems.

Klir and Valach (1965) have defined a system S such that

$$S = (A, B),$$

where

$$A = (a_1, a_2, ..., a_n)$$

and

$$B = (a_0, a_1, ..., a_n).$$

So that $A \subset B$ since $a_0 \in B$ $a_0 \notin A$ and where a_0 depicts the environment of S. We also have a set of values r_{ij} $(i, j = 0, 1, ..., n)$, which we denote by R, as the relators between A and B so we say that r_{ij} is the manner in which the input quantities of elements a_j depend upon the output quantities of a_i. ($\subset$ means "is contained in", and $\in$ means "is a member of".)

The relation

$$y = T(x)$$

relates the stimuli x to the responses y by the transformation T. T may be single or many-valued and we have partial responses which are the responses to partial stimuli. The situation can be depicted as follows:

$$y_1 = f_1(x_1, x_2, ..., x_p)$$
$$y_2 = f_2(x_1, x_2, ..., x_p)$$

$$---$$

$$y_q = f_q(x_1, x_2, ..., x_p).$$

Or in general

$$y = f(x),$$

where $f_1, f_2, ..., f_q$ are functions of p independent variables $x_1, x_2, ..., x_p$, and f is the vector function of the independent variable vector x. The behaviour exhibited by the system may be random, sequential, parallel, etc., and may be determinate or probabilistic. We supply these definitions in a formal manner mainly to remind the reader that cybernetics is very much concerned with formal systems. The definitions given here of a system will in fact be repeated in the chapter on automata theory in a slightly different form; there they will specifically refer to automata, which are equivalent to what is here called a system.

We now define cybernetics as the study of arbitrary systems capable of receiving, storing and processing information and utilising it for purposes of control and regulation (Kolmogorov, see Ashby, 1956).

Much of what this book is concerned with is the more detailed analysis of this definition of a system (or automaton) for a series of particular cases.

2.2 SERVOSYSTEMS

One potent force that has led to modern cybernetic theories of adaptive systems is that of servosystems, with closed-loop control. We shall say a few words about the theory of such systems, but not attempt to develop it in any detail.

Figure 1 shows an open-loop system where there is no correcting feedback. This simply controls the indoor temperature as a function of the outdoor temperature (Porter, 1969) but does not feedback and change the internal temperature as a function of itself.

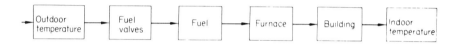

Figure 1   Open-loop control system where the amount of fuel sent to the furnace is a function of the outdoor temperature.

Figure 2 shows the closed loop version of the system where the indoor temperature variation itself feeds back against the desired temperature level. This has the effect of diminishing the amount of heat allowed into the system if the temperature internally is too high and increasing the heat allowed in if the internal temperature is too low. Such closed loop systems form ·a branch of differential equations as far as their mathematical description is concerned.

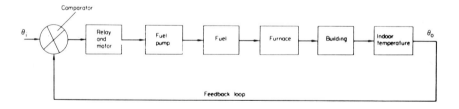

Figure 2   Closed-loop control system where the temperature needed (θ_i) is compared to the actual indoor temperature (θ_o) and the heat increased or decreased accordingly.

Let us consider briefly how the mathematical description is built up. If we apply a Force F to a spring of elasticity K, and let us assume our y-coordinate reads 0 when no force is applied, Hooke's law of elasticity says that the force F_k when applied will be proportional to the displacement y, i.e.

$$F_k = K_y,$$
(1)

where F and K are both functions of time. The equation of motion is:

$$y = \left[\frac{1}{K}\right] F$$
(2)

or

$$K_y = F.$$
(3)

Figure 3 shows this simple sort of open-loop system.

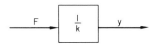

Figure 3

Let us next suppose that our spring has guides with frictional forces F_r which are proportional to the velocity dy/dt. We now have:

$$F_R = R \frac{dy}{dt}$$
(4)

and for the equation of motion

$$R \frac{dy}{dt} + Ky = F.$$
(5)

If we next hand a mass M on the end of our spring we generate a third force which by Newton's second law is proportional to the acceleration $d^2 y/dt^2$. This gives

$$F_M = M \frac{d^2 y}{dt^2},$$
(6)

F_M is the opposing force due to the mass M. The equation of motion of the system becomes:

$$M \frac{d^2 y}{dt^2} + R \frac{dy}{dt} + Ky = F.$$
(7)

We shall not here indicate how we derive the solutions to such differential equations. But the reader who is interested can consult any elementary textbook on differential equations.

Now consider Figure 4 which shows another closed-loop system.

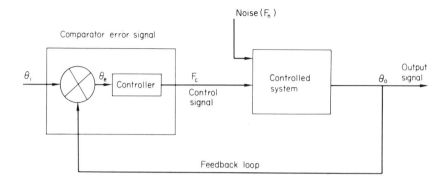

Figure 4 A generalized closed-loop system as in Figure 2, except that here we have not specified the details, but include a disturbing input F_n, which we can call *noise*.

We wish to relate θ_0 to θ_i and we consider both the control and the controlled system. The former is given by

$$r\frac{d\theta_0}{dt} + \theta_0 = \frac{1}{K}(F_c + F_n).$$ (8)

The latter is given by

$$F_c = k(\theta_i - \theta_0).$$ (9)

The controlled system is identical with out spring with frictional guide lines and with the equation of motion.

$$R\frac{dy}{dt} + Ky = \dot F$$ (5)

and if we let $s(y) = dy/dt$ we can rewrite (5) as

$$(Rs + K)y = F.$$ (10)

Combining R and K then gives the time constant τ such that $\tau = R/K$ and we get:

$$(\tau S + 1)y = (\frac{1}{k})F$$ (11)

so that

$$y = \left[\frac{1/k}{\tau S + 1}\right]F.$$ (12)

The amount $(1/k)/(\tau S+1)$ is called a *transfer function*, where a transfer function is the amount the system multiplies the input to derive the necessary output.

We return now to the mathematical description (8) and (9) of Figure 4.

We can now define $\theta_c \equiv Fc/K$ and $\theta_n = Fn/K$; we can rewrite (8) as

$$\tau\frac{d\theta_0}{dt} + \theta_0 = \theta_{\hat c} + \theta_{\hat a}$$ (13)

and if we define $k_1 \equiv k/K$ we can rewrite (9) as

$$\theta_c = k_1 (\theta_i - \theta_0). \tag{14}$$

If we next substitute (14) in (13), we get

$$\frac{(\tau)}{1 + k_1} \frac{d_{\theta 0}}{} + \theta_0 = \frac{(k_1)}{1 + k_1} + \frac{(1)}{1 + k_1} \theta_n. \tag{15}$$

(15) is the equation which defines the system of Figure 4.

We should, if we were persuing this mathematical treatment further, next analyse the solution of such equations, and we should go on to study the transient analysis of such systems which considers inputs to the system, and the *frequency* analysis which considers inputs of a special kind called periodic sinusoidal functions which reveal the dynamic properties of the system. At this point, we leave our brief comment on servosystems which can be followed by the interested reader by reference to a large volume of literature on the subject. We shall in the next chapter start with a brief example of hardware systems which are servosystems.

2.3   IN PARTICULAR

As long ago as 1951, J. O. Wisdom (1951) had pointed out that the basic hypotheses of cybernetics were:

1) Feedback in general and negative feedback in particular, represent a vital condition for the self-correction or adaptation necessary to any "learning" system.

2) Watt's governor, the thermostat and the human operator in such roles as cyclist or car driver are examples of such feedback systems, and are all systems which are in some sense stability seeking systems. It should be emphasised that this includes human and other organismic systems, and subsystems, as well as artificial systems. The artificial systems also include artificial limbs and the like, as well as models of systems.

3) In their goal-searching activities, most "intelligent" systems need to amplify signals (communications) in order to achieve the necessary "purposive" control.

4) Physiological descriptions of human and lower organisms had long emphasised the purposive nature of behaviour, embodied in such principles as *homeostasis* (Cannon, 1929; Hill, 1910, 1932, 1936).

5) At the behavioural level of activity, the perception of processes, especially, the ability to generalise and perceive *universals* is critical (McCulloch and Pitts, 1942).

6) At all levels of organismic activity, but especially at the energy level of description, "open systems" were seen to be relevant (von Bertalanffy, 1951, 1952).

2.4   SELF-ADAPTING SYSTEMS

Cybernetics is inter-disciplinary, insofar as it has its background in a variety of different sciences as well as as in philosophy. In fact, we can pinpoint the background of cybernetics in mathematics, physiology, electrical engineering, especially with respect to computer technology, as well as psychology and, to a somewhat lesser extent, sociology. Indeed, the whole of biological theorising is to some extent a forbear of cybernetic thinking. At the same time logic has played a major part in determining the development of cybernetics. We must be forgiven for re-emphasising this mixed heritage, but it is vital to remember it, in the process of understanding cybernetics.

However, the inter-disciplinary nature of cybernetics has created some difficulty for it. It is inherent in our knowledge that anything that is very general and cuts across the accepted boundaries of science should leave its followers in something of an exposed position because they are dealing in established sciences and must necessarily deal with them in a somewhat more superficial way than the particular specialist scientists themselves, and even more important, since it is looking at the subject from a different vantage point, it extracts different sorts of problems from it. This is a difficulty that confronts the cybernetician in the same way as the philosopher of science or the scientific theorist.

One of the results of this general inter-disciplinary background of cybernetics is that more than most subjects it has a variety of different viewpoints attached to it which seem, at least at first sight, to be quite different from each other. One of the reasons for these apparent differences of viewpoint is the fact that the different theorists have used their own terminology and notation.

One could, for example, talk about cybernetics in terms of feedback, especially negative feedback, feedforward, stability or ultra-stability and think of stability as implying points of equilibrium in a system, and it is this equilibrium of a system which gives it its control on the one hand and allows it to be described adequately on the other. One thinks straight away of something relatively simple like a Watt governor which is one of the earliest of feedback devices, in which a signal indicates the speed of the steam engine. This signal is conveyed to a power amplifier device in the form of a steam throttle so that as the engine accelerates so the steam applied to it is reduced; as a result of course, the speed of the steam engine is kept steady. It is worth noting that the signal is independent of the energy and therefore it is a form of information control, and in a sense this is the prototype of all cybernetic systems. It is indeed an example of precisely the type of closed-loop system described in the last section but one (2.2).

It is the negative feedback of information flow (and its storage) which, in controlling systems which are self-adapting and evolving in an environment, are the basic features of cybernetics (Wisdom, 1951). In a sense, as was suggested in the first chaper, this means that the search for artificial intelligence is the principal ingredient of cybernetics.

It must be emphasised again that the whole problem of learning and adaptation, as well as problems of thinking (George, 1970) can be tackled from a variety of different standpoints. This does not only mean that various methods could be used to actually affect the study, but more so that rather different models can be envisaged for different purposes. It is really at this point that it is necessary to make another important distinction in cybernetics.

2.5   GROWTH AND PRE-WIRED SYSTEMS

One of the distinctions that has sometimes been made in the field of cybernetics is that between *growth* models and *pre-wired* models. It has often been argued that if one is simulating organic self-adapting systems, then the model itself must grow and change. On the other hand, it has been argued with equal cogency that if we are simulating adapting systems we can do this perfectly well by means of fixed or pre-wired systems such as in a computer. The reason why it is thought by the adherents of the pre-wired model that the computer is a perfectly adequate model for self-adaptation is that it is, of course, a universal model since it is never in any case complete until its program has been inserted, and that the choice of programs allows for change and self-adaptation to take place within the computer. Such programs have sometimes been called "underspecified"†
(Mackay, 1951, 1956).

Adherents to the growth view of simulation will sometimes argue that one must have a system, ideally built of chemical and protoplastic materials, such as the models that have been suggested by Pask (1959) on one hand and Mackay and Ainsworth (1964) on the other. Such models literally change their structures as a function of the environment in which they live. This is not a contradictory situation, but if one is interested in functional, or as one might say physiological, variations and adaptions, then a pre-wired model having variation within it is perfectly adequate for certain purposes and certain circumstances.

On the other hand if one is interested in anatomical variation, then one must admit that ideally one should use an organic or some sort of physically changing

---

† The word "underspecified" was specifically used by Professor Mackay in private discussions and in some papers delivered at symposia. The references give some idea of Mackay's views.

model. What is important from our point of view is to recognise that these are not inconsistent points of view; rather they are complementary. Perhaps what is more important, and what in some measure underlies the discussion about growth and pre-wired models, is the question of how much the maturation and evolution of a model affects is state at any later time. In other words, should one attempt to build ready-made models of some aspect of the adult human being, such as the ability to think? Or should one, on the other hand, construct a system which slowly evolves the ability to think. The answer presumably is that sooner or later both should be done. Whereas the second is clearly necessary for anything like a complete biological model, the first is completely adequate to an understanding of learning or problem-solving, planning, etc., especially where the attempt is to synthesise, not primarily to simulate, human behaviour.

2.6   SIMULATION AND SYNTHESIS

One of the points already made in the first chapter and made again in the last section of this chapter should be further emphasised in this section. It is that there are at least two distinct types of cybernetic problem; sometimes though they have not been sufficiently distinguished. Firstly cyberneticians have been interested in the simulation of organismic behaviour. They have been interested more often than not in trying to simulate human intelligence, but on the other hand cyberneticians have also been interested in constructing systems which were capable of learning, thinking, problem-solving and performing the whole range of human-like ability, without any interest whatever in simulating human intelligence as such; this latter is what we have called the problem of synthesis.

It is possible to argue that any attempt to build an artificially intelligent system necessarily means copying human beings. This is rather the point of view taken by the people who work in the field of bionics; they openly copy organismic behaviour in the design of engineering materials, among many other things. This is as may be, but it is certainly true to say that we can construct artificial systems which clearly work on quite different materials from those used in human beings. For example, a computer which can perform many, if not all, human-like activities, operates on the basis of elements like transistors which are manifestly different from human neurones in their material construction, although they are functionally very similar in certain ways.

It is the functional similarity of artificial to natural systems which is perhaps the most important feature of cybernetic development. Cyberneticians are not generally so concerned with having their models made of the same materials as the original − although sometimes they are − they are usually concerned that they have a method which is functionally similar. Although, in the extreme case, there is the cybernetician who does not care whether his model has any resemblance whatever to the human being, and judges its effectiveness *only* in terms of the end results. It is here that in practice there must be some functional similarity to human intelligence, because in trying to construct a model one is bound in some part to copy the human being and his methods. Indeed this copying of the methods is usually quite explicit. The fact remains that we have to distinguish very carefully between cyberneticians who are specifically trying to understand human behaviour or biology by means of simulation, and cyberneticians who are only interested in synthesising artificial intelligence systems for planning, or other control purposes, in society. It is natural to think that the first group who are interested in simulation should be interested in growth models to a far greater extent than the second group, who are primarily interested in the use of computers.

All that has been said so far in this chapter must be taken to be typical of the sort of distinction that is made throughout a subject like cybernetics, or indeed in most sciences, and it is important for the reader to clearly understand this point.

2.7   THE BIOLOGICAL SCIENCES

We shall in the course of this book be meeting and discussing some of the principal methods that cyberneticians have been using, and two later chapters deal explicitly with the physiological and psychological problems from a primarily cybernetic point of view.

A point to notice is that much of biological science in the past has been mechanistic in viewpoint, which will mean that explanations have tended to be machine-like in character. Strangely enough, in spite of this, even mechanistic biologists have tended to reject, at least in part, cybernetic development and its relevance to biology. At the same time, of course, many biologists have taken a keen interest in cybernetics and tried to follow its developments and to utilise its ideas. But the fact remains that cybernetics is not recognised as a natural outcome of mechanistic-type thinking. Nor is it widely appreciated that it is the effective constructability or general effectiveness of a system that springs from cybernetic designs, as well as the precision of description.

It is not necessarily hardware models, simulating some aspect of organismic behaviour that is looked for in cybernetics, but also an effective blueprint whereby anyone could build the model suggested from the blueprint plans alone. This is what is meant by *effectiveness;* this is the property of being able to follow in detail and carry out some operations without fully understanding them. This is the same as what mathematicians call an *algorithm* or a *decision procedure.* We shall be saying a great deal more later on about algorithms and decision procedures, and especially the contrast between them and *heuristics.*

Many people from within the biological sciences have used cybernetic ideas for a very long time; one should mention here again the name of von Bertalanffy (1951, 1952) whose work on system theory is a good example of the application of mathematical methods to biological systems, and is thus in the general tradition of cybernetics. He also noticed, what is so important for a cybernetician, that many apparently wholly dissimilar systems have many features in common; this, of course, is one of the main points of cybernetics, when we talk about "machines" and their similarity to organisms. What we tend to mean here, and certainly what von Bertalanffy meant, was that they could be described by the same sort of model. In von Bertalanffy's case the model was of a mathematical form, and this again is consistent with the development of cybernetics. In talking of mathematics, one should, of course, accept symbolic or mathematical logic, as well as computer programming, as being within the domain of mathematics.

General systems theory has taken a long time to establish itself, although von Bertalanffy and other workers in the field have had a growing following. There is though no doubt that similar viewpoints percolated through to the heart of the cybernetic movement under the leadership of Wiener, Bigelow and Rosenbleuth (Rosenbleuth, Wiener and Bigelow, 1943; Wiener, 1948) when they first publicly formulated cybernetic ideas in the 1940's. Their whole attitude regarding the organisation of a system, and the system's characteristic of stability and feedback, indicate clearly the close resemblance of their cybernetic ideas to the ideas of general systems theory.

As far as psychology is concerned, ideas like *homeostasis,* first proposed as early as the twenties by W. B. Cannon (1929), is precisely cybernetic in point of view. Homeostasis states that *needs* in organisms set up patterns of activity, which are then directed, as far as it is possible, by the ability of the organism, to the removal of that need. In other words, hunger sets up a state of activity in an organism which leads it to seek food to satisfy its hunger and bring back a stable state, a state of contentment or homeostasis.

One of the direct outcomes of the homeostatis point of view is a model which will be described in the next chapter; it is due to W. Ross Ashby (1952, 1956) and is called the *Homeostat.* This is precisely a system which adapts to changing circumstances and adapts in different ways as a function of the circumstances at the moment the change first takes place. Basically this is an attempt to show variability which comes into the homeostatic type of control pattern. Ashby, in describing the homeostat and various related systems, finds it necessary to use the notion of ultra-stability. One may think of ultra-stability in terms of state-determined behaviour. By "state-determined behaviour" we mean to say that behaviour is state-determined if an observer knowing the state at time T is able to predict the state at time $T + 1$ with certainty. In practice we may suppose that most organismic models are not state-determined, but are rather better described statistically, or as being probabilistic, and we can only predict future states from past states or present states — in terms of uncertainty.

State-determined behaviour tends to converge onto a stable state or enter into a behavioural cycle. Both of these are states of stable equilibrium, because without external disturbance the behaviour remains invariant. Ashby described state-determined behaviour and the stability of patterns of state determined behaviour in terms of a space and certain types of mathematical notation, which we need not go into here.

The aim of models based on these concepts of state-determined behaviour, ultra-stability and homeostasis, is that of looking for something which is general and is not primarily concerned with specific aspects of human behaviour such as perception, learning, etc. but rather with general forms of self-adaptation. Many people have tried to start with modules or randomly connected elements, and have asked themselves what environmental conditions are necessary to bring about the state of patterning as well as ultra-stability in those models. Many principles have been drawn up, and theorems proved, to show something of the nature of the necessary conditions that must exist for the subsequent evolution of intelligence systems.

We will not attempt to follow out in any detail the complete range of self-adaptive models. In the next chapter, some of the actual hardware models that have been constructed will be described; many of these illustrate points which are being made in this chapter. At the same time we will have to be content with giving some general summary of the type of principle that was being searched for.

One last point should be made to underline the question of *growth* in a system. Many cyberneticians, including Turing, have tried to show that randomly connected elements can acquire a definite pattern and lead to all the necessary characteristics of stability which allow control and learning to take place. It is important to note that whereas this is a most important exercise from the point of view of evolution, it is not important to anything like the same extent from the point of view of the development of an individual. Individual organisms whether of the simplest kind or of the most complex in the form of human beings, never start with random assemblies of cells. They start with detailed blueprints from genetics, which allow the maturation of the system, which is at the same time acquiring information about its environment (Apter, 1966).

It is this last point which is perhaps fundamental to understanding cybernetics. Many people have discussed the growth and the evolution of systems, and many others have discussed the development of a selectively planned individual. All too often, cyberneticians themselves have not made it clear which it is they are describing and discussing, and what its relevance is to human biology. As long as we keep these two types of models separate in our minds, then the sort of confusion that has sometimes occurred in the past should not occur again in the future.

This chapter has attempted to make some more of the distinctions that cyberneticians wish to make, and clear the ground in part for a point of view which in this book will be primarily one of regarding cybernetics as a model-constructing procedure where the principal models will be those of logic, information theory, automata (both finite and infinite), and computers, all of which are equivalent to each other in some sense. These methods are used in the context which regards the primary problems of cybernetics as those of simulating problem solving, general intelligence and learning. It should be emphasised, however, that the more evolutionary and more biologically determined viewpoints also exist in cybernetics and we are mentioning them here although not developing them to the same extent.

2.8   CURRENT RESEARCH

In this chapter we have taken one step towards the particular, but have intentionally repeated some of the more important generalities of Chapter 1. Current research in this field of defining systems still continues and is part of the movement called general systems theory (Mesarovic, 1972; Mesarovic and Takahara, 1973; Pennacchi, 1972). Many of the definitions of systems turn out to be equivalent, even though presented in different form, but the basic search is for generality.

Servosystems are a particular type of feedback control system and research is constantly going on in this field to embrace ever more complex types of feedback control, and recently special emphasis has been placed on biological and chemical control systems (Grodins, 1963). Apter (1966) has also developed systems of an automata-like kind that grow and bear some relation to genetic forms.

Increasingly work is going on at a mathematical level (Barnett and Storey, 1970; Porter, 1972) which deals with the stability characteristics of complex dynamic systems and in this respect there is a trend towards an integration with systems theory and the theory of abstract systems mentioned above. Such work has tended to take a definite mathematical form although the reference is still to the characteristics of systems which are still also the domain of control theory.

Negative feedback is still a key feature of cybernetic systems, but the most recent development of "feedforward" systems is a reminder that, with human-like intelligence, anticipatory behaviour is in many ways as important as a "knowledge of results".

2.9   SUMMARY

Self-adapting systems can be thought of as total systems in any fabric which adapts to changing circumstances. They may be "natural" or "man-made".

Self-adaption must be built into any synthesis or simulation of human intelligence. This chapter has been primarily concerned with the first view which tends to emphasise the system as a whole.

Homeostasis, stability, ultra-stability are some of the concepts introduced into a discussion of negative feedback systems, and it has been emphasised that, from the point of view of general self-adaptive systems, cybernetics cuts across most existing scientific disciplines.

Feedforward is another feature of intelligent behaviour which emerges from the higher levels of organismic intelligence.

CHAPTER 3

Models in hardware

Argument

Many models have been built in hardware to demonstrate properties of organismic behaviour. Surprising as it may seem at first sight, most people are impressed more by a simulation of human behaviour that entails actual physical movement than they are by much more complicated theories which have no such immediate visual impact; the theories, however, may often be more valuable in predicting and understanding human behaviour.

The simplest sort of basic organismic-like system is one that illustrates *tropistic* capacities. Thus a machine that will follow a light source, or a machine that will learn to run a maze efficiently after a few trials, or a machine that will learn to run away from a light source or some other stimulus tends by the very nature of things to look more like an animal than a computer which, for all its complexity of structure and intricacy of detail to say nothing of its enormous potential abilities, utterly lacks visual appeal.

We must accept the fact though that models, both in hardware and software, are a vital part of the driving force underlying cybernetics.

The idea of "man as a machine" has long ago stimulated people to talk and think in terms of robots or automata, and this in turn has stimulated the manufacturers of models — whether electrical, mechanical, chemical or manufactured by any means whatever. These models are sometimes of "whole organisms", sometimes of parts of organisms such as eyes and ears, or they may be attempts to show the principles which are thought to be used, say, in the fields of human intelligence.

The eventual aim may be to build a human being artificially, but such an aim must still be a long way from being fulfilled. This though is what is ultimately needed — at least a functional blueprint for a human being. Cybernetics often involves the process of model construction, and one form of model is the hardware model.

In so far as models have traditionally been constructed by scientists, and in so far as models are helpful both for pedagogic purposes and the clarification of the scientist's own ideas, their construction is obviously to be encouraged. In the field of cybernetics in recent years, there has been a gradual move away from hardware to theoretical (software) models. The reason for this is that it is difficult to build a sufficiently large and instructive hardware model in the amount of time available to each individual scientist. Also, when we bear in mind the money available for such an undertaking, software provides a much more economic approach. It is for this reason indeed that computers, which are then controlled suitably by (software) programs have increasingly tended to be preferred to hardware models.

The advantage of the hardware model, however, is that it has a persuasive force and an appeal to the human eye which no purely theoretical model can ever have. Therefore, it is not surprising to find that a number of hardware models have been built over the years and we shall describe a few selected ones with a view to trying to clarify the general process of hardware modelling.

When we consider hardware models in cybernetics, we consider especially servosystems and computers. Digital computers are the most important and these are discussed separately in Chapter 8, while analog computers are only discussed in this and the last chapter, and they are discussed only in so far as they fall within the class of cybernetic models of servosystems.

We have already said something about servosystems and we have made clear that closed-loop control systems can be built for various purposes, usually for the control of some quite specific system such as a domestic water or heat supply, a gun turret on land or at sea, an automatic pilot and so on and so forth. We shall accept all such systems as cybernetic, but will not want to argue too much about the classification arrangement which delineates cybernetic from non-cybernetic systems.

A servosystem can be described in terms of the equations that depict it and then we seek to define a transfer function which depicts the nature of the control relationship, along the lines we described in the last chapter. We shall be giving as our first example of a hardware model one selected from the large set of such closed-loop servosystems.

Before we do so though there are one or two points that must be made clear. In general, cybernetic models are very much more complicated than the control of the water supply or of a gun turret. As a result, we can no longer treat the problem of supplying such cybernetic models as merely a search for the mathematical definition of the system, or as a search for a suitable transfer function. It is all much too complicated, at least at this stage, for these sort of methods to be applicable. As a result, we have to develop other methods which fall into two main categories. The first is of hardware models, a sample of which are described briefly in this chapter, and are usually very simple and demonstrate certain cybernetic principles and that alone. The second category is inevitably theoretical and includes paper-and-pencil models of both a mathematical and a statistical kind, computer programs and blueprint automata which depict very complex systems. These complex systems, which may include the human brain or a large industry, call for special methods. The most important of these is that of *heuristics* and we shall discuss heuristic methods in a later chapter.

The reader will realise from what we have just said that the present chapter is concerned only with a discussion of simple unpretentious models. It would be a mistake for him to read too much into what have been historically interesting and what have been helpful illustrations of the methods under discussion.

We now look at some simple servosystem models. We shall not, as we did in the last chapter, attempt a mathematical description of the systems, but merely give block diagrams which illustrate their function.

3.1   SERVOSYSTEM MODELS

We first deal with a simple model of the economy as illustrated in Figure 1. Here we shall not attempt to give the detailed mathematical description but merely remind the reader that the servosystem type of model has a much wider application than merely the control of physical systems.

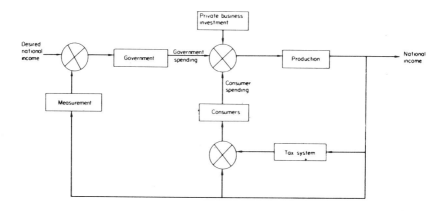

Figure 1

We should add once more that control theory has also been applied to biological systems (Grodins, 1963), but the descriptions become very much more complex and involve non-linear differential equations.

Grodins describes a respiratory chemostat and a cardio-vascular regulator which, by virtue of fairly complicated chemical means, controls the breathing and heartbeat of the human. We shall now move on to other simple cybernetic models which are essentially analog computers.

3.2   GREY WALTER'S MODELS

Grey Walter (1953) produced two of the first cybernetic models since cybernetics became a field of study in its own right, indeed since its formal introduction as a separate science in 1947. He built a simple conditioned reflex analog model called *Cora* and he also built a machine which is popularly known as a "tortoise" which is capable of moving around and imitating the tropistic act by following a light source.

Cora is a type of conditioned response machine and its response unit is a simple neon tube which flashes when responses are being made to a particular stimulus. If a whistle is sounded as a sign of a forthcoming light stimulus, then *Cora* can be made to flash in response to the whistle whereas originally it responded only to the flash of light. This illustrates the basic process of association which is so necessary to simple conditioning.

The tortoise on the other hand is a more complicated system with two sensory elements in the form of a simple contact receptor and a photo-electric cell. The tortoise is in a mobile frame which together move around the floor, the whole system is driven by an electric motor. It carries an accumulator on its chassis, two valves, registers, condensers and a pilot light. The behaviour of the tortoise is tropistic in that it follows a light source.

In complete darkness the steering of *Speculatrix*, which is its more formal name, is continuously rotated by the steering motor, while the photo-cell scans all the time. When a certain amount of light enters the photo-cell, the scanning rotation stops, and as the light increases so scanning starts again, but more slowly. This way the system acts quickly to any change in the environment and then acts slowly to avoid over-response. It should be added that *Speculatrix* makes an impressive sight as it searches, in effect, for light in the same way as an organism might search for food.

3.3 UTTLEY'S MODELS

A.M. Uttley has built two hardware models, of which one is the classification model and the other the conditional probability model. These are rather different from Grey Walter's models in that they are passive or lack mobility, and are built more to illustrate the basic principles of classification and conditional probability.

The idea of classification which is thought of by many people including Uttley (Hayek, 1952; Uttley, 1954, 1955a, 1955b), as basic to perception is simply that of having a number of different stimulus units which can classify inputs as they occur. Thus to take the simplest example, if one has an input made of three input elements, say, *a, b* and *c*, we can say that either they all fire or only some of them (possibly non) fire. So we may say an object which fires all of *a,b* and *c* is one sort of object, an object which fires *a* and *b* alone is another sort, an object that fires *a* and *c* alone is another sort, and so on. There are reasons for doubting that such an overall classificatory method is suitable as a model of the human sensory system, but it has a close resemblance to it in principle, and is one that demands a highly constrained type of classification system. We shall be discussing this matter in more detail later..

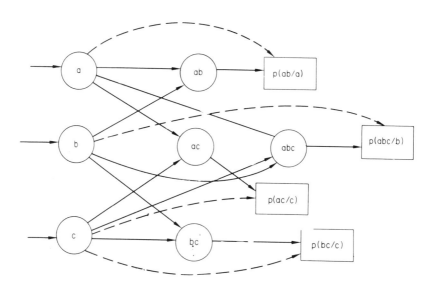

Figure 2   *a, b* and *c* are classified completely into *ab, ac, bc* and *abc.* We also show *some* of the conditional probability counters, where, for example, *p(ab/a)* means "the probability of *ab* given *a*".

The second model built by A. M. Úttley is one based on his own ideas and those of Hayek (1952) which suggest the fact that if a complete count is kept of the frequency occurrence of previous events, then the necessary prediction can be made about current happenings. For example, if *A* is followed by *B* on every single occasion, then we can write the probability of *B* following *A* in the form $P(B/A) = 1$, which is another way of saying that *B* will always follow *A* . It is not the case, of course, that such a sequence of events is really "certain", only that it has always occurred that way in the experience of the system doing the computing. In the same way the probability of any event following another can be recorded and thus an estimate can be given of the chances of some event X, say, following some other event Y.

This concept of conditional probability computers seems to bear a close relationship to the way human beings store and utilise information for predictive purposes. To this extent Uttley himself in building his own conditional probability machine was indeed simulating a very important aspect of admittedly somewhat idealised human behaviour.

The difficulty with Uttley's model (we call it *one* model since both classification and conditional probability systems can be put together to make one large model) comes about when we try to generalise it to show how the whole of human behaviour, and perhaps also the structural features of the nervous system, is simulated adequately by this sort of modelling. The truth is that we have now to weigh and constrain so many different features of this conditional probability model, which makes it so complicated that it is difficult to be sure that the original principle is still really being utilised in any important sense in the model.

However, there remains a lot of evidence that the conditional probability and the classification method is basic to artificial intelligence. What one has to accept is the fact that conditional probabilities become very much more complicated than merely a record of one event following another; such events have to be recorded in hierarchical order, and therefore one event may be said to follow another event at one level of description (a *molar* level, say) whereas this implies the most detailed analysis of a complex of events following a complex of events at an even more detailed level of description (a more *molecular* level).

It is not only that the ability to describe an artificially intelligent system demands some sort of hierarchical treatment, involving many different levels of detailed description, it is also that many events are related to other events in a fairly complicated fashion. Thus we may expect certain events A to happen if B happens or if, and only if, C happened before B. This example is meant to illustrate the complicated conditions which will pertain in many cases. Furthermore there will be changing circumstances which make a complete record of the past unsatisfactory in estimating what is likely to happen in the immediate future. Uttley recognised this in his conditional probability model, and weighed probabilities in terms of *recency*. The difficulty is that recency is not the only factor that weighs probability considerations in the light of making immediate decisions.

Uttley's models are capable of description as stochastic processes, and in particular by a particular type of process called a Markov net. Other writers in the field have specifically developed stochastic descriptions of intelligent organismic behaviour (Bush and Mosteller, 1951a, 1951b, 1955). Such models are software rather than hardware and will be discussed later. Nevertheless the point that such hardware models can be described in such mathematico-statistical terms is of the utmost importance.

Perhaps the biggest difficulty for Uttley's version of a stochastic model is the fact that a sufficiently clearcut distinction is not made between symbols and the things that symbols denote. We have, in intelligent automata, to distinguish sharply between linguistic considerations and so called "factual" considerations. A failure to recognise this distinction is a failure to recognise the full range of artificial intelligence. It is no criticism of Uttley that his models have not, as yet, been taken to this next stage, which is an extremely difficult one to achieve. It is to be hoped that they will be revised in the light of these more complicated weighting situations, which we see now to exist. However it seems to the author that conditional probability computers are essentially correct in principle and are almost certain to be pursued further. Indeed Uttley himself (1966) has suggested further revisions to bring them more into line with apparent facts.

Another consideration should be mentioned at this point, and that is that any model of human intelligence, even if at its more lowly levels, is liable to be probabilistic or statistical rather than deterministic. By this we mean that the complexities of the world as such, and the way we need to process these complexities, is almost certainly on a probabilistic basis rather than on a precise deterministic basis. In other words, complete precision derived by a one-to-one contact of elements or neurons in the nervous system is unlikely alone to be a realistic modelling; it could however be the basis to serve for higher level more probabilistic models. This may be taken by some readers to mean that the whole concept of a deterministic model is wrong and that we should have approached the matter probabilistically in the first place. Whether this be true or not, the reasons for approaching it in a deterministic fashion are that it is then easier to see the consequences of such models clearly depicted, and this includes the whole logic of the situation.

3.4 ASHBY'S MODEL

Ashby's best-known model is the Homeostat (1952). This is a machine which is designed to illustrate the principle of ultra-stability. The Homeostat, like Uttley's models, is a machine which is not a "moving" machine, and is built primarily to illustrate a principle rather than to demonstrate the outward show of organismic type of behaviour. The Homeostat consists of four boxes with magnetic needles pivoted on the top of each. The magnets can be deflected from their normally neutral positions after which they may return to that position as a position of equilibrium. The main feature of this homeostatically controlled system is that the return of the needles to the neutral position can vary as a function of the circumstances in which the original deflection took place.

Ashby's system − a form of analog computer − is an illustration of an adaptive purposive machine which seeks stable, or "ultra-stable", states which are in a sense solutions to problems. It is intended to show how variable goal-seeking behaviour can be achieved by even a relatively simple system of appropriate design. From one point of view this model is illustrative of human-like needs causing the organism to seek a homeostatic state of equilibrium; once discovered, the stable state causes the organism to stop its searching activity and the method used is a function of the original degree of displacement as well as the overall state of the system.

3.5   PASK'S MODELS

Gordon Pask (1960, 1961) has built a whole series of models, or automata which represent different aspects of organismic structure and function. Many of these have been concerned either with teaching on a group basis, or learning on both an individual and group basis; Pask has long been concerned with different aspects of self-adaptation and the evolution of systems in an environment.

Perhaps the best known model of the many ingenious models suggested by Pask is the one showing the growth of threads in an electrical field. The idea is that there is an actual growth process going on and the threads can go back to solution or be reformed as threads in making the most complicated of patterns. This occurs as a function not only of their own state at the time that their own regeneration takes place, but also according to the distribution of the electrical field in which the whole operation takes place. This clearly is one of the types of model which was mentioned in the last chapter, as attempting to simulate the growth aspects of organisms from a cybernetic point of view. Mackay and Ainsworth (1964) have produced somewhat similar models (indeed it is believed that these have prior claims) in simulating the growth aspect of an organismic process. But from our point of view they illustrate much the same principle.

Pask's model consisted of a shallow perspex dish containing an acid solution of a metallic salt which was moderately conductive and an aqueous solution of ferrous sulphate. He had inert platinum wire electrodes and then by energising one of the electrodes there was a dendritic growth towards that electrode from one of the other electrodes. This growth was the result of electrodeposition. This is accompanied by an acid back reaction which tends to dissolve the dendrite. The complex growth process involved states of stability where growth occurs, and states where growth diminishes. But certain non-reversible growths may take place which permanently change the network set up. The analogy between this and the growth of nervous tissue is fairly clear even in terms of our simplified description.

3.6   MAZE RUNNING MODELS

There have been many different kinds of maze running models and we shall not attempt to discuss the full range here. We shall merely mention that among the best known ones are those built by Shannon (1951) and Deutsch (1954). Both of these maze running models were based on essentially the same principle of simple *selective reinforcement*. It is easy enough to see that if you have something that can record the fact that it is blocked or not blocked at a "choice point" in a maze, and can record and retain this fact so that the next time through the maze instead of going to the turning which leads to a lane that is blocked (if it is a two-choice point) it goes to one that is open, then it can record and remember such information. Therefore learning in this somewhat simple sense is a fairly obvious feature. Consider the maze shown in Figure 3.

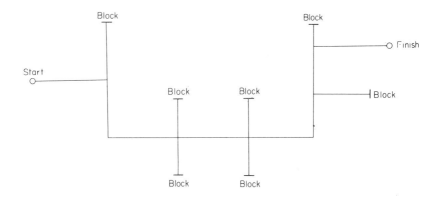

Figure 3   Maze with seven blind alleys shown by blocks.

It will be seen that at choice point one, if it turns left it is blocked. It records the fact and has to return and then has the choice of "straight on" or right, and if it goes right it goes back to the original point when it has to turn around. But now it has no choice point with which to proceed up the maze again at which point it must go right at the first choice point rather than left, since the left turn has already been blocked. The second choice point is now the third choice point so it might make two mistakes before it learns to go the correct way, and so on, dealing with choice point after choice point through the maze until the end of the maze is reached. It need hardly be added that this represents no very complicated logical principle. It is simply a matter of deciding how to store the information and how the interaction between the machine and the outside world should be achieved. It is usually achieved in the model by something quite simple like a photoelectric cell or a selenium disc, and a simple store to allow it to record the memory of failures and successes.

Maze running machines have the advantage of illustrating clearly to an observer the simplicity of some simple learning process. On the other hand, they have the difficulty attached to them that having gone so far in the correct direction and certainly in the most dramatic manner, there is a limit to the actual effectiveness of the process by such methods. This limitation is clear when the need arises to generalise on these simple beginnings and to show more complex learning.

We should mention in this section the work of Oettinger (1952) which, although it did not involve a separate working model, was an early type of maze running program for a computer. Oettinger thought of his computer program as a "shopping" program. It went from shop to shop gradually acquiring the goods it needed, and learning where to go to get a particular thing. Learning was speeded up because even when looking for an article A and finding, say, that the shop had not got A, it noticed that it did have B, C and D. This shows learning which is not wholly controlled by goal-seeking; it is what psychologists sometimes call "latent learning".

3.7   CHAPMAN'S SELF-ORGANISING SYSTEM

The principle of Chapman's (1959) classification system is more of the Uttley kind than of the maze running kind. Chapman's model differs from that of Uttley's earlier models in that it does not require *complete* classification. It demands that any number of elements can be gathered together into several of the *possible* sets of combinations of their elements. There is then the further condition that the several combinations of elements which can be gathered together shall be those which occur most frequently.

At first sight, the limitation on the number of combinations that can be classified appears to be a simplification imposing an unjustifiable constraint on the system. However, if we consider a situation similar to that of visual perception, where the number of elements is so large that only a tiny fraction of the possible number of combinations occurs, the useful economy of Chapman's system becomes obvious. The condition of relating priority of classification to frequency of occurency inevitably means that the system does not classify elements immediately, and at this stage is not therefore strictly a classifying system, in the same sense as used by Uttley. Its structure is such that, by operating on it with groups of elements, it *grows* and *learns* to classify them. There is a sense in which we can say that Chapman's system learns to classify; Uttley's system classifies to learn.

The technique by which this is achieved in the hardware model is that of inhibition. Each of the inputs to the machine representing an element, or primitive stimulus, is connected to every one of the outputs. These outputs represent events by a number of barely conducting paths consisting of threads of cotton moistened with lime water.

When a group of elements is "fired" by application of a positive potential to the ends of the cotton threads, the event is registered by the lighting of several of the output lamps. For each such event, all conducting links connecting inputs which were not active to outputs which were active, are rendered less conducting by the passage of a large current, and the consequent evaporation of moisture. In addition, the active links are rendered less conducting, at a different rate, unless or until the output on which they terminate only just fires (i.e. its threshold is only just exceeded by a small quantity). In general if a number of different events occur, a tendency is observed for the outputs to distribute themselves among the events, and eventually to represent each event uniquely. However, with suitable adjustment of the rates at which the sets of conducting paths for each event are modified, it is possible for certain outputs to respond, not to separate, events, but to several events all containing a common subset of elements. In a sense the machine has recognised a general characteristic of its environment.

By careful control of the vapour surrounding the cotton threads, the machine can be made to "forget" events which have not occurred recently, or whose frequency has diminished and so allow more recently frequent events to over-write them. Although a system which allows over-writing would cause confusion if used to store detailed information, it has very obvious advantage as an early warning system in an organism whose environment is changing, and it seems likely that a system of this type plays an important part in important organic processes such as "directing attention".

Chapman's machine is significant in itself as a pointer to the way in which economy can be achieved in a large classification system; but what is of more importance is that he, like Pask, has demonstrated that a highly organised specific system can grow from a non-specific medium with a relatively simple structure, obeying generalised rules of growth. His system invites some comparison also with that of Mackay and Ainsworth.

3.8   STEWART'S MODELS

Classification is also the basis of an automaton made by Stewart (1959) which he has called "Flebus". Stewart's aim in building this automaton was partly influenced by the inverse of the Turing game (Chapter 1) which was concerned with answering the question: "Can automata behave like humans?" Flebus has four input channels, each of which may be in one of two discrete states

The programming of the automata sets up plugboard connections between the sixteen output sockets of the input net, and the fifteen input sockets of the output net, but of course the automaton can be programmed in a variety of different ways. Stewart then used the automaton for a series of experiments involving the human operator. The automaton was used to simulate a number of different situations such as the use of binary controls in a binary display situation, routine checks, fault diagnosis, and so on. Here we have a system that is comparable to a type of teaching machine (see Chapter 12).

The use of the automaton as a simulator involves further special input and output material, and the realisation of simple logical functions and stochastic processes, and can be made as complicated as we like. The automaton has great versatility, and realises some of the properties we should expect to find in a human organism, although in a very simple form. One of its most interesting features is that it was constructed directly from logical net diagrams.

3.9   GEORGE'S MODELS

These models, like Flebus, were built directly from logical nets (1961). The first model shows a particular classification and conditional probability system. Only two inputs are classified, and the memory is only over six events, but the model can easily be extended, by the use of additional relays, to include any number of inputs and any length of memory. It can also be extended to deal with temporal sequences and logical associations.

This brief statement applies to the first model made by George (1965). The second model was built in units whose memory was subsequently extended to something near to eighty events. There were some twelve of these units available and they could be connected in any way whatever to realise a wide variety of different automata. These automata are capable of realising all the characteristics already described, and could be shown to demonstrate many of the characteristics of simple learning. Some of the units could be regarded as motivational units, and thus the effectiveness of any association may be made to depend on their firing at specific times. This means that the modular model was based on selective reinforcement which allowed adaptation to changing "organic needs" as well as to changing circumstances.

A third and fourth model were made, and they were intended to be models of the eye and the visual system, on one hand, and simple learning on the other; they are both designed on the basis of blueprints in logical net forms. The models were constructed with the idea of trying to find a workable and inexpensive method for constructing large scale automata in hardware. It is clearly easy enough to draw neural (or logical) nets (see Chapter 7), but though these are sufficient to illustrate effectively the principles of behaviour for a large scale experiment, a hardware system is far easier to build than to describe in its logical form.

3.10   GOLDACRE AND BEAN'S MODEL

Our last example of a hardware model is strictly a biological simulation (Goldacre and Bean, 1959) and could perhaps have been featured in a later chapter concerned explicitly with biological models. However, we shall describe it here.

The model consists of an artificial "tissue", or group of artificial electronic "cells" which can communicate with and influence one another. Its behaviour resembles, in some respects, the behaviour of groups of cells in the animal where communication between cells seems to be important, such as in the co-ordinated growth of a developing egg into an adult animal; and in the behaviour of nerve networks in the brain.

The co-ordinated growth which occurs in a developing embryo, and which involves the control of pattern and shape and determines whether the fertilized egg will grow into, say, a frog, fish or snail, contrasts with the unco-ordinated growth seen in malignant tumours. The hypotheseis was developed that co-ordinated growth in the normal animal was to some extent a result of the passage of information and growth-controlling impulses from cell to cell by direct contact, growth proceeding by a sort of brain-like interaction of the cells of the organism.

The model was built to show the feasibility of this hypothesis, simulation coming from recent findings that tumour cells have different cell surfaces from the normal, and do not form firm connections with one another and so would escape from this kind of control. With the Goldacre and Bean model it is possible to imitate and illustrate various processes in morphogenesis. It is possible, for example, to show how such a model is capable of generating a head-end or head-tail polarity in a developing egg from a group of cells which are all equivalent and connected together in a symmetrical way; how shape could be controlled in a growing pattern of tissue, according to a built-in "heredity"; how cells could become different from their neighbours; how regeneration of a lost part could occur; how reproduction of organisation could occur; and a possible basis of left- and right-handedness. In order to make it possible to follow easily the changing patterns of activity of the model it was arranged for each cell to emit a different "musical" note as it became activated.

The group of interacting cells in the model has some properties associated with nerve networks in the brain, and can be used to illustrate some "brain-like" phenomena. Such "brain-like" phenomena is obviously suited to modelling by neural nets. One example of their possible application is of Freud's theory of art where a tension in the brain seeks to find some outlet in useful activity, or if these channels are blocked, it may express itself in some artistic way.

In the model, tensions may be represented by electric charges in condensers which can be made to actuate a device for connecting up "nerve cells" in various pathways (as if seeking an outlet), and for firing pulses into such networks; and the pattern of activity generated can be followed by the musical sound emitted.

Various interesting "melodies" and "rhythms" can be generated and, by introducing disturbances, these "tunes" can be made to change and gradually find their way back to the original theme. In several other ways the neural nets are interesting in connection with music; for example, if connections between the cells are made and broken in various ways, as if exploring various avenues for discharge, pulsation can be generated in various cells with certain networks, the property of the networks is such that the frequency of pulsation changes (on changing the connections between the cells) in the ratio of small whole numbers, as is the case in the pitch and rhythm of music.

Such a model, which has a broad molar biological interpretation is typical of models of a biological kind that are still being manufactured to illustrate basic principles of organic systems. The bulk of the rest of such models are still couched in terms of tape automata.

3.11   IN GENERAL

It is difficult to draw any firm conclusions from what we have said about hardware models, except perhaps to remind the reader that we have selected just a few illustrative models out of a whole wealth of such models, and that most of the models described are now fairly old. Other names such as those of Harman, Minsky and Selfridge are associated with the building of models which have illustrated different aspects of human or organismic growth, development and intelligence. But most significant perhaps is the relative dearth of recent models which could be called "second generation" models. Such models that have appeared recently are much more "special purpose" in their design, and we might mention here the "computer controlled arm" (Paul 1972) and the tactile receptor design by Kinoshita, Aida and Mori (1972). What stands out most prominently is the need, in the development of cybernetic hardware, for a large scale model. This suggests the use of the large scale digital computer and the reasons for this are fairly obvious.

A computer may cost up to half a million pounds or more, but is universal in the sense that it is not a model of anything specific until a program is written for it. This means that you have available at a cost far beyond the reach of the normal research institute something that offers the only possible large size of model; to specifically simulate the complexities of human behaviour would be so costly and so time consuming that it is unlikely to be tackled until we have taken huge steps in simulating this intelligence and problem solving ability and the like on the computer itself. These are the reasons for supposing that, although many more models will inevitably be built dealing with different aspects of organismic development and structure, more of cybernetics in the future than the past is likely to be concentrated around the use of the digital computer and the use of theoretical, especially mathematico-statistical, models.

3.12   SUMMARY

In this chapter we have described various hardware models which one may subsume under the name cybernetics. In particular we have referred to the Ashby Homeostat, Grey Walter's tortoise and Speculatrix and Uttley's classification and conditional probability machine. We also have other models of classification and conditional probabilities and these are briefly described, and many of the hardware models of Gordon Pask are also described. Shannon's maze running machine and Deutsch's maze running machine are taken as representative of this group of hardware models. Chapman's, Stewart's, George's and Goldacre and Bean's models were also briefly described.

This chapter is aimed to illustrate by selecting a few of the better known hardware models the type of construction that has gone on in the field of cybernetics, which is primarily aimed to make clear to the student what is being achieved, on one hand, and to clarify the ideas of the scientist on the other.

CHAPTER 4

Logic, semantics and pragmatics

Argument

This chapter provides on one hand the foundation for the next chapter on automata theory, and on the other hand it provides a link between the simulation and synthesis of intelligent behaviour.

Logic (or syntax) is concerned with the basic operations of a linguistic system and thus is vital to the description of any science, while semantics relates the terms used to features of the empirical world. "London" is the name for London, and, in general, semantics is the subject which relates words to the things that words represent or denote. *Semantics* is concerned with meaning (primarily of sentences but also of words) and the use of words as labels. Semantics, as far as cybernetics is concerned, is closely bound up with natural language programming (Chapter 15) and, of course, the philosophical foundations of any science, and cybernetics in particular.

Even more general than semantics is *pragmatics*. Pragmatics is concerned with the relation between people in general and is concerned with the users of language in particular. There is a clear sense in which syntax of logic is included in semantics, which is itself included in pragmatics. Pragmatics is directly related to the cybernetic modelling of human behaviour (Chapter 10) and artificial intelligence (Chapter 13).

The word "automaton" (or "robot") is often used to describe artificial systems or artificial models of humans (or other organisms) and indeed one of the most important types of model which has been used by cyberneticians to try to simulate the function, and indeed to some extent the structure, of the human being is the set of models called finite automata. Finite automata may be variously defined, but can best be described as systems constructed according to certain rules whereby the systems may take on only a finite number of different states. In the next chapter we shall make these ideas more precise.

One way we can conceive of finite automata is as paper tape machines, as was mentioned in the first chapter. We can think of a tape as being ruled into squares and placed on rollers moving backwards and forwards, or perhaps in one direction only, beneath a scanner. Turing machines (also an example of infinite or non-finite automata) are tape automata of the two- way kind, i.e. they may move backwards or forwards under the scanner.

But let us look more carefully at *logic* before we discuss automata further, since it is from logic, by and large, that artificially intelligent systems spring. Indeed we shall make logic the subject of this chapter and follow it with a discussion of finite automata in the next chapter (Chapter 5). Logic is also necessary to an understanding of neural nets (Chapter 7).

4.1   LOGIC

In this section we shall develop formal logic, as it is sometimes called. The reason why the word "formal" is used is because certain logical relationships, such as the relationship of inference from one statement to another, depends on a purely formal relationship which exists between those statements. For example, if I say "Jack is the son of Charles", then I am saying something about a relationship between two people; it could have been between two things, so that I could say "X is to the left of Y", or "Jack is married to Betty". These are relational statements and we could say that the relation between two people could be represented by the letter R and the two people by x and y. Then we have Rxy, and it does not matter what we replace x and y by, provided they are capable of being in the relation R to each other.

What we are saying is that there is a certain relationship between two people or things and this has a form which does not depend upon the particular nature of the things, at least this is true within certain limits.

To be more specific, let us take a relation such as "to the left of" and say "Jack is to the left of Charles" or "Jean is to the left of Joan", and the sentences do not depend upon who the particular people are. What is important is simply that certain relationships "to the left of" (from some particular point of view, of course) is independent of the particular items named.

The above example brings out the main point about the *formal* nature of logic, and is important to an understanding of its basis. We shall now try to develop some part of formal logic, where formal logic applies to the development of formal propositions or statements (or sentences) drawn from a linguistic background.

Before we do this we should say that words like "term" and "proposition" will be used very frequently, and although the word "proposition" is probably familiar, the word "term" should be explained. The word "term" is equivalent to the word "class". In other words, a *"term"* is the name for some class of objects. Furthermore, we must remind ourselves that sentences or statements in English are generally capable of being split up into subject and predicate. The subject represents a *term* and the sentence in which the subject occurs will also involve a relational statement (a verb) and may, of course, represent all sorts of connectives such as *"and"*, *"or"*, etc.

One of the principal logical forms, obviously in a linguistic background, which has been fairly systematically investigated, is the *syllogism*. The *syllogism* is a form of argument where a direct inference is made from two propositions to a third proposition. We shall treat the syllogism in some detail as an example, since by its very simplicity it is easy to see how a computer program can be written to implement it.

The propositions which make up the syllogism are all of the form:

"All S is P"
"No S is P"
"Some S is P"
"Some S is not P".

Or, to give more concrete particular examples:

"All men are foolish"
"No man is foolish"
"Some men are foolish"
"Some men are not foolish".

We wish now to put different propositions of these four types together to form an argument of the kind:

If a and b then c.

Let us give an example:

If "All men are foolish"
and "Frank is a man"
then "Frank is foolish".

This is a syllogistic form of argument which allows the deduction of a conclusion from a major and minor premise.

Now it is clear that propositions or statements as we sometimes call them (and think of sentences in English) have a subject and a predicate. So that in the statement "All men are foolish", we say that "All men" is the subject and "are foolish" is the predicate. To understand the syllogistic form of argument more completely, we must now define the notion of <u>distribution</u>.

A subject is said to be *distributed* if it refers to all the possible members of some class of objects or people. As has been said, the word "term" is used to refer to the name of some class of objects or people, and now we ask the technical question as to whether it is distributed. For example, in the statement "All men are foolish", "men" (the subject) is clearly distributed because it refers to the class of all men, whereas the predicate "are foolish" is not distributed because it can refer to women, children, perhaps even dogs or cats.

To follow deductive arguments in syllogistic form, it is essential to understand the notion of distribution. Also it is vital to understand the notion of terms. In the statement, "All men are foolish", "men" and "foolish" are both terms. In the statement "Some dogs are bad-tempered", "dogs" and "bad-tempered" are both terms. So terms are words or phrases defining a class of objects or people.

It must be said again that a subject or predicate that is distributed refers to the whole of a class, or the whole of whatever a term refers to.

Look again now at the general forms of proposition:

"All S is P"
"No S is P"
"Some S is P"
"Some S is not P",

and simply classify them as having distributed subjects and predicates according to their form. So the following table applies:

Proposition	Subject	Predicate
All S is P	distributed	undistributed
No S is P	distributed	distributed
Some S is P	undistributed	undistributed
Some S is not P	undistributed	distributed

To summarise the table in general terms we say that "some or anything" is always undistributed and that when either the S or the P (i.e. subject or predicate) is negative then the predicate is always distributed.

Next we must look at the *valid* forms and *moods* of the syllogism, remembering that all syllogisms are of the form:

If X and if Y, then Z,

where X, Y and Z are statements that may take certain forms. Prior to stating these rules we must notice the use of the words "middle term".

"If Rome is in Italy   (major premise)
and I am in Rome   (minor premise)
then I am in Italy"   (conclusion) .

This is a deductive argument and clearly in syllogistic form, and the term that occurs in both the major and minor premises, but not in the conclusion ("Rome" in this case) is called the "middle term". For what follows, we use the words "general" and "particular" where by general statements we mean statements starting with the words "all" or "no"; by particular statements we mean statements starting with the word "some". We shall, it should be noticed, use single quotation marks for words and double quotation marks for terms (which may also be words) or for statements, and we shall also use double quotation marks to draw attention to somewhat ambiguous terms. Italics are normally used for emphasis.

The rules for valid syllogisms are as follows:

1) The middle term must be distributed once at least in a syllogism.

2) No term must be distributed in the conclusion which was not distributed in one of the premises.

3) You can make no inference from two negative premises, or two "particular" premises.

4) If one premise is negative (or particular), the conclusion must be negative (or particular) and vice versa.

These four rules limit the possible combinations of statements that would otherwise make up valid syllogisms. It means that we cannot permit as valid, syllogistic forms such as:

"If I am not in Rome and if Rome is not in Italy then..."

It is easy to see that no conclusion can be drawn from these two premises.

We shall not attempt to show which syllogisms are valid moods but clearly the ones we have already used, such as:

"If Rome is in Italy
and I am in Rome,
then I am in Italy"

is valid because it does not offend against any one of our four rules of validity. The same test of validity should be made by the reader on the syllogistic argument on page 46.

We have one further constant, or set of rules to apply to our argument before we can eventually be sure it is a valid syllogism. This last consideration is about *figures*, which further restricts the range of possible moods.

We know that syllogisms are deductive arguments involving three statements and each statement involves two terms. So a syllogism is of the form YX, ZY, ZX or any combination of X, Y and Z where Y (or X or Z) is the middle term. But YX, ZY and ZX is not the only form. We must supply a simple table, where Y is always the middle term, i.e.

	I	II	III	IV
Major premise	YX	XY	YX	XY
Minor premise	ZY	ZY	YZ	YZ
Conclusion	ZX	ZX	ZX	ZX

All valid moods must also be capable of being put into the form of this table of figures. If this cannot be done, even after rearranging the order of the statements but without changing the nature of the argument, the form is not syllogistic. All *valid* arguments involving just three statements are not, of course, necessarily syllogistic. The syllogism on page 46 can be seen to be of Mood I.

A further restriction occurs now so that 5 of the 24 possible valid moods which can be put into these figures are weak arguments. This means that they may be of the form:

> "If all Scots are clever and
> all clever people are brown-eyed,
> then some Scots are brown-eyed."

This is clearly a weak argument, because one could have inferred that *all* Scots are brown-eyed. No more will be said about this form of argument, although the interested reader could now work out for himself the remaining 19 valid syllogistic moods and figures. In fact, he would probably be better advised to save his efforts for the greater demands of symbolic logic that are yet to be made upon him.

We must now turn to a brief discussion of logic that takes a more mathematical or symbolic form. We shall outline next the basic principles of Boolean algebra (B^*) — or "the calculus of classes", as it is sometimes called.

We shall say that any well-defined collection of objects is a set or a class. We can thus talk of the class of all red or all green objects, the class of all polar bears, or all spoons, of all circular objects, and so on. We can represent a class by a circle and for convenience represent the whole universe of all possible classes by a rectangle. So:

This diagram represents a class of objects A, and this may, of course, be used to represent any set of objects of any colour, shape or any other property.

If we now call the complete universe of all possible classes by the number 1, we can then say that everything that is not A (A') and everything that is A, makes up the whole of the universe.

$$A.A' = 1,$$

where . means "and" and the prime sign ' means "not". So we can think of A as "all red objects" and A' as "everything that is not red". We assume, of course, that everything in the world can be described as red or not-red, and we resolve every doubt by such conventions as become necessary.

4.2   SYMBOLIC LOGIC AND EULER-VENN DIAGRAMS

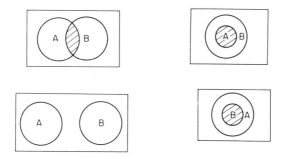

Figure 1

Let us now look explicitly at Euler-Venn diagrams, the first of which appeared above. They represent classes named *A, B, C,* ... as the areas contained within circles. So:

Figure 2

A is the class of objects such as all *red* objects, all *blue* objects, all circular objects, all women and so on.

If we represent the whole universe of all possible classes by a rectangle, we say that everything inside the rectangle, but outside the circle *A*, is called not -*A* (and written *A'*) so:

Figure 3

If we add a second class *B*, then we may have *A* overlapping *B* or not, or *A* may be included by *B*, or vice versa, as depicted in the four diagrams of Figure 1.

If we define the value 1 as representing the set of all possible classes and the value 0 as being the null set (the class with no members), and then we can write $A \cap B$ for "the overlap of *A* and *B*". So:

$$A \cap B = 0 \tag{1}$$

means "A and B do not overlap" (the third drawing of Figure 1) and:

$$A \cap B \neq 0 \tag{2}$$

means "there is some overlap between A and B" (the three different overlaps possible are shown in Figure 1). Equation (1) represents such statements as "No object can be both triangular and square at the same time", and (2) may represent some such statement as "some objects are both green and square at the same time". We can define anoth connective $\cup$, and write $A \cup B$ to mean A and B together ($A \cap B$) and A *and* B alone.

Now we can build up other logical relations involving either and or or, where we must define *and* and *or* as follows:

$$A \cdot B \tag{3}$$

means "A and B", and

$$A \vee B \tag{4}$$

means "A or B or both", so that $A \vee B = 1$ is represented in the same way as $A \cup B = 1$, then again it is the same as $A \cap B = 1$ where the overlap of A and B alone is conceived.

We can represent these basic logical formulae in what are sometimes called truth tables.

The truth table for "not" ($'$) is:

A	A'
0	1
1	0

and for "and" (.) it is:

A	B	$A \cdot B$
1	0	0
0	1	0
1	1	1
0	0	0

and for "or" (v) it is:

A	B	A v B
1	0	1
0	1	1
1	1	1
0	0	0

We can define the truth tables for v and ' (or "or" and "not") to define a new connective for material implication. By "material implication" we mean that some statements materially imply some other statements. They take the general form "If ... then ---". We say:

$$A \supset B = \text{df. } A' \text{ v } B, \tag{5}$$

where "df." means "by definition" and we write the truth table:

A	B	A ⊃ B
1	0	0
0	1	1
1	1	1
0	0	1

The reader should try and derive this truth table himself by combining the truth table of v and the truth table for '.

The combination of A and B to give $A \supset B$ is achieved by looking at the definition of $A \supset B$, which is A' v B, so we need the truth table for "or" (v), and instead of A v B, we substitute A' for A.

We can now state a postulate set to serve as an axiomatic basis for B^*, such as the following:

For any classes A, B ..., 0 belonging to Boolean algebra B^* where 1 is the universal class and 0 is the null class,

1) $A + B$ is a class belonging to B^* written $A, B \in B^*$ and also $(A + B) \in B^*$ where $\in$ means "belonging to". (+ is the same as . or "and".)

2) $A, B \in B^*$ and also $(A \times B) \in B^*$ ($\times$ is the same as v)

3) $A + 0 = A = 0 + A$

4) $A \times 0 = A = 0 \times A$

5) $A + B = B + A$

6) $A \times B = B \times A$

7) $A \times (B \times C) = (A \times B) + (A \times C)$

8) $A + (B \times C) = (A + B) \times (A + C)$

9) $A + A' = 1$ (′ is not, as before)

10) $A \times A' = 0$

11) A Boolean algebra B^* is composed of at least two classes A and B from which theorems in Boolean algebra about any number of classes may be derived.

We shall do no more than introduce these basic statements about logic at this stage, except to add that we can, if we wish, interpret the classes $A, B, ..., N$ as propositions $p . q, ..., w$ where we now change the values 0 and 1 to f and t, which stand respectively for *falsehood* and *truth*.

We can, of course, formulate other systems of logic, such as many-valued (which is not limited to the values 0 and 1) and probabilistic logics, and we can define such other operators as are needed to produce and enrich the precise languages we need.

As far as cybernetics is concerned, logic plays a very important part, since it has the necessary precision for descriptive purposes and this can be used to define a process or machine, and it clearly bears some relation to the way organisms, or certainly machines, "think". A computer operates on a logical basis and models of behaviour can be described in logical terms, whether that logic be of a precise or of a probabilistic form. We next say just a little about the propositional calculus (P), the functional calculus (F), the calculus of relations (R) and something of their relation to each other.

4.3   THE PROPOSITIONAL CALCULUS

The interpretation we place on a symbolic system may vary according to its use. Thus we can take Boolean algebra and interpret the variables as propositions rather than classes.

We need now also to make our ideas a shade more precise. One step that results from this search for precision is to say that all the rules which *formalise* our system (of symbols in this case) are really in a higher language which we call a meta-language. If this meta-language is to be formalised, then the formalisation should be carried out in a meta-meta-language which would not itself be formalised. This process can go on indefinitely, and underlines the point that however much we may formalise a system, there must remain unanalysed or non-formalised concepts, etc. underlying the formalisation. It is in this sense that all of logic, and the syntax for languages of any sort, come within the domain of semantics — which associates symbols with "reality" and which in turn is part of pragmatics which is concerned with the human beings who are thinking and communicating in the language. We shall return to this matter later, but in the meantime we must develop a brief description of our formal models.

There are many versions of the propositional calculus ($P*$) since we can have different axiom sets to start from and different rules of inference, since these are axioms stated in the meta-language of $P*$. We now describe one particular of P, which we shall call $\bar{P}$ (Church, 1944).

4.3.1   The symbols

The primitive symbols of the system are the propositional variables

$$p, q, r, \ldots$$

(with suffixes as needed), and constants

$$[\, ,] \, , \supset \, , \sim \, ,$$

which are "left bracket", "right bracket", "material implication" and "negation".

> $A, B, \ldots, N$ are meta-variables
> $(\, ,) \, , \overset{.}{\supset} \, , \psi$ are meta-constants.

In practice, we shall hardly need to use $\overset{.}{\supset}$ or ψ, but we are making the point that these symbols should be distinguished from their equivalents in the language P itself. For typographical simplicity we shall use in the few relevant cases the same symbols for constants in the meta-language as we use in $\bar{P}$ (e.g. in the formation rules).

4.3.2   The rules

A formula is said to be well-formed (wff) if it satisfies the following conditions: Any variable alone is well-formed (wf.); if both A and B are wf, so are $\sim A$ and $(A \supset B)$, and nothing is wf. other than it follows from these rules.

Examples of wff are obvious enough, so that if $\sim \sim p \supset p$ is wf, then so is $\sim (\sim \sim p \supset p)$, and if $\sim p \supset p \supset q$ is wf so is $(\sim \sim p \supset p) \supset (\sim p \supset p \supset q)$.

4.3.3   Dot convention

We should notice straight away the use of brackets in the above wff. Let us make these rules clear.

One of the axioms of $P*$ is

$$p \supset q \supset p, \tag{1}$$

where the same formula in brackets is

$$p \supset (q \supset p) \tag{2}$$

as opposed to

$$p \supset q \supset p, \tag{3}$$

which in the bracketed version is

$$(p \supset q) \supset p. \tag{4}$$

We can if necessary use : to take priority over . and .: to take priority over : and so on.

In the above example we use the notion of association to the left which means that where brackets and dots do not exist we bracket off from the left. The transposition of (3) to (4) in the above provides an example of this. We now supply one more example in going from (5) to (6) and two further examples of the use of dots for brackets going from (7) to (8) and (9) to (10).

$$p \supset p \supset p \supset p \supset p \tag{5}$$

is read as

$$((((p \supset p) \supset p) \supset p) \supset p) \tag{6}$$

and

$$p \supset p \supset : p \supset p \supset . p \supset p \tag{7}$$

is read as

$$(p \supset p) \supset ((p \supset p) \supset (p \supset p)) \tag{8}$$

and

$$p \vee : q \supset r . \equiv p . : \supset q \supset r \tag{9}$$

is read as

$$((p \vee ((q \supset r) \equiv p)) \supset (q \supset r)) \tag{10}$$

so it can be seen that the   main connective is associated with the largest number of dots.

4.3.4   Axioms

The axioms of $P*$ are

A1) $p \supset (q \supset r) \supset . p \supset q \supset . p \supset r$

A2) $p \supset . q \supset p$

A3) $\sim p \supset \sim q \supset . q \supset p$.

and it should be noticed that we use brackets mixed with dots where convenient to our purpose; we could write A1

$$p \supset . q \supset r \supset . p \supset q \supset . p \supset r,$$

where the dot replaces the left hand bracket in each case. If we had wanted to write

$$(p \supset (q \supset r)) \supset ((p \supset q) \supset (p \supset r)) \tag{11}$$

we could have written it as either

$$p \supset . q \supset r . \supset . p \supset q \supset . p \supset r$$

or

$$p \supset . q \supset r \supset : p \supset q \supset . p \supset r,$$

where we now replace the right hand bracket by a dot as well as the left one
We will now repeat the axiom set for P^* in bracket form only:

A1) $(p \supset (q \supset r) \supset (p \supset q) \supset (p \supset r))$

A2) $(p \supset (q \supset p))$

A3) $((\sim p \supset \sim q) \supset (q \supset p))$

where we obviously can omit the extreme left end and right end bracket without ambiguity.

4.3.5   Rules of inference

I1) From A and $A \supset B$, to infer B (this rule is known as *modus ponens*).

I2) From A to infer $S_C^B A$ (this rule is called *substitution* and involves the substitution of C for B at all occurences of B in A).

4.3.6   Definitions

We can introduce any number of new constants defined in terms of our basic list, e.g.

D1) $(A \not\subset B)$ $=$ df. $\sim . B \supset A$

D2) $(A \lor B)$ $=$ df. $(A \supset B) \supset B$

D3) $(A . b)$ $=$ df. $(A \not\subset B) \not\subset B$.

D2 and D3 are especially important because they represent disjunction (inclusive or) and conjunction (and) respectively, and, as before, "= df." means "defines" or "can be replaced by". Note the danger of ambiguity that may occur because a dot is used for conjunction as well as for a bracket.

Before discussing very briefly the properties of our formal axiomatic system, we shall draw attention to an alternative symbolism that is sometimes more convenient to use in the computer rendering of logical formulae — this is the so-called Polish notation.

4.3.7   Polish type notation

The Polish type equivalents of the axiom set of $P*$ are as follows:

A1)   *IpIqrIpqIpr*   (12)

A2)   *IpIqp*   (13)

A3)   *IINpNqIqp.*   (14)

We place the I (for implication and symbolised $\supset$ above) where the dot occurs to replace the left hand bracket. The new notation is easy to follow if we look again at (1) or (2) and (3) or (4). They are written in Polish notation as (13) above and

      IIpqp

respectively. To complete our examples we can write (11) as

      IIpIqrIIpqIpr.

So much for the definition of the axiom set for $P*$. We now let the rules of inference work on the axioms to produce the theorems. We shall show only one example theorem since proofs are complicated and we only show one to prepare the reader for a brief later example on theorem-proving by computer.

4.3.8   Theorem

To prove $p \supset p$

Start from A1:

$$p \supset . q \supset r \supset . p \supset q \supset . p \supset r$$

and substitute p for r i.e. S_p^r A1. This gives

$$p \supset . q \supset p \supset . p \supset q \supset . p \supset p.$$

The first part is $p \supset . \ q \supset p$, which is A2, so we use *modus ponens* (if A and $A \supset B$, then B), so that taking $A = p \supset . \ q \supset p$, then $B = p \supset q \supset p \supset . \ p \supset p$ and we have

$$p \supset q \supset . \ p \supset p.$$

We then substitute $q \supset p$ for q in this

i.e. $S^q_{q \supset p} \ p \supset q \supset . \ p \supset p$

which yields, by using A2 and *modus ponens* again, the theorem $p \supset p$.

The proving of theorems by such means is laborious and there is no guarantee of success, even by machine (Newell, Shaw and Simon, 1963; Wang, 1960), (see Chapter 14 for a further discussion) but we do not need to use such methods since there is an *algorithm*, or what we sometimes call a decision procedure, for proving theorems in P^*.

The decision procedure is as follows:

"Every theorem is a tautology and every tautology is a theorem"

By a tautology we mean that if the truth table is given for any wff in P^*, then for all combinations of t and f for each variable of the wff, the final column is always made up entirely of t's. An example will help. Just look at $p \supset p$, and we write its truth table, remembering $p \supset p = $ df. $\sim p \ v \ p$.

p	p	$\sim p \ v \ p$
f	t	t
t	f	t

Notice that only t's occur in the final column. Look now at a more complicated example.

$$\sim p \supset . \ p \supset q. \tag{15}$$

Rather than write the truth table in full, it is often easier to say what condition would make the wff false. (15) would be false only if $\sim p$ were t while $p \supset q$ was false. For $p \supset q$ to be false, p must be true, so now $\sim p$ must be false and this is not possible. In other words $\sim . \ p \supset q$ is a theorem. The reader who is doubtful of this result could write out the complete truth table.

One limitation on the propositional calculus is that it treats classes or propositions as a whole, and for some purposes we want to separate the subject from the predicate of a sentence, or the variables from the function in a functional description. This leads us to a whole group of calculi called the functional calculi. A few words will be said about these and other formal languages before we have a brief discussion of semantics and pragmatics.

4.4   OTHER FORMAL LANGUAGES

The first order functional calculus includes all of $P*$ as a part and also contains additional features. We now have individual variables.

$$x, y, ..., x_1, y_1, ..., \text{etc.}$$

and functional variables

$$F^1, G^1, ..., F^2, G^2, ..., F^3, G^3, ...,$$

where the superscript indicates the number of arguments admitted by the function. So F^2 (x,y) is a diadic functional variable. We have universal and existential operations:

$$(Ax)F(x)$$

and

$$(Ex)G(x),$$

which are read as "for all x, the function F holds" and "there is at least one x for which the function G holds". We could also, of course, have expressions such as:

$$(Ax)F^2(x,y)$$

where we say x is a *bound* and y a *free* variable.

We shall not attempt to define the formal system F, as we shall call it, but the usual rules of formation and axiom sets and rules of inference are needed, and theorems are proved in the usual way. Difficulties occur with F over the relatively complicated rules of substitution, partly because of the possibility of variables occurring in both a *free* and a *bound* state in the same wff.

We now should add that with any formal calculus, questions arise as to its *consistency, completeness,* and the *independence* of the axioms, as well as the possible existence of a decision procedure. The propositional calculus and first order functional calculus are consistent, which means you cannot prove a theorem and its negation in the same system. We say a system is complete if for every wff A, say, then either A or A' is a theorem and this would be undesirable, since we do not wish such an undiscriminating language; neither $P*$ nor F is complete. Axiom sets can be chosen such that the axioms can be shown to be independent and finally whereas $P*$ has a decision procedure which depends on the notion of a tautology, it can be shown that F has no decision procedure, nor can it have one.

These last results which are now famous should not be interpreted to mean that all parts of F have no decision procedure since many parts have, but the complete system has not.

4.5   QUANTIFICATION

Something of the significance of quantification should now be made explicit.

If one says that $3 > 2$ or $3 = 2$ or $3 < 2$, this can be written in a logically based manner as:

$$(3 > 2) \text{ v } (3 = 2) \text{ v } (3 < 2)$$

and, apart from the relative triviality of what is asserted, there is no special difficulty in making and understanding the statements.

If, however, we wish to say that every real number is either greater than, equal to or less than zero, we cannot similarly translate it as:

$$(x > 0) \text{ v } (x = 0) \text{ v } (x < 0),$$

where x stands for "every real number" and the reason is that they now simply do not assert the same thing; the symbolic version asserts that x falls entirely into one of three classes which is false and not what was intended by the verbal statement.

The correct symbolic version of the verbal statement should read:

$$(Ax) \text{ Number } ((x > 0) \text{ v } (x = 0) \text{ v } (x < 0))$$

which means "whatever real number you select it will be either greater than, equal to or less than zero".

The functional calculus uses this type of quantifier as we have seen and we can illustrate its use again by a few simple examples.

>"All women are wise" becomes
>(Aw) Woman (w is wise),

or

>"No woman is a man" becomes
>(Aw) Women $\sim$ (w is a man).

This should serve to remind us that the syllogism which we dealt with earlier is correctly located within the domain of the functional calculus and its general form is:

$$(Ax)(F(x) \supset G(x)) \supset ((Ax)(G(x) \supset H(x)) \supset (Ax)(F(x) \supset H(x))).$$

The above argument is really saying that a general statement of a form such as "$x + 3 = y$" is not a sentence, and therefore does not express a proposition. It is rather a sentence form which only becomes a sentence when we substitute particular numbers for x and y, e.g. "$2 + 3 = 5$". The notion of a variable, such as x and y above, is linguistic rather than logical.

The difficulty is that the rules of substitution (also linguistic rather than logical) are very complicated when we move into the functional calculi. This is a matter which has been given a lot of attention by logicians, and it gives rise to the question of whether or not one can build a logical system sufficiently strong to provide a foundation for mathematics. The problem has been solved, and the principal equivalent solutions have been provided by Curry (1942, 1949) and Church (1941).

Only the flavour of the method can be given here, but we will follow it up further than we have F because it seems likely to be more relevant than F to the use of logic in computing. Such a field is sometimes referred to as combinatorial logic.

4.6   COMBINATORY LOGIC

We must define first of all our operators, which are here called Combinators. We have a class of entities of which two special ones are called A and K, and there are two binary operations called "application" and "equality" and symbolized by "X" and "$=$".

We say that a string of symbols is wf. which means it names an entity if it has rank -1 and the rank of each proper leading subpart is non-negative. *Rank* is the number of X's minus the number of letters. For example, $AXXAXKK$ is a word since there are three X's and four other letters and $3-4 = -1$. Furthermore any proper leading subpart of it has non-negative rank, e.g. $AXXAXK$ has rank 0.

Now we write some postulates:

1) If $(a,b) \in C$, then $Xab \in C$ and is unique.
2) If $a \in C$ then $a = a$.
3) If $a = b$ then $b = a$.
4) If $a = b$ and $b = c$ then $a = c$.
5) If $a = b$ and $c = d$ then $Xac = Xbd$.
6) If $(a,b) \in C$ and $Xac = Xbc$ for all $c \in C$, then $a = b$.
7) $(A,K) \in C$.
8) If $(a,b,c) \in C$ then $Aabc = acXbc$.

The operator XKa when applied to an entity b yields the constant result a. We can write I for AKK, B for A/KAK, and so on as necessary. This allows us to derive simple theorems, e.g.

T1) $Ia = a$

$Ia = AKKa \; (I = AKK)$
$\quad = KaXKa \; (Aabc = acXbc)$
$\quad = a \;\; (Ka \text{ applied to any entity gives } a)$

So $Ia = a$

T2) $Ba = AXKa$

$Ba = AXKAKa$
$\quad = XKAaXKa$
$\quad = a/Ka$

The purpose of this is to provide a progressively clearer description of a system *without* the use of functions. I is clearly the identity operator, and so we can derive other operators B, C, ... etc. which perform the same role as various functions. Indeed we can build up in this way a powerful calculus without the accompanying problems of complex substitution. The best known version of this is the calculus of lamda conversion but we shall not try to derive that here. We shall merely note that it has come in for a great deal of attention from workers in the computing sciences.

We look briefly now at another calculus called the calculus of relations (R).

4.7   THE CALCULUS OF RELATIONS (R)

It is clearly possible to regard any primitive operation in the calculus of classes (Boolean algebra or the propositional calculus) as a relation. We could write, for example, any of the following equivalent forms:

$$a \cap b = a.b = aAb = Aab$$
$$A \cup b = avb = a0b = 0ab$$
$$\sim a = a' = Nb$$
$$a \cup b' = a \supset b = aIb = Iab,$$

and so on.

We can also think of a function $f(x)$ as a relation between an individual variable and its equivalent functional variable, and we could easily write it in the form xmf, xMf or Mxf. So R represents a convenient alternative form for writing formulae without the obvious need for parentheses. The notation could be further simplified by placing the operators to the left of the wf. strings.

However, we do not eliminate the need for quantifiers by the use of R; to do this we should need to use a combinatorial logic.

A development of the calculus of relations leads to relations between relations. A typical example is the relative product $R|S$, where

$$(R|S)\,xy = (Ea)\,(R(x,a).S(a,y)).$$

Note the need for the existential operator in the definition.

Relations may have all the usual properties of being *symmetric, reflexive, transitive* and the like, so that if, for example:

$$Rxy = Ryx$$

we say the relationship is transitive in R. Here x and y could be interpreted as "Alex" and "Ian" where R is the relation "... is the brother of ---". If R was the relation "... is the father of ---" then the relation R would be assymetrical and

$$Rxy \neq Ryx$$

or

$$Rxy \rightarrow \sim Ryx = NRyx.$$

If we take the relative product of R and R, e.g. "... is a cousin of a cousin ---" then we can introduce a convenient shorthand and write

$$R|R = R^2$$

R^{-1} is such that $RR^{-1} = I$.

We can then write such powers as

$$(R^{-1})^2 = (R^2)^{-1} = R^{-1}|R^{-1}$$

$$R^3 = R^2|R$$

and so on.

From the point of view of a descriptive language, R is particularly convenient, and it may be simply conjoined with probabilities in one form or another to provide a description of empirical facts under conditions of uncertainty. Indeed since any empirical statement is uncertain, probabilities are implicit in them.

It is perhaps worth mentioning that much of mathematical logic has been developed as a foundation for mathematics and for logical systems capable of providing an analysis of natural language and its logical entailments. In thinking of empirical descriptions we are considering mathematical logic in a somewhat different capacity. The reason now for its precision is not only to tighten our descriptions (Woodger, 1937, 1939) but also to provide a formalism for easy use on a computer. The ease of the use stems partly from a close resemblance that exists between mathematical logic and computer languages (see Chapter 8).

It is obvious that we are not talking about mathematical logic for the sake of mathematicians, but for cyberneticians, and for them it is no more than an introductory way. Let us now move on to a discussion of semantics and pragmatics.

4.8   SEMANTICS AND PRAGMATICS

By semantics we mean the science that connects symbols to their referents. "Chicago" refers to Chicago. When we wish to refer to the word "Chicago" we write it in quotes and when we wish to refer to the city of Chicago, we write it without quotes.

Words are not the same as the things which words represent and semantics is concerned with precisely this major point (Carnap, 1937, 1952, 1943, 1958; Korzybski, 1933). It may be obvious that a pencil is not the same as the word "pencil" which is used as a label to refer to it, but this becomes much less obvious and more difficult to remember when we use words like "fundamental", "relation", etc., which may not have a simple physical object as its referent. The implications of this vital subject should be borne in mind whenever any discussion is taking place on any matter at all (George, 1963).

Here however we are only concerned to point out that sets of symbols can be used to describe something else only when some association is set up between the symbols and the something else. Formally one may say we mean "x" to stand for X. We name this ship "Queen Elizabeth" etc. We could have formal rules of designation so that we have:

1)   "Chicago" *des.* Chicago.
2)   "port" *des.* All places with sea or water adjacent and where ships may be harboured.

and so on.

We see immediately that such semantic rules, or rules of designation, may be complicated when they refer to classes of objects, as opposed to merely naming an individual object. An individual is named, as it were, with a label and although the referents may have hazy boundaries, generally speaking one finds it relatively easy to see the limits on the referent. When we refer to a class of objects like "all ports" or "all pens", etc., we have to try and overlook certain differences and emphasize certain similarities; the problem is as to where one should draw the line.

In any event, the field of semantics is concerned with the interpretation of formal symbolic systems. We want to say, for example, that the symbol "1" means the same as "one", "2" means the same as "two", and so on.

This whole matter can also be thought of in the context of a conversation between people and this can include the behavioural reactions of the people concerned. This is the field called pragmatics, and we shall be discussing pragmatics (Morris, 1946; George, awaiting publication), semantics and syntax in more detail in Chapter 15, prior to a discussion of programming natural language ability on a digital computer.

4.9 SUMMARY

This chapter has dealt with formal logic. It has described the rules which govern the use of the syllogism, which is one of the simplest and best known forms of logical argument.

Valid syllogisms such as "Paris is in France and I live in Paris, therefore I live in France" has mood I, and satisfies all the rules about having a properly distributed middle term (Paris) and so on.

From formal logic which links directly with language, we go to symbolic forms that may be linked with ordinary language or mathematics or any interpretation at all. Here we met Boolean algebra, the propositional calculus, and saw something of the different notation and different uses to which such formal logical models could be put.

All of this needs to be thought of by the cybernetician as essential to his logical thinking and providing by automatic (or machine) theorem proving to be part of the subject matter of artificial intelligence. Logic is closely associated with ordinary language by way of semantics and pragmatics, each of which plays an important part in cybernetic thinking.

CHAPTER 5

Finite automata

Argument

Finite automata are developments of logical systems. They were devised in the first instance primarily, as in the case of Turing Machines, to provide a definition of an algorithm within mathematics and then in turn to be used for defining the notions involved in "effective computability".

Cyberneticians are interested in automata mainly because the human being can be regarded, in a highly abstract way, as a finite automaton. The properties necessary to his effectiveness as a problem solver and thinker, as well as a computer, can then be assessed in some measure.

The type of automata which have been most frequently investigated by cyberneticians are those of the logical or neural net type which we discuss in a later chapter; they are, however, equivalent to the tape automata discussed in this chapter.

5.1 INTRODUCTION

What we have said about logic in the last chapter leads naturally to a consideration of automata, since a Boolean algebra such as B^* is capable of being described in terms of an algorithm, and an algorithm is, in effect, an automaton.

We can think of automata as tape machines as described in Chapter 1, and we can think of the automaton as composed of a reader and a tape ruled into squares and capable of having symbols on each square. The automaton scans the squares one at a time, and as a result we say it generates or proves theorems, performs computations or solves problems.

The field of automata theory has now a long and important history. Such methods were used to prove theorems about the formations of mathematics and lie at the foundation of what is known to be *computable.*

In recent years we have come to consider automata with many different tapes, and with tapes that go both left to right and right to left, or tapes that go one way only.

The upshot of much of this work has been of purely mathematical importance but one kind of automaton has been of special cybernetic interest; these automata are called *neural nets* and will be described in the next chapter but one.

In this chapter we shall now describe automata in more general terms and subsequently we shall consider particular interpretations of some of these automata. The situation here is exactly the same as it is with formal calculi and their interpretation, through semantic rules, as descriptive systems.

5.2   AUTOMATA THEORY

We shall now discuss a version of finite state machines; we are assuming the word "machine" is now sufficiently understood for our purpose, and will not discuss it further. We are concerned with a machine (model or black box are adequate alternative names which are sometimes used) that is interacting with an environment. A stimulus or input to the machine (M) is a response or output from the environment (E) and vice versa.

We need now to distinguish more precisely between a deterministic and a non-deterministic machine. A *deterministic* machine, and these are the ones we are mainly concerned with, is defined so that its output, at time $t + 1$, $R(t + 1)$ is determined by the input at t, and the previous history of the machine.

We can write this:

$$R(t + 1) = F(H(t), S(t)), \tag{1}$$

where H is the previous history and S is the input. F is some function relating the two to the output. This and the following descriptions are alternatives to the definitions supplied in Chapter 2.

A non-deterministic machine is one whose output is *not* determined by the previous input and its history. A particular kind of non-deterministic machine which is of special interest is one where, for example, the input and history determine the probability of some response. This last type of machine is called *probabilistic*.

The internal state (Q) of the machine is defined as being dependent upon its previous internal state and on the previous input. We write this:

$$Q(t + 1) = G(Q(t), S(t)). \tag{2}$$

G is some function relating the previous state and the previous input.

We can further distinguish between automata that can *grow* (and are potentially infinite) and *fixed* automata which includes virtually all those that have been referred to so far. It seems that automata that can grow but cannot do so beyond some specified size can do no more than an automaton that is fixed. We shall call these last automata *growth* automata, and the potentially infinite ones we shall call *growing* automata. Turing machines can be thought of as being either "growth" or "growing" automata.

It should be noted in passing that when we say that a growth automaton can do no more than a fixed automaton we are thinking in terms of computations, but this does not mean that, from a psychologist's or neurophysiologist's point of view, for example, growth automata are of no interest. There is some good reason to suppose the brain comes precisely into this group.

We can further classify automata as *continuous* or *discrete* (McNaughton, 1961); they can also be classified as *synchronous* or *non-synchronous* according to whether or not their input and output history can be described completely as occurring during certain discrete moments of time.

In general, we shall say that automata are devices of finite size at any particular time such that the defined output is a function of what has happened at the defined input. Our equations (1) and (2) make this concept more precise.

We shall later say something about infinite-state machines and this naturally leads to a discussion of Turing machines and infinite automata, and the closely associated matters of computability and recursive functions. This is the domain *par excellence* of the mathematician and metamathematician. The results however would seem to have importance for all cyberneticians, whether their interest is in computers, physiology or social problems.

To return now to *finite automata,* we would remind the reader that our brief description of these systems is meant only as a general summary. There is no intention of dealing with mathematical proofs, although references will be given to some of the more important proofs. Much of the mathematical foundation of the theory can be found in the following references (Davis, 1958, 1965; Minsky, 1967; Arbib, 1965; Rogers, 1966) for those who are especially interested.

The key notion of a finite automaton is that by its present and future behaviour only some finite number of classes of possible histories can be distinguished. These histories are what we have called the "internal states" (q_1, q_2, ... q_n) of the machine; and for "distinguished" we might have used the word "recognised".

Let us try and be clear about the recognition of a machine's history. Before doing so however, let us follow Minsky (1967) and describe some representations of such nets. The first is a simple tabular form where we represent our two defining functions F and G.

A simple "memory machine" has the following definition:

		State	
G		q_0	q_1
	s_0	q_0	q_1
input	s_1	q_1	q_1

	State	
F	q_0	q_1
s_0	r_0	r_1
s_1	r_0	r_1

input

and this same automaton can be represented by a state-transition diagram as follows:

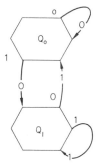

So that given input 1 (at base of arrow) in state q_0 (or Q_0) the hexagon, the output is 0 (written on the arrow itself), and the new state is q_1 (or Q_1). We could write this same description in the form of a set of quadruples:

$$
\begin{array}{cccc}
q_0 & 1 & 0 & q_1 \\
q_0 & 0 & 0 & q_0 \\
q_1 & 1 & 1 & q_1 \\
q_1 & 0 & 1 & q_0
\end{array}
$$

Where the first q gives one state and the last q_1 gives the next state, and in between occurs the input and then the output. We can also rewrite our tabular description more simply as:

	State	
G	q_0	q_1
0	q_0	q_0
1	q_1	q_1

input

		State	
F		q_0	q_1
	0	0	1
input			
	1	0	1

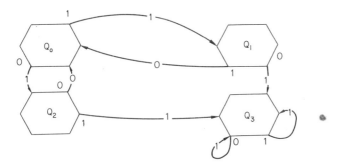

The quadruples are as follows:

q_0	0	1	q_2
q_0	1	1	q_1
q_1	1	1	q_0
q_1	0	1	q_3
q_2	1	1	q_3
q_2	0	0	q_0
q_3	0	1	q_3
q_3	1	1	q_3

Now if this machine is to avoid the "deadend" of state q_3 from which it cannot escape then it must, if started at q_0, have an input tape that carried to q_1 or q_2 and then back to q_0. So 1 at q_0 will send it to q_1 which *must* have a 1 to send it back to q_0. Thus it is that for an 0 to appear on the output, the inputs must all be in pairs of 0's or 1's. There is, of course, nothing to exclude the possibility of going to q_3 and this can be achieved (again presuming we start at q_0) if we started with inputs 10 or 01. These would take us to q_3, *via* q_1 and q_2 alternatively.

From this automaton, it is easy to see that if at any time t, we in fact get an output 0, which can only occur in states q_1 or q_2, then we can say that the history of the automaton is a set of pairs of either 0's or 1's.

It is in this sense that automata can distinguish or recognise certain features of its previous history (its previous internal states). It obviously cannot do the job completely since our automaton cannot distinguish between such histories as (0000110011) and (1100001100).

We should remind the reader again that the *theory* of automata is abstract and is concerned with the logical and mathematical consequences of precisely formed concepts. In fact, while this is true, we can at the same time make the point that the full adder is a finite automaton, and its realisation or synthesis is precisely the full adder used in digital computers. This sort of relationship is one reason for our discussion of automata. The others are: (1) the intrinsic mathematical and logical interest and (2) the significance of the results for brain and behaviour models.

This last comment is a reminder that we should distinguish between the structure and behaviour of an automaton. The structure is precisely what we would expect — the anatomy of the system, while its behaviour is the observable change of activity with respect to its input and output. Clocks are just the sort of black box we have here in mind. They may have many different mechanisms (structures or anatomies) but their behaviour is equivalent. At least to put it more carefully, there are whole sets of clocks with equivalent behaviour, however different their anatomy.

There are two further points which are next worthy of mention: (1) an isolated finite automaton, (2) the question of initial states.

It can be shown that if an automaton is isolated from all external stimuli, it will fall into a perfectly periodic pattern of behaviour. This may take some time but must sooner or later occur. This is the sort of result that is of interest when considering the experiments that have been carried out in keeping people in isolation (as far as is practically possible) for periods of time (Heron *et al.*, 1955) when their behaviour seems to lose its usual critical faculty and becomes increasingly repetitive.

The second point seems to have no special consequences for behaviour. It is the fact that some automata have not assumed initial states — in other words it is assumed that they have in infinite past. Such an assumption is biologically unrealistic and must not (Kleene, 1951) be used other than to simplify, as it might, problems of neural modelling; it is a device comparable to the use of complex numbers in the description of electrical circuits.

We shall in fact return to this problem when we consider that class of automata called neural nets (Chapter 6). E. F. Moore (1956) considers automata with an infinite past in his discussion of whether such automata are equivalent to each other. Moore, in what he describes as *Gedanken* experiments, selects inputs for machines which are equivalent if in return they produce the same outputs.

The point about Moore's work which is worthy of mention here, is that because his automata do not have an initial state his results are distinctly more complicated. So what might be a simplifying condition for some purposes seems to be a complicating condition for others, and perhaps this is especially so in the general theory of automata. We shall not though in this book generally be concerned with either "isolated" or "infinite past" automata.

5.3   SOME RESULTS IN AUTOMATA THEORY

We shall now give a different sort of definition of finite automata in terms of set theory and provide a few results that have been discovered by people working from this point of view.

McNaughton (1961) defines finite automata as follows:

It is an ordered quintuple $\langle S, I, U, f, g \rangle$ where each of the five items is itself an abstract mathematical entity. S, I and U are finite sets of abstract entities called elements; f is a function that maps SxI into S, and g is a function that maps SxI into U. Thus for every element s in S and i in I, $f(s,i)$ is an element of S and $g(s,i)$ is an element of U.

S is here the set of states, I is a set of input values, U is a set of output values, f is a transition function that defines the next state given the input value and present state (the same as our G of 1.1) and g (same as F of 1.1) defines the output value given the input value and present state.

It is of interest to compare the above definition with a slightly differently worded but equivalent definition due to Arbib (1965). A finite automaton is a quintuple $A = (I, O, S, \lambda, \delta)$ where I is a finite set of inputs, O is a finite set of outputs, S is a finite set of internal states, and where λ $SxI \rightarrow S$ is the next-state function and δ $SxI \rightarrow O$ is the next output function. Here λ is the same as f before (our G) and δ is the same as g before (our F). Otherwise the word "ordered" is omitted now and indeed the order of variables is different but they are directly given their interpretation in automata terms. These definitions obviously amount to the same thing, and there are many others which differ slightly in wording but are also essentially the same. To all these definitions, the usual point applies; they are abstract and we must not confuse the abstract definitions and theorems with the interpretation we place upon them.

Let us look now at some results for tape automata. We can think of tapes as being two-way, as in the Turing machine, or one-way; we can also think of them as being single-tape or multi-tape.

Rabin and Scott (1959) suggested and Shepherdson (1959) proved that for every two-way automaton there exists an equivalent one-way automaton. The equivalent one-way automaton is usually more complicated and needs more internal states. The essential and perhaps fairly obvious condition for the equivalence is that a one-way automaton must carry with it all the information it will subsequently need, precisely because it cannot go back.

If we think of human beings as one-way automata, where the direction is through time, then it saying, in effect, that the human must have a memory store if they are to be capable of dealing with a certain class of activities. Memoryless robots, so-called, have been discussed (Culbertson, 1956) but although they can exhibit a degree of apparent intelligence, there are serious and obvious limitations on their abilities.

Rabin and Scott (1964) have shown that two-tape and multi-tape automata which are one-way are equivalent to single-tape one-way automata in the computations they can perform, although once again the methods used may be different.

Two-way two-tape automata (Rabin and Scott 1964) have no decision procedure and we have no way of deciding whether the set of tapes (computations) it can accept are empty or not.

Another comparison is between real-time and general (non real-time) automata. This is a field which has been extensively researched by Yamada (1962).

Yamada defines a divice which is capable of a limited number of operations at any time on a fixed number of tapes. But again the general finding does not seem to be of great theoretical importance, since for every set of operations done by a real time automaton we can always devise an equivalent general automaton, and vice versa. Exactly the same argument applies, of course, to digital computers. Everything that can be done on-line can be done off-line and vice versa.

Yet another kind of automaton is called a *linear-bounded* automaton (Myhill, 1960). It is an automaton which is two-way and can do what a Turing machine can do — it can write and erase symbols on tape. This type of automaton is not strictly finite, but rather potentially infinite, since the tape which is, in effect, an additional memory store can be made as long as is necessary to compute the problem. It is because the amount of memory is a linear function of the length of the problem that the title "linear-bounded automaton" was bequeathed it. From the cybernetic point of view such automata may prove just as interesting as finite automata, but this chapter is intended to be limited to finite automata. In any event few results have as yet been achieved by linear-bounded automata.

It is possible that a domain of application for linear-bounded automata can be found in modern linguistics studies and we shall bear this in mind in our later discussion of natural language programming (Chapter 15).

McNaughton (1961) in his discussion of finite automata describes the relation between automata theory and cybernetics in the following terms:

It might seem that cybernetics should be identical to the theory of automata. However, Wiener's (1948) theory is based on probability and statistics, and especially on the statistical theory of communication. The theory of automata, as should be clear ... is based on logic and discrete mathematics.

McNaughton accepts the fact that the two purposes are different, but in this and in the above quotation he seems to be taking a narrow view of cybernetics. Cybernetics is concerned with the modelling of natural and artificial systems, especially those concerned with intelligent behaviour, varying from the simplest learning to the most complicated human thinking. It is also rather especially concerned with the structure and function of nervous systems. It is here we find the beginnings of the neural net type of automata.

That the two approaches are closely related is clear, and they may indeed, at some later stage, become parts of some more general theory. In the meantime we would expect cyberneticians to take the closest possible interest in the development of automata theory.

We shall cite one last example of results derived from automata theory that have a direct interest for cyberneticians.

Automata theory has tackled the problem of immortality. The problem so tackled is stated as follows. We have a machine that is capable of replacing all its parts as they wear out. Each part has a probable life expectancy and the problem as posed by E. F. Moore (McNaughton 1961) is to construct a machine that has a greater life expectancy than any of its parts.

The answer given is as follows: If a machine has no more than w parts and the probability of survival of each part is greater than some constant k (>0), then the probability that all the parts will fail at once at some time is at least $1-(1-k)^n$, so sooner or later all parts will fail together.

Since it is an abstract theory, we may take it seriously to the extent of saying that is does not, as McNaughton suggests, follow "that no individual biological organism can live for ever", since it does not necessarily follow that the failure of all the parts causes death. The sensing process which is presumed to be vital can be made external, if necessary to the system, and artificial or new parts introduced

This sort of result although theoretically interesting is in fact irrelevant to cybernetics.

5.4   CURRENT RESEARCH IN AUTOMATA THEORY

In this section we shall say nothing about current research in automata theory *per se*, since this would entail a deeper introduction than this chapter has supplied and would be of primary interest to those whose interests are of a mathematical or meta-mathematical kind. In fact, the whole field of automata theory has proliferated to such an extent in the last few years that all sorts of different automata are now under consideration, some of which refer to linguistic problems and which directly relate to our discussion of Chapter 15. One recent summary of one important aspect of automata theory which will be of relevance to those interested in this more mathematical approach is supplied by Arbib (1969).

One development in automata theory which has cybernetic relevance is that of Varshavsky (1969). He has followed up the work of Tsetlin on the control processes of complex systems. This involves the study of the interaction of collections of automata who use strategies and play games against each other. In particular this bears on the work of self-reproducing automata (von Neumann, 1966) and is also related to the travelling salesman problem and the synchronization problem such as is involved in the Firing Squad problem. The development of the theory, although referring explicitly to automata, is also developed in a formal mathematical manner.

A recent attempt to develop automata which have brainlike properties is due to Aleksander and Fairhurst (1972). They start from an E. F. Moore (1964) type of automaton and hope to describe such activities as learning, adaptation, recognition, recall and types of response activity. They use automata theory in precisely the way one would expect from a cybernetician, by laying out a precisely defined functional framework which provides a basis for experimentation.

Aleksander and Fairhurst proceed in a manner analogous to those using the neural net approach by positing an electronic logical synthesis of their automata. They then proceed to define cognitive activities in terms of associative action within the cells, and they establish a framework for further brain-like studies. This approach seems likely to prove most fruitful as an alternative framework and description to neural nets which we will discuss in Chapter 7.

This chapter has discussed elementary automata theory as represented by various categories of formal systems. Automata have been shown to be deterministic or non-deterministic, some of the latter being probabilistic. There can also be fixed (pre-wired) or growth automata, and they may be synchronous or non-synchronous, continuous or discrete. Furthermore, as in the case of E. F. Moore, all automata do not have initial states; this can be a source of considerable additional complication.

Various definitions of finite automata are given, all of which are more or less equivalent, and some attention is given to recent research on the use of automata for cybernetic types of research.

It has been made clear that automata theory has, in recent years, become such a vast subject — much of it of purely mathematical interest — that any attempt to summarise all aspects of the current state of the subject is impossible.

CHAPTER 6

Infinite automata and mathematics

Argument

This chapter is concerned with infinite automata, which means primarily it is concerned with Turing Machines and Universal Turing Machines.

The discussion also inevitably bears upon axiomatic systems in general and their various properties of decision procedures, completeness, consistency, etc. It must be remembered here that an axiomatic system with a decision procedure is, in an obvious sense, a "machine", while any axiomatic system can be thought of as a "machine" in the wider sense in which cybernetics is interested.

Recursive functions also appear at this point and we develop in some depth one aspect of the general cybernetic argument of Chapter 1; this is where mathematics and cybernetics meet.

6.1 METAMATHEMATICS

In a sense we are dealing with primarily the world of the mathematician, or the meta-mathematician, although not from his point of view. For this reason we shall not pursue this subject in the same depth as some of our other topics. There exist many excellent books that have already dealt with these matters (Kleene, 1952; Rogers, 1966; Minsky, 1967). We shall, however, try to outline some of the main results both for their own interest and also because some of the concepts and notions involved bear on the problems of cybernetics; it is, in a sense, another example of the mathematician's approach to cybernetics.

What can machines do? Here we use the word "machine" in the sense of something mechanical. We know something of the limitations of finite machines. If we make our machines infinite in memory, say, can they solve more problems? Are there still limitations on what infinite machines can do?

There is certainly a sort of limitation introduced by our ability to describe our problems sufficiently precisely. If we cannot precisely describe a process, we cannot be certain of carrying out the operation involved, since we cannot, as we might with a human being, ask him to improvise or to learn from experience. This does *not* mean that we cannot build a *machine* to do these things, but we are in *this chapter* considering the concept of machines in a narrower context of the more conventional automatic operation.

We have discussed *effective procedures* (decision procedures or algorithms) and we know roughly what is entailed by them and we know that Turing (1936) (and most others since him) believed that what a Turing machine can do (or compute) is the same as what is "machine-like. This argument applies especially to the theses of Church (1936) and Post (1943). We shall now look briefly at the notion of Turing Machines and then Universal Turing Machines.

6.2   TURING MACHINES

We can think of a Turing Machine as being made up of a tape ruled off into squares (see Fig. 1, Page 13) and capable of writing a symbol onto a square, reading a symbol from a square and moving either left or right along the tape. There is also the program for the automaton, which is the set of quadruples or quintuples which define as a function of the initial set of symbols on the tape (the input) the operation or computation of the machine. At the end we are left with the output which are the symbols remaining on the tape after its operations are completed.

We assume that the Turing Machine is capable of being in only a finite number of distinct internal states and that the next operation at any time is a function of its internal configuration at the moment and the finite expression which then appears on the tape. Following our earlier definitions of machines, we can define a Turing Machine more formally as follows:

$$Q(t+1) = G(Q(t), S(t))$$
$$R(t+1) = F(Q(t), S(t))$$
$$D(t+1) = D(Q(t), S(t))$$

As before, G is some function relating the previous state and the previous input, while F is a function relating the same two functions as G. G determines the change of state as before while the output R writes on the square it is scanning; this writing may include over-printing the symbol already there, *and* also moving the tape either to the left or to the right. The new function D simply tells us which way the tape moves.

The set $S_0, S_1, ..., S_n$ is the alphabet of input symbols, $r_0, r_1, ..., r_m$ are output symbols and $q_0, q_1, ..., q_p$ are internal states.

The machine so far described is finite, but can be thought of as "potentially infinite" in that should it be about to run off either end of the tape, more tape can always be added. Nevertheless, at any particular time the amount of tape is finite.

Formal mathematical description of Turing Machines are available in Turing (1936), Post (1943), Kleene (1952), Davis (1958), Arbib (1965), and Minsky

(1967). We are not concerned here with the various different notations which are all equivalent to each other; but we show two of them briefly as an example of the differences.

Davis talks about quadruples

$$q_i S_j S_k q_l$$
$$q_i S_j R \; q_l$$
$$q_i S_j L \; q_l$$
$$q_i S_j q_k q_l$$

which imply that given the internal state q_i and scanning symbol S_j we can either expect to overprint S_k, move right, move left or in the case of the last quadruple ask, in effect, a question as to whether a particular integer n, say, belongs to a set such as A. Turing Machines which include this fourth quadruple are called Interrogation Machines. Those that exclude it are called Simple Turing Machines.

The above quadruple notation, in Minsky's terms, become quintuples:

$$(q_i, S_j, Q_{ij}, S_{ij}, d_{ij}.)$$

The first pair are identical with Davis' first pair, and the new state symbol is q_{ij} and the new symbol scanned is S_{ij} and d_{ij} gives the direction of movement . We shall feel free to use either of these two notations, but will generally use the first (Davis, 1958).

We next add some formal definitions:

An *instantaneous description* A is an expression containing only one state symbol and contains neither R nor L. It must have at least one symbol to the right of the state symbol.

A *tape expression* contains only one alphabetic symbol and we shall write the number of 1's. For example, $6 = 111111$ or $4 = 11S_4 S_5 S_6 11$. All other symbols now apart from 1 are being ignored.

A *computation* on a Turing Machine Z is a finite sequence $A_1, A_2, ..., A_p$ of instantaneous descriptions where $A_1 \rightarrow A_2$, where $\rightarrow$ means "yields" or "leads to". A_p is the terminal instantaneous description. Now we give a simple example of a Turing operation:

Purpose   Starting at the left end of the tape the purpose is to eliminate S_3 and S_5 and replace them by S_2 and S_4 and then return to the left end of the tape. The quadruples are:

$$q_0\ S_0\ R\ q_0$$
$$q_0\ S_1\ R\ q_0$$
$$q_0\ B\ R\ q_1$$
$$q_1\ S_2\ R\ q_2$$
$$q_2\ S_2\ R\ q_2$$
$$q_2\ S_3\ S_2\ q_2$$
$$q_2\ S_4\ R\ q_2$$
$$q_2\ S_5\ S_4\ q_3$$
$$q_3\ B\ L\ q_3$$
$$q_3\ S_4\ L\ q_3$$
$$q_3\ S_2\ L\ q_3$$
$$q_3\ B\ L\ q_3$$
$$q_3\ S_1\ L\ q_3$$

The successive instantaneous descriptions (one giving rise to the next) that are used to carry out our simple purpose above are as follows:

$$q_0 S_0 S_1\ B\ S_2 S_3 S_4 S_5\ B \to S_0 q_0 S_1\ B\ S_2 S_3 S_4 S_5\ B \to$$
$$S_0 S_1 q_0\ B\ S_2 S_3 S_4 S_5\ B \to S_0 S_1 B\ q_1 S_2 S_3 S_4 S_5\ B \to$$
$$S_0 S_1 B\ S_2 q_2 S_3 S_4 S_5\ B \to S_0 S_1 B\ S_2 q_2 S_2 S_4 S_5\ B \to$$
$$S_0 S_1 B\ S_2 S_2 q_2 S_4 S_5\ B \to S_0 S_1 B\ S_2 S_2 S_4 q_2 S_5\ B \to$$
$$S_0 S_1 B\ S_2 S_2 S_4 q_2 S_4\ B \to S_0 S_1 B\ S_2 S_2 q_3 S_4 S_4\ B \to$$
$$S_0 S_1 B\ S_2 q_3 S_2 S_4 S_4\ B \to S_0 S_1 B\ q_3 S_2 S_2 S_4 S_4\ B \to$$
$$S_0 S_1 q_3\ B S_2 S_2 S_4 S_4\ B \to S_0 q_2 S_1\ B\ S_2 S_2 S_4 S_4\ B \to$$
$$q_3 S_0 S_1\ B S_2 S_2 S_4 S_4\ B.$$

In the above computation the successive positions of the scanner on the tape are shown by the movement of the state symbol in each successive instantaneous description.

6.3   TURING MACHINES FUNCTION

We should remind the reader that by a *function* we mean something that depends in a certain way on something else. The amount of rainfall is a function of the volume of raincloud; the golf score you make is a function of your ability at golf. In mathematics we tend to talk of a function as a rule, whereby for a given argument you can compute the value of the function for that argument, e.g. If $x = 2, y = 3, F(x,y) = x^2 + y = 7$. We have already seen in our discussion of logic roughly what is meant by a function, so together with what we have said above, this should be sufficiently clear for our purpose.

As far as Turing Machines are concerned, we can think of a function as being defined by the Turing Machine's behaviour. The argument occurs on the tape before computation starts and the value of the function for that argument is what is left when the computation is complete.

We now show two examples of Turing Machines computations. Our first example is the trivial one of subtracting one number from another. Let us take 5 - 2. So the function $f(x,y)$ to be computed 5 - 2 and the quadruples needed are as follows:

$$q_1 \ 1 \ B \ q_1$$
$$q_1 \ B \ R \ q_2$$
$$q_2 \ 1 \ R \ q_2$$
$$q_2 \ B \ R \ q_3$$
$$q_3 \ 1 \ R \ q_4$$
$$q_3 \ B \ L \ q_9$$
$$q_4 \ 1 \ R \ q_4$$
$$q_4 \ B \ L \ q_5$$
$$q_8 \ 1 \ B \ q_5$$
$$q_5 \ B \ L \ q_6$$
$$q_6 \ 1 \ L \ q_7$$
$$q_7 \ 1 \ L \ q_7$$
$$q_7 \ B \ L \ q_8$$
$$q_8 \ 1 \ L \ q_8$$
$$q_8 \ B \ R \ q_1$$
$$q_8 \ B \ L \ q_9$$
$$q_8 \ 1 \ R \ q_8$$

$$a_1 = q_1 \quad (111111, 111)$$
$$= q_1 \quad (111111 \ B111)$$

where the number is initially represented by one more 1 than occurs in the actual number e.g. 1 is represented by 11 and 2 by 111.

So if q_1 starts at the left end digit and we get the following set of I.D.'s:

$$q_1 111111B111B$$
$$q_1 B11111B111B$$
$$B \ q_2 11111B111B$$

$B \, 1 \, q_2 1111B111B$

$B11q_2 111B111B$

$B111 \, q_2 11B111B$

$B1111q_2 1B111B$

$B11111q_2B111B$

$B11111Bq_3 111B$

$B11111B1q_4 11B$

$B11111B11q_4 1B$

$B11111B111q_4 B$

$B11111B11q_5 1B$

$B11111B11q_5 BB$

$B11111B1q_6 1BB$

$B11111Bq_7 11BB$

$B11111q_7 B11BB$

— — —

and this cycle is repeated until only 111 is left on the tape.

Our second example is a simple proof as opposed to a numerical example. The successor function is simply:

$$S(x) = x + 1$$

with particular examples such as $S(8) = 9$, $S(11) = 12$, and so on. The successor function plays a very important part in the foundations of mathematics and is by the nature of things particularly easy to show as being computable.

Proof: Take a Turing Machine Z and let $q_1 \, \bar{m}$, which is the initial instantaneous description to be terminal for all m. Z needs only one quadruple:

$$q_1 BBq_1$$

and then for $\langle q_1 \, \bar{m} \rangle$ we have output $m + 1$.

We now define a Turing computable function $f(x)$ as that function which can be computed by some Turing Machine T; the tape of T is initially blank except for the conventional representation of the argument x, and where the value of $f(x)$ is the number of 1's that remain on the tape when T stops.

The reference to 1's as the form of the output is a reference to the representation of numbers by their total number of 1's, e.g. 6 = 111111, or when stated conventionally as an argument 6 = 1111111.

Let us look at one more example of a Turing Machine computation. It is the identity function.

Let $I(x) = x$; we must then show that $I(x)$ is computable. Z can consist of the single quadruple $q_1 \, 1 \, B \, q_1$. Then we have;

$$q_1\, \bar{n} = q_1\, 1\, 1^n$$

which yields

$$q_1\, B\, 1^n$$

and this is terminal, hence

$$\varphi\, Z^{(n)} = \langle q_1\, B\, 1^n \rangle = n.$$

The important point that Turing Machine demonstrated is that there exists a Turing machine that can, subject to conventions of input representation, comput any Turing computable function whatever, and such a machine is called a Universal Turing Machine.

6.4   UNIVERSAL TURING MACHINES

A Universal Turing Machine is something often referred to in metamathematical and cybernetic literature, and we should say something here about the nature of a Universal Turing Machine and also something about its significance.

A Universal Turing Machine is a little like an interpreter in computer programming, where by an interpreter we mean a symbolic language which describes a machine code program where there is some simpler code in the interpretrive language and, as opposed to compilers, where there is a (1,1) correspondence between interpreter and machine code language, and where the translation (if there is a translation at all) and programming generally occur in the same step.

If we think of a function $f(x)$ which is Turing-computable, then we can find, by definition, a Turing Machine Z, which can compute the function f. This means that for each value of x on the tape of Z a computation occurs leaving a string of symbols $Sf(x)$ remaining on the tape.

We have in the last section of this chapter done precisely this sort of thing, and in doing we have behaved like a Universal Turing Machine. The technique used for translating the description of a Turing machine onto the tape of the Universal Turing Machine will not be described here; a description can be found in Minsky (1967).

6.5   RECURSIVE FUNCTIONS

We have already mentioned recursive functions and discussed recursive definitions. There is indeed a whole branch of mathematics known as the theory of recursive functions. The theory is a part of metamathematics but it has an immediate bearing on computing and automata, and is therefore related to cybernetics.

We shall remind the reader again that we are not here interested in taking a mathematician or meta-mathematician's view on the subject, so we shall not attempt to develop the theory or show theorems beyond the few necessary to give some feel for the subject.

There are a certain set of functions which play an important part in recursive function theory and provide a particulary convenient description of most of mathematics. One of these is the successor function which we have already mentioned, another is proper subtraction $x \cdot y$, which we illustrated by a simple numerical example. If we add four further functions and two operations (called "composition" and "minimilisation") we have an axiomatic type of system from which we generate recursive functions. We can show that all the functions and two operations are Turing-computable, so it follows that recursive functions are computable. The question then is as to whether there are any functions of classical mathematics which are not recursive, and if there are, are they computable? The answer is that there are such functions of which x^y is an example. To deal with this we widen our concept of recursive functions to that of primitive recursive functions. We then find that such functions as x^y are included and can also be shown to be computable.

This brings us to the final very complicated issue of whether all well formed formulae of classical mathematics are computable, to which the answer, as shown by Church (1936) and Turing 1936), is "No". It is possible to construct formulae which are acceptable within the domain of classical mathematics and which can be shown not to be computable. The details of these results and the closely associated results of Gödel (1931) take us beyond the scope of this book, but we shall devote a brief final section to Gödel's theorems.

6.6   GÖDEL'S INCOMPLETENESS THEOREM

It is worthwhile for us to dwell for a moment on this famous theorem, or to be more accurate these famous theorems, since more than one is involved. One reason for looking at this matter carefully is that it has sometimes been thought to have special reference to the comparison between machines and brains (George 1962, 1972; Lucas 1970)

It must be remembered first of all that we are dealing with axiomatic systems. We want, for example, to know whether the axiomatic systems we are considering have certain properties such as completeness, consistency or a decision procedure.

It is a matter of history that the classical theory of sets was shown to be inconsistent, and this inconsistency was only removed by the addition of Russell's theory of types. But the theory of types is itself *outside* set theory and in effect involves additional principles. When we talk of the properties of consistency and completeness in an axiomatic system we mean to investigate them from an algorithmic point of view. We want all true statements about a domain of activity to be included and all false statements excluded; this is a complete system.

If we take *any* axiomatic system rich enough to provide a foundation for mathematical logic then Gödel first showed that such a system would be incomplete. It is always possible to find true statements about mathematical integers which cannot be proved within such an axiomatic system. Gödel went on from this to show that it was also impossible to show that such a system was consistent by methods which could be represented in the axiomatic system itself. The analogy with set theory and the theory of types is obvious.

Equivalent to the role played by the theory of types, we now have Gentzen's (1938) non-finitist extension of the axiomatic system which permits of a proof of the consistency of the axiomatic system; but once again the proof is outside the system itself.

Gödel's methods of numbering and his use of such concepts as ω-consistency take us beyond the scope of this text. But we should add the fact that these results turn out to be special cases of the more general results of Turing and Church to the effect that such an axiomatic system as we have been describing not only has no decision procedure, but it cannot have a decision procedure.

We must now mention briefly that some writers say that this work sets a limit to computers and machines which do not apply to the brain. But this is not so unless one limits the computers to axiomatic systems and quite obviously there is no reason for doing so. They can be programmed to "make jumps" in their logical processes when making inductions and using other probabilistic methods. So, we assert that the results of Gödel, as well as those of Turing and Church, have no bearing whatever on any limitation that applies to the machine but not to the brain; the limitation is on axiomatic brains, whoever has manufacturered them, and by whatever means.

The importance of infinite (or non-finite) automata to cybernetics is twofold. On the one hand the same argument applies here as applied in the last chapter to finite automata, and this is concerned with the analogy that exists between automata and human beings, and especially between automata and the brain. On the other hand the work on Turing Machines, in particular, is connected with the philosphical foundations of cybernetics. It is thought by some to provide a limit to what artificial systems can do, and thus to answer in the negative the question "Could machines be made to think?". We believe that Turing machines do provide limits to computability, but these same limits can be applied to the human brain and provide no justification for arguing that machines could not be made to think, so we shall make the opposite assumption (George, 1972).

6.7 SUMMARY

This brief chapter provides a further stage in the discussion of automata and formal logical systems. We have now talked in terms of non-finite, or infinite automata, where an automaton is equivalent to an axiomatic system.

Turing Machines were developed far enough to see the basic principles upon which they worked, and a few of their properties were demonstrated. The most important feature of Turing Machines lies in their supplying algorithms for various axiomatic systems, and then with Gödel's theorem, showing all axiomatic systems may not have such axioms. Such representations of logic and set theory lead directly to a consideration of Recursive Function Theory.

The basic argument about the ability of "machines" (artificially constructed systems) to think is closely bound up with Turing Machines and their capabilities. We are clear that Turing Machines do not in fact supply any evidence that contradicts the belief that "machines *could* be made to think".

CHAPTER 7

Neural nets

Argument

Neural nets are particular types of finite automata. They are designed partly to investigate the mathematical and logical properties of certain systems and partly as models of the human nervous system, and although they differ from the human nervous system in many obvious ways, they nevertheless allow us to study the properties of systems like the human nervous systems. We can, if necessary, in the course of time make our neural nets more and more like actual nervous systems, but the gulf between actual nervous systems and what have been called conceptual nervous systems is anyway, in the end, one of degree.

Neural nets, or logical nets as they have been called, show the structure and function of a system that can be described by mathematical logic. So that logical systems, such as Boolean algebra, discussed in Chapter 5, are also descriptions of automata. Such automata can be made as complicated as we please.

We have so far discussed hardware and software models, and we have also discussed logic and mathematics which lead on to a consideration of theoretical automata. It is known that these automata can be actually manufactured since they are based on algorithms or effective procedures. We know also that automata are synthesised as digital computers as well as other simpler models. We now turn to automata that are especially designed to simulate the structure of human nerves, or neurons. Such automata are capable of being translated into tape automata, or can be programmed onto computers. But we shall consider them in this chapter purely as collections of neurons obeying certain well-defined rules.

We should add that such neural nets can be thought of as alternative forms of tape automata, by which we may discuss the properties of logic and mathematics, and indeed any events that can be described in logico-mathematical terms. But first let us think of them as idealised nervous systems.

Look first at Figure 1 which lists different sorts of automata including neural nets.

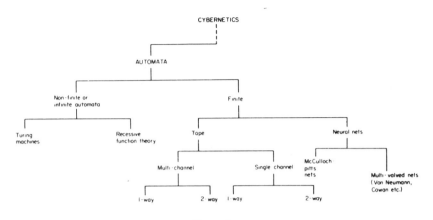

Figure 1

7.1   NEURAL NETS

The first people to construct models, or automata, of the neural net kind were Warren McCulloch and Walter Pitts (1943), and they first called such models "neural nets". The name obviously stems from the intended interpretation of the elements and their connections. What they ·had in mind was an artificial nervous system, which could be. constructed theoretically, in this well-defined way, and from which models could actually be constructed.

It is easy enough to construct neural nets in "hardware", if necessary; and there are indeed various ways of doing it ·as well as various ways in which it has actually been done.

McCulloch and Pitts drew up neural nets as blueprints for the special senses (the senses of sight, hearing, touch, taste and smell) as well as the central processes of the human brain which involves the ability to learn, think and solve problems.

We will describe briefly how neural nets are constructed. We shall not in the first place use the original Pitts—McCulloch notation, because other simpler and more elegant notations have emerged since. The points of resemblance to the human nervous system though are obvious in each case from the way the nets are drawn up. It should be added that there have been many other contributors to neural net theory (George, 1956, 1967; da Fonseca, 1966; Culbertson, 1950, 1952, 1963; Blum 1962; Verbeck, 1962; Cowan 1962; Lofgren 1962).

Figure 2 shows four neurons (or elements) represented by circles, connected in a simple net. The reason for calling them elements rather than neurons is to avoid any misunderstanding as to its representing actual neurons, or being called literally the model of actual neurons. A logical element is, in many ways, obviously different from a neuron. The circles represent the neurons or elements; and on the right we usually, by tradition, draw the output to the neuron, while the inputs are on the left.

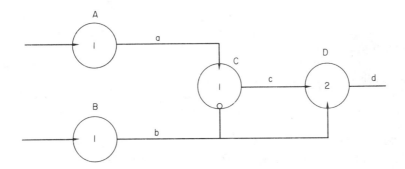

Figure 2   *a* fires at *t* + 1 if input to *A* fires at *t*, and the same for *b* with respect to *B*. *a* will excite *c* and *b* inhibit *c* so if both fire together *C* will not fire. *D* only fires if *c and b* fired the instant before. Arrowheads represent excitatory inputs and small circles represent inhibitory inputs.

This net is of the kind which we sometimes call a finite automaton and it is represented in this bit-by-bit form, where have several elements connected with lots of other elements. These elements can be connected in quite a complicated manner and they must be connected according to certain well-defined rules and the rules for the connection of neural nets are relatively simple; we shall state them now.

The first rule is that an output (on the right) must either contain an impulse or not, at any instant of time. In other words, the output may ramify and go to various other elements, but these other elements all either receive a single pulse at any instant or no impulse at all. There is no possibility of mixing the outputs so that some carry pulses and some do not; they must all be of one kind.

The second rule is that the inputs (on the left) can be pulse-carrying at any instant of time and you can have any pattern of 1 (which represents a pulse) and 0 (which represents the absence of a pulse) in a set of input fibres. Now these *neural nets are really a geometrical rendering of Boolean algebra*, at least in the first place. The only difference between the Pitts–McCulloch neural nets and the ordinary formulae of Boolean algebra lies in the fact that these nets have time co-ordinates attached to them, so that we have to think of this element firing at time *t*; and subsequent elements at *t* 1, *t* 2, ..., etc. Indeed we say that each element holds up the firing one instant of time. Now the instant of time can be any sort of unit one wishes. We should add though that we can make our nets sufficiently complicated to take us beyond Boolean algebra, although we still remain in the domain of mathematical logic.

All elements take one instant of time to fire, so that if there is one obviously non-realistic feature in the system, it is that all neurons in the human nervous system are not identical in this respect. Each neuron has a threshold, represented by the letter h where we say that the number of excitatory inputs firing at time t must at least equal the number of inhibitory inputs firing at time t plus the constant threshold h. We assume, also contrary to fact, that the threshold for every neuron is the same.

We can represent pictorially excitatory inputs by little filled-in triangles and we usually use open circles for inhibitory inputs.

Let us label the inputs a and b, and a single output we will label c. The threshold of this element is 1, and we can state the condition for this element to fire as follows.

We say the c fires at t, if and only if (which is represented by the three lines $\equiv$) a fires at $t-1$, or b fires at $t-1$. If we reproduce the same element with the threshold of 2, instead of 1, then our condition of firing changes so that we say that c fires at t if and only if a fires at $t-1$ and b at $t-1$.

Both inputs have to fire simultaneously to fire the neuron in the second case, whereas in the first case either of them *alone* would be sufficient to fire the neuron. The thresholds of elements are all real numbers and they may thus include negative numbers or zero. If, however, you have a threshold of zero, an output c for an input a (we want an inhibitory input this time), we say that c fires at t, if and only if a does not fire at $t-1$ In other words, the element is "live" and fires all the time unless there is an inhibitory input; and this represents the logical operator "not".

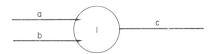

Figure 3 c fires at $t+1$ if a fires at t *or* b fires at $t-1$, and so on.

One of the things that is important about neural net models is that hardware systems can be built from them, so that they are clearly blueprints, and are therefore effective. Neural nets can also be represented as diagrams with elements or neurons connected by fibres, and they can be made as complicated as you like, but we can always think of them as being represented by *not* and *and* or *not* and *or*, even though in practice we use devices and elements which are far more complicated. We can always, however, show that these more complex nets can be reduced to combinations of those which we know to be effective.

To complete our picture, we want one other particular type of element for storing information, because one obvious property of any intelligent system is that it stores information and the storage element often used is neural nets. It seems likely that this is neurophysiologically realistic, although on current evidence unlikely to be the way in which all information is stored in the human nervous system. The element is a loop element which fires back on itself.

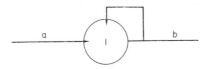

Figure 4   A simple looped element which once having fired continues to fire itself indefinitely.

Hence the output, b for example, fires at $t - 1$ if a fires at t, and continues firing indefinitely, unless of course there is some inhibitory input available. If such an input is not available, then it will never stop. b will stop at some future time, and only if c fires at t, and not a (a^1).

As we have said, all elements are virtully the same in the neural net system; they could of course, be made to be different, but they will all be the same in one model. All such systems as this are *pre-wired*. This is a matter which some people have objected to, but it represents two different approaches to cybernetic problems; both these approaches were mentioned in Chapter 2.

The drawing of realistic neural nets can become tiresome, but one can, for example, represent all neural nets in forms of matrix, and there are a number of matrix algebraic operations which represent realistic properties of the neural net representation. This algebraic representation of nets by matrices is one way in which you can put neural nets onto a digital computer. There is usually a language especially constructed to represent matrices on a digital computer; which is one reason why the matrix representation is useful. Although it is artificial and is only one way of representing neural nets on a computer, we are not necessarily committed to it. Whichever method we choose, we can handle very large collections of elements and their connection on a computer, and this is one possible approach to cybernetic modelling. Indeed a matrix representation of a neural net is simply a blueprint for an automata. We shall discuss this matter briefly in a later section of this chapter.

It is true to say that once our logical net system has been placed onto a computer it will have taken up most of the storage space on most computers. This leads to the question as to whether one can drop the well-defined connectivity of the neural net system and simply represent the net by something both terser and more flexible. One way to this is to represent the conditional probabilities which are going to affect neurons.

At this point we lose any attempt to reproduce anatomical similarity to the nervous system. On the other hand, we gain a large amount of space so that it may be profitable not to represent neural nets in matrix form on a computer, but to program the computer directly to simulate what is now a more artificial and functional nervous system — an automaton which is synthesising function, but not structure. We shall be saying something in the next chapter about the efforts to program computers directly to simulate behaviour.

It should be said that there are now many different renderings of neural nets, some of which are designed to show how by duplicating or triplicating information in the net we can ensure that the system is error-free. (Von Neumann, 1951; Cowan, 1964; and others), and we shall be saying more about this shortly.

We can simulate or synthesise almost every biological system and in doing so many scientists have not only used the computer to represent the relevant neural nets, but they have also related neural nets to information theory. Information theory is an attempt to analyse and measure, in mathematical terms, the flow of information in any system. When the reader remembers that cybernetics is the science of control and communication it will be easy for him to understand why information theory is relevant to cybernetics. We shall be discussing information theory in Chapter 9.

7.2   PROPERTIES OF NEURAL NETS

We have so far merely introduced the basic ideas of neural nets. Before we take the discussion any further we shall have to make the point once more that there are two different views of the importance of neural nets. One is that these are just other forms of finite automata. Indeed it is perfectly true that we can as well study the properties of finite automata through neural netas as through tape automata, and we shall be saying something about results that bear directly on finite automata. The other half of this coin is to be aware that McCulloch and Pitts had the actual nervous system in mind. It is obvious from the choice of elements and their connections that an idealised nervous system was envisaged. At the same time, it can obviously be made explicit that no one believes for one moment that such networks are identical with actual nervous nets. Perhaps we should from the start enumerate just a few of the many differences:

1) Actual neurons differ from each other in size and firing time

2) The actual nervous systems of organisms when they fire are accompanied

by chemical changes which may directly affect the overall properties of the system.

3) Neurons in the human being are thought to fire "across" the cells directly to each other, as well as along synapses and dendrites.

4) Some theorists have thought there were (electrical) field affects operating in the nervous system.

So far, we have introduced neural nets with the equivalent logical formula, and although we shall include some of the formulae for the sake of those who are interested, we shall generally assume that the system is a simple network whose behaviour can generally be followed quite easily.

We will remember also that neural net automata can be synthesized as digital computers and to bring this point home clearly let us look at a gating network with simple memory.

The formula for Figure 5 is

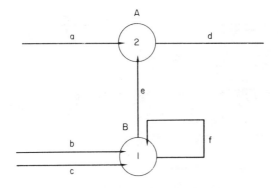

Figure 5   This figure shows B as having a loop f which fires back on itself, acting as a simple memory.

$$d_t \equiv a_{t-1} \cdot e_{t-1} \tag{1}$$

and since

$$e_{t-1} \equiv (e_t c_{t-1}) \vee (b_{t-1} \cdot c_{t-1}) \vee (e_{t-1} \cdot b_{t-1}) \tag{2}$$

we can substitute (2) and (1), which gives

$$d_t \equiv a_{t-1} \cdot ((e_t \cdot c_{t-1}) \vee (b_{t-1} c_{t-1}) \vee (e_{t-1} \cdot b_{t-1})). \tag{3}$$

The logical formulae defining the firing condition of even simple nets soon become extremely complicated so we shall omit this part of the description after the *next* figure (Figure 6). We shall show the logical formulae for that if only to show the alternative logical description in Polish notation. Figure 6 is a serial binary adder.

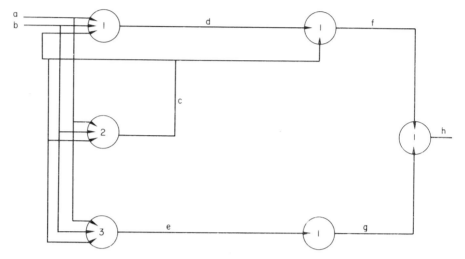

Figure 6   A six element *n*, without loops.

$$h_t \equiv f_{t-1} \; v g_{t-1}$$

$$f_{t-1} \equiv d_{t-2} \cdot c_{t-2}$$

$$g_{t-1} \equiv e_{t-2}$$

$$d_{t-2} \equiv a_{t-3} \; v b_{t-3} \; v c_{t-3}$$

$$c_{t-2} \equiv (a_{t-3} \cdot b_{t-3}) \; v \; (a_{t-3} \; v c_{t-3}) \; v \; (b_{t-3} \cdot c_{t-3})$$

$$e_{t-2} \equiv a_{t-3} \cdot b_{t-3} \cdot c_{t-3}.$$

So

$$h_t \equiv ((a_{t-3} \; v b_{t-3} \; v c_{t-3}) \cdot ((a_{t-3} \cdot b_{t-3}) \; v \; (a_{t-3} \cdot c_{t-3})$$
$$v \; (b_{t-3} \cdot c_{t-3}))) \; v \; (a_{t-3} \cdot b_{t-3} \cdot c_{t-3}).$$

$E h (t) O((AOa\,Obc)\,NOAah\,Oacbc)\,(AaAbc)$ is the equivalent in Polish notation for the last formula defining *h*.

7.3 REGULAR EVENTS

We must now use neural nets as a mathemetician does to categorise a class of events which such nets depict. We want to be able to draw a limiting boundary around such nets and see what they can and cannot do, and then see how they relate to other automata.

Look first (Kleene, 1951) at Figure 7:

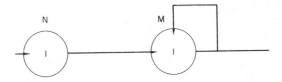

Figure 7   This simple loop element has another element (*N*) firing into it.

This depicts a simple loop element and we know only that if *M* is firing, then *N* has fired sometime in the past. If we assume that the past is finite, all we know is that *N* fired at some time, but we do not know when; Such an event is *indefinite*.

A *definite* event occurs in some finite period of time $p - S + 1, ..., p$ for $S + 1$ and where p is the present. There are 2 definite events of length S. We say that each of the tables 2 tables would constitute an occurrence of an event of length S with the input neurons in our neural net.

What we have in mind here is a matrix of the following form, where $k = 3$, and $S = 5$:

t	A_1	A_2	A_3
P	1	0	0
$P-1$	0	1	0
$P-2$	1	1	1
$P-3$	1	1	0
$P-4$	1	1	0

and the combination of 0's and 1's refers to every possible combination of firing (1) and non-firing (0).

We call a definite event *positive* if it occurs when at least one input neuron fires during the period covered by the event. This means there are ks entries in the matrix, 2^{ks} possible matrices and $2^{2^{ks}}$ possible events.

We can now define a prepositive event as one that occurs only when an input neuron fires in its first moment $p - S + 1$.

We now say that a *regular* event is an event which has a nerve net which when started in a prescribed way, represents the event by firing a certain inner neuron at time $p + 2$, if and only if that event has occurred ending at time p.

If the event is prepositive, the net may start with all inner neurons quiescent. Now to a much more general definition of regular events. A regular event is described by a regular expression. A *regular* expression is such that:

1) Any letter symbol x, say, alone is regular.
2) If E and F are regular expressions, then so is (EF).
3) If $E, F, ..., G$ are regular expressions, so is $(E \vee F \vee ... \vee G)$.
4) If E is a regular expression so is $E*$

It must also be added that regular events are those described as above and no others. An expression is a well-formed formula which describes a legitimate net or part of a net.

A word should perhaps be said about *recursive definitions* at this point, since we have already discussed recursive functions. A recursive definition is a sort of inductive definition where we use the thing to be defined (or its definition) in the definition itself and thus create an impression — sometimes justified — of circularity. We state a *base*, a *recursion* and a *restriction*. In other words, we have a starting set (*base*) e.g. all tall men, and then a recursion such as all *collections* of tall men, and tall men of all colours and finally the *restriction* which says *only* those described are accepted — e.g. tall women are not acceptable. These ideas are not implicit in what has been said about *recursive functions*.

We can now use a neural net to show one of the recursion features of the definition of neural nets.

Let us look at the condition 4 which says if E is a regular expression so is $E*$. By $*$ we mean "any number of occurrences of" and therefore by $E*$ we mean E repeated a finite number of times where E is a regular expression. So if a is regular, so is $a * a$, which includes such sets as a, aa, aaa, $aaaa$, ... etc. If $(a \vee b) *$ b is regular it includes abb, ab, bb, ..., etc.

Look now at the following neural net (Figure 8) which depicts a net that realises the regular function $(a \vee b) * b$.

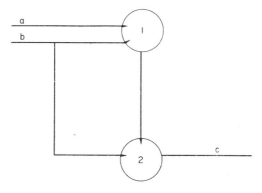

Figure 8 c fires if a or b is always followed by b, i.e. $c_t \equiv (a \vee b)_{t\text{-}2} * b_{t\text{-}1}$.

We can draw nets that recognise any of the class of regular events, or to put it another way finite automata generally can recognise *only* regular sets of sequences. So we know exactly what finite automata can do, and we therefore know that an event that is not regular cannot be "recognised" to be a finite automaton. This does not mean that non-regular events cannot occur in finite automata, only that if they do they will not be recognised.

7.4   EQUIVALENCE

We now will specifically add that all finite automata of the tape form are equivalent to all finite automata of the neural net form. Either is equivalent to a digital computer provided the finite past of the computer is always available to it. This sort of equivalence has already been mentioned. We shall not prove these statements as theorems; those interested should consult Minsky (1967, page 55).

What we have been discussing is concerned primarily with the properties of neural nets (and finite automata) in general, and will now move on to discuss a few of the tricks of their use which are important, especially from the point of view of behavioural and biological modelling.

Let us mention next a particular equivalence which exists between every finite state machine and a neural net. If a machine exists with m inputs, p internal states and n outputs, the equivalent neural net has m input fibres, n output fibres and an mp array of inner elements, each cell of threshold 2, where there are m cells for each of the p states. It remains to connect up the neural net to simulate the behaviour of the machine whatever that behaviour may be, and this can always be done.

The above argument which is illustrated in more detail in Minsky (1967, page 55 *et seq.*) does not purport to provide an efficient equivalence; it merely purports to show that the possibility of equivalence is always there.

Let us turn now to a more cybernetic view of neural nets.

7.5   NETS AND CYBERNETICS

An illustration will now be given of the use of neural nets from the cybernetic point of view. Here we are using the neural nets to construct models for intelligent behaviour with respect to the environment.

If the environment is a simple maze then our neural net represents an automata capable of running the maze. This is not itself very complicated but raises certain questions of interest and leads cumulatively to neural nets of greater behavioural interest, and raises problems too.

It will be realised clearly that the neural nets — perhaps better thought of as logical nets here — are the abstract version of the sort of hardware models described in Chapter 2.

Consider a simple maze such as the following:

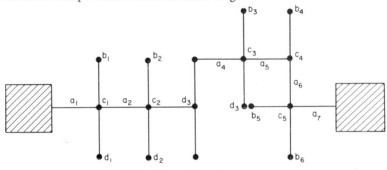

Figure 9   A simple maze

For convenience we now label the choice-points a_1, a_2, a_3, a_4, a_5 and a_6. We shall also label the routes at each of the choice points (they are all "three-choice" points) b_1, c_1, d_1, b_2 c_2 d_2, ... etc. The problem now is what sort of neural net can solve this maze.

If we assume that the discriminations needed between a's, b's, c's and d's is given and that the net incorporates the principle of getting from start to finish as quickly as possible, then our net must simply establish the connections

$$a_1 \ c_1 \ a_2 \ c_2 \ a_3 \ b_3 \ a_4 \ c_4 \ a_5 \ d_5 \ a_6 \ c_6$$

which gives the correct solution.

The sort of association net which we have used before (George, 1961) could be the basis for such a model. Here we show the net in abstract form:

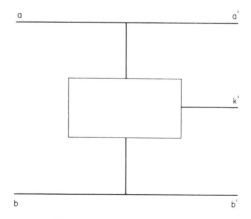

Figure 10   An abstract association net or B-net.

a activates a^1, b activates b^1, and if a and b have occurred together more often than not in the *recorded* past, then a alone or b alone will fire k^1 as well as a^1 or b^1.

The counters are made up of looped elements which are wired to do whatever job we need, and using c for the positively firing looped counter (d would be used to depict it if its score was negative), we can write the logical formula as follows:

$$k_t \equiv (a.b)_{t-1} \text{ v} (a.c)_{t-1} \text{ v} (b.c)_{t-1} \qquad (4)$$

We write $(a.b)_{t-1}$ as shorthand for $a_{t-1}.b_{t-1}$ to save labour.

Now we can use a notation which is more "molar" than (4) to represent the same state of affairs, i.e.

Aab or *A*(*a* v *b*) *k*.

Since ca^1 and bb^1 are given connections as in our example what may be learned is that a and b are positively associated, or what amounts to much the same thing a or b is associated with k. In other words, the firing of k tells us that a and b are positively associated. If k does not fire when either a or b fire alone, then we know that a and b have been negatively associated.

From the behavioural point of view we must now ask a few basic questions. Suppose we have a large scale system with inputs.

$$s_1, s_2, ..., s_n$$

and outputs

$$r_1, r_2 ..., r_m$$

and we allow positive or negative association for all combinations of s's and r's. We have then a completely classified association system, wherein a subset of s's, s_1, s_2, s_6 and s_7 are associated with r_7, r_8 and r_{10}. So overlooking the behavioural implausibility of complete classification, which we discussed earlier, we still have to consider the question of whether the inputs and outputs must always stand for the same organic activities. The most plausible answer to this question is "yes" at the sensory and motor level of activity, but "no" at the central level.

If we have a centrally organised "brain" which asserts that a will be "interpreted as ..." or "stand for ...", and b will "stand for ..." and so on, we need to be able to clear such sets of neurons from time to time and reassign them to new duties. This clearly implies the need for a sort of hierarchical organisation, so that a meta-system exists whose duty is to *name* the variables so used.

In neural net terms we now need a set of layers of elements making up a three-dimensional array if we are to simulate the more intelligent types of human behaviour.

Let us illustrate the point with a simple example of "concept formation". If in our lower net level we find such states as

$$A(a_7\ a_8\ a_9)(b_1\ b_2) \tag{1}$$

$$A(a_9\ a_{10}\ a_{11})(b_1\ b_2) \tag{2}$$

or in general

$$A(a_n\ a_{n+1}\ a_{n+2})(b_1\ b_2) \tag{3}$$

then some recoding is possible, by clearing all the particular associations (1), (2), etc. and retaining at the higher level only the association (3). (3) represents a statement (or concept) about the state of the lower level of elements.

In such a manner we must try and build upon the earlier work on neural nets and make them more effective from the cybernetic point of view. We shall be returning to these matters from time to time.

7.6   MATRIX REPRESENTATION OF NEURAL NETS

The matrix representation of neural nets (Landahl and Rung, 1957) splits the description into structure and function. Consider a matrix $A \equiv a$; this represents all the anatomical connections in our neural net. Consider a simple net.

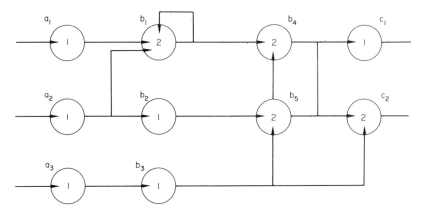

Figure 11 a_1, a_2, a_3 are input elements; b_1, b_2, b_3, b_4 and b_5 are inner elements; c_1 and c_2 are output elements.

The structure matrix is composed of a square 10×10 matrix which shows the complete interconnectivity possible in the system. It is as follows:

	$a_1\ a_2\ a_3$	$b_1\ b_2\ b_3\ b_4\ b_5$	$c_1\ c_2$
$A \equiv a_1$		½ 0 0 0 0	0 0
a_2	0	½ 1 0 0 0	0 0
a_3		0 0 1 0 0	0 0
b_1		1 0 0 ½ 0	0 0
b_2		0 0 0 0 ½	0 0
b_3	0	0 0 0 0 ½	0 ½
b_4		0 0 0 0 0	1 ½
b_5		0 0 0 ½ 0	0 0
c_1	0	0	0
c_2			

The structure matrix can have pulses occurring only where real numbers appear in the structural matrix. We must now take a table of inputs:

	$t_0\ t_1\ t_2\ t_3$
a_1	1 0 1 1
a_2	1 1 1 1
a_3	0 1 1 1

and these give the following function matrices, where we deal with only Lij, which is the set of non-zero matrices from A above. We get:

$t_0 \equiv$

½ 0 0 0 0 0 0
½ 1 0 0 0 0 0
0 0 0 0 0 0 0
0 0 0 0 0 0 0
0 0 0 0 0 0 0
0 0 0 0 0 0 0
0 0 0 0 0 0 0
0 0 0 0 0 0 0

$t_1 \equiv$

0 0 0 0 0 0 0
½ 1 0 0 0 0 0
0 0 1 0 0 0 0
1 0 0 0 0 0 0

$$
\begin{array}{ccccccc}
0 & 0 & 0 & 0 & 0 & 0 & 0 \\
0 & 0 & 0 & 0 & 0 & 0 & 0 \\
0 & 0 & 0 & 0 & 0 & 0 & 0 \\
0 & 0 & 0 & 0 & 0 & 0 & 0 \\
\end{array}
$$

$$
t_3 \equiv
\begin{array}{ccccccc}
\tfrac{1}{2} & 0 & 0 & 0 & 0 & 0 & 0 \\
\tfrac{1}{2} & 1 & 0 & 0 & 0 & 0 & 0 \\
0 & 0 & 1 & 0 & 0 & 0 & 0 \\
0 & 0 & 0 & 0 & 0 & 0 & 0 \\
0 & 0 & 0 & 0 & 0 & 0 & 0 \\
0 & 0 & 0 & 0 & 0 & 0 & 0 \\
0 & 0 & 0 & 0 & 0 & 0 & 0 \\
\end{array}
$$

$$
t_4 \equiv
\begin{array}{ccccccc}
\tfrac{1}{2} & 0 & 0 & 0 & 0 & 0 & 0 \\
\tfrac{1}{2} & 1 & 0 & 0 & 0 & 0 & 0 \\
0 & 0 & 1 & 0 & 0 & 0 & 0 \\
1 & 0 & 0 & \tfrac{1}{2} & 0 & 0 & 0 \\
0 & 0 & 0 & 0 & \tfrac{1}{2} & 0 & 0 \\
0 & 0 & 0 & 0 & \tfrac{1}{2} & 0 & 0 \\
0 & 0 & 0 & 0 & 0 & 0 & 0 \\
\end{array}
$$

and so on. A few theorems can be proved with respect to the relation between structure and function matrices, but the proofs will not be given here.

The fact that such nets can be placed on computers is fairly obvious, and the matrix representation of neural nets is particularly appropriate for this purpose.

If the structural matrix is dropped, and only the function matrices are considered then the anatomy of the system is no longer described and the remainder is in effect a stochasic process.

Probabilistic nets (Rashevsky, 1948) are a natural corollary to deterministic nets but they will not be described in this chapter.

7.7   CURRENT RESEARCH IN NEURAL NETS

The field of neural nets has been the subject for sporadic developments in the last year or two, but not perhaps as much as most of the other sections of cybernetics.

Nemes (1969) describes the logical background of neural nets and also discusses their application to modelling the visual system. Lerner (1972) also mentions neural nets but neither author contributes anything new to what has already been done.

Glushkov (1969) also analyses neural nets and in particular discusses and adds to our understanding of the Perceptron (Rosenblatt, 1958), but little is really added to neural networks as such.

da Fonseca (1966) has carried out the most detailed application of neural nets in recent years. He gives a most detailed application of neural nets to all aspects cognition and has made a major contribution to our understanding of cognitive processes.

George (to be published) has also attempted to derive cognitive descriptions in neural net terms, and the most recent of these attempts was designed to show how language and concepts can be fitted into neural net terms. By and large this is a field which is wide open for further experimental and theoretical investigations.

7.8   SUMMARY

We have summarised neural nets in their simplest form, showing some conventions which allow us to draw network diagrams and write the logical formulae which describe those diagrams.

Deterministic nets can be used to compute probabilities and can be represented in matrix form. Probabilistic nets can also be drawn.

The notion of *regular events* tells us something about the events neural nets can depict. This also provides a link with recursive function theory.

This information will be relevant to the chapter on computers (Chapter 8) and the chapter on information theory (Chapter 9).

The digital computer in cybernetics

Argument

The digital computer plays a central role in cybernetics since it is the only fast, large universal machine available which is capable of providing models of such complex systems as the human brain, or of human behaviour.

The digital computer is an automatic calculating machine. It was designed to perform arithmetic operations and mathematical calculations at very high speeds. This in itself has transformed science and knowledge, and as we discover that more and more things can be mapped on to arithmetic so the transformation turns into a major revolution.

The computer is a storage and data retrieval device which is incomplete until a program is placed in its store. Then with the program in store it becomes an autonomous system and proceeds automatically to perform the computation. in its store. Then with the program in store it becomes an autonomous system and proceeds automatically to perform the computation.

Computers are realizations in hardware of finite automata, and thus their behaviour comes within the compass of our discussion of finite automata in Chapter 5

A great deal of research is being carried out all the time in the field of computer science and three of these fields that are most relevant to cybernetics are list processing, interactive programming and heuristic programming.

The digital computer is a tool for storing and retrieving information, as well as for performing mathematical calculations automatically at very high speeds. Its behaviour is specified by the particular programs which may be fed into it

The computer holds a position of central importance in cybernetics, partly because it provides facilities for simulating and synthesising complex systems like the human nervous system, and partly because most applications of cybernetic ideas to practical problems have so far involved computers. Computers are by far the largest and fastest universal machines and this alone gives them a vital significance for any form of large scale modelling operation. It is essential, if one is to understand much of cybernetics, to have some understanding of computers and the way in which they function; this is the main purpose of this chapter.

Digital computers are directly related to automata. Turing (1936), who is famous for his work on Turing Machines, some of which we have discussed, also played a major part in deveoping modern digital computers. Digital computers are one *hardware* equivalent of finite or potentially infinite automata. Indeed we say again that the Turing Machine is equivalent to a digital computer, if, and only if, the digital computer has access to all the punched cards or punched tape that has passed through it during its total period of use, or during the period which applies to the equivalence relation.

8.1   TYPES OF COMPUTERS

Computers can be classified in many different ways. As a first step we can differentiate between calculators and computors. A calculator may be said to be a hand-driven, non-automatic, computing machine. An example of this would be any sort of desk calculator in which there is a continual interaction between the person using the calculator and the machine itself. The calculator is not capable of storing information over a long period and this ensures that it is not automatic. Strictly speaking, it can store numbers, but not orders. A digital computer on the other hand can be programmed to perform sequences of operations, the program specifying the orders and their sequence being stored in the computer. Nevertheless the calculator has played a very important part in the devlopment of the modern computer. It is of interest that the first calculator was designed by Pascal in 1642 (when he was only 19 years old) and modified some thirty years later by Liebniz.

Having distinguished the computer and the calculator, by noting that the computer is automatic rather than manual, we may now subdivide the class of computers. A computer may be *digital* or *analog*. A digital system is one which works on a discrete number basis, so that a number is represented formally inside the system. To illustrate the difference between digital and analog in very general terms, a piano, we may say, is a discrete system wherein you either play or do not play a given note since each note is divided discretely from the next. An analog system, on the other hand, is continuous in its scale and in the case of the analog computer represents its numbers by physical variables, such as currents and voltages. By analogy with our example of a piano, the violin is an analog system, since it can vary its pitch continuously. Furthermore, whereas the desk calculator is discrete in its operation but not automatic, so the slide-rule is ·continuous in its operation and also not automatic, i.e. the slide-rule bears the same relation to the analog computer that the calculator bears to the digital computer.

Analog computers have existed for a long time and undoubtedly will play a large part in the development of cybernetics and the simulation of various aspects of living organisms. However, they are usually smaller than digital computers and less flexible; they have certainly so far played a less important part in cybernetics than digital computers. We shall not, in fact, in this particular book be discussing analog computers at all, except to say that in the opinion of many people the human brain is both analog and digital in its operation, and also to the extent that we have mentioned such analog computers as Ashby's Homeostat and some servosystems (Chapters 2 and 3). It is because the brain is thought to be both analog and digital that any attempt to simulate the whole system in digital terms may have its limitations, although digital systems can always be made to approximate to analog ones. For many purposes there is no problem involved here because if we are building a model in terms of a computer program, then the actual structure of the model is obviously going to be so different from that of the system simulated that the question of whether the simulation is digital or analog may be comparatively unimportant. We shall, from now on, restrict our description of computers to that of automatic, electronic, digital computers.

The earliest digital computers were mechanical, as indeed was the original computer envisaged by Charles Babbage, who is in many ways the founder of modern digital computers. Indeed the very first digital computers to be produced were of a design similar to that which Babbage had suggested. The main reason Babbage's own computer designs failed to come to immediate fruition in his own time was the lack of development of precision engineering at the time his work was being done.

Digital Computers can be further subdivided in a variety of ways. For example, there can be one-address, two-address, three-address or n-address computers. This distinction over the number of addresses that occur in the order words of the computer will be explained later. There can aslo be serial or parallel computers. This means that they can perform their operations one at a time or many at a time; for the purposes of simulating human behaviour the latter type of computational machine is the more likely to be accurate, although this is a matter for some debate. However, the majority of computers in commercial use at the present time are serial rather than parallel.

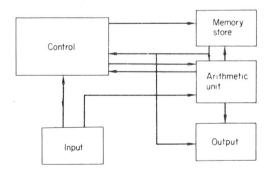

Figure 1   A simple block diagram of a digital computer.

Figure 1 shows the relation which exists in a computer between the control, input, output, arithmetic unit and store. (Although it is true that not all modern computers have arithmetic units as such, the majority of them do.) The store of the computer contains both the list of instructions (program) and the numbers which are to be operated upon by these instructions. The control unit then operates on the instructions which send the numbers to the Arithmentic Unit for the operation to be carried out. After the operation is carried out the numbers are returned to the store. Unless otherwise specified, the instructions constituting the program are normally obeyed in their natural sequence.

Instructions need to be stored as computer "words" which are themselves in numerical form; numbers also need to be stored as words and, as a result, we have in the machine computer words which are capable of representing both instructions and numbers. Different computers may use different codes for this purpose ·of representing instructions and a number of modern computers use decimal code. Most of the older computers, and some of the modern ones, use binary. Various other codes are used as alternatives to, or in addition to, binary or decimal machines, and for particular purposes. These other codes are usually either octal, duo-decimal, hexa-decimal, "excess three" or binary-coded-decimal. We shall say just a little about these codes shortly. It suffices here to say that the ordinary English and decimal number scales of everyday conversation are usually translated into a binary or some other scale. The instructions (e.g. add, subtract, etc.) are usually coded into the same code as that used for the numbers.

Let us now assume that we have instructions and numbers in store. As the instructions start operating on the numbers they are put into the Arithmetic Unit, the operations are performed and the resulting numbers returned to the Store. Now to be able to phrase the instructions which are to operate on the numbers in store we have to be able to describe which instructions we are referring to, and we do this by referring to the address of the registers in which the numbers are placed. We can imagine, for our purpose, a simple three-address computer. A three-address computer is one whose instruction word contains three addresses: the address of the two numbers to be operated upon and the one where the result has to be put when the arithmetical operation is completed. One-address and two-address computers operate slightly differently, usually in conjunction with what is called an accumulator. In the latter cases, instructions simply put all numbers which are to be operated upon into the accumulator. There are also separate instructions for putting the numbers back again from the accumulator into store.

Suppose we lay down the following code for our three-address computer instructions:

Add	01
Subtract	02

Multiply	03
Divide	04
Conditional jump	05
Load	06
Print	07
Stop	08

There will be many more instructions than this in a computer, but we need not discuss them in order to show how the basic operations function. Load and stop orders are input-orders, while the print and jump instructions are organisational orders.

Let us now concentrate our attention on some simple arithmetical program. Suppose we wish to multiply 4 and 7 together and then divide by 2 to get an answer. We place the numbers 4 and 7 in particular registers, which we shall call 200 and 201, so that we now write 200(4) and 201(7). We now need to use the two orders multiply (03) and divide (04). As we are using a three-address computer the structure of the instruction work is $I/A_1/A_2/A_3$, where the I (two decimal digits) tells us what operation to perform and A_1, A_2, A_3 are the three addresses involved. The first two addresses tell us where to take the numbers from the store and the last address tells us where to put the numbers back into store. The three A's are addresses of the numbers to be operated upon. We can easily see now which orders we need and how to write them. They are as follows:

    03/200/201/202
    04/202/200/202

These two instructions (which we can place in storage registers 000 and 001, say) are the two instructions which will multiply 4 by 7 to give us 28 and then divide 28 by 2 to give us 14. The computation itself is obviously a trivial one, but it shows in fact how we write our instructions, indeed how we write a program. We program the computer to perform the operations (however complex) for us.

In the use of digital computers, many programs, especially those of cybernetic interest, may turn out to be extremely long and complicated. Under these circumstances the program is best (even necessarily) tackled in stages. First of all we clarify our ideas as to how the arithmetic should be done. It must be remembered that this may be quite complicated, demanding the solution to differential equations or asking for the inversion of a set of matrices, or some other quite complex piece of mathematics. Having decided upon the mathematical technique to be adopted, the programmer makes out his flow-chart, which will show clearly each step that needs to be taken to reach the end of the computation.

The programmer completes his flow chart before he writes out his instructions and codes them. Eventually he punches the instructions on tape (in binary code if necessary), so that the programmed tape (the set of instructions) and the other punched tape, the data tape (the set of numbers to be operated upon) are separately punched. Some machines use cards, others use tape, while some may use both, or even other methods altogether.

Many different arithmetical codes are used in computers. We should say now that in the "static representation" of numbers and instructions we think of holes punched in tape or cards. Thus a hole in a particular square of the tape or card represents a one, while the absence in a square represents a nought. The usefulness of the binary code lies in the fact that it can be represented by any two-state switch or indeed anything which is capable of representing only distinguishable states. The main reason the binary code was in fact developed in computer hardware is the relative ease with which the hardware can cope with the representation of only two distinguishable states. (It is interesting to notice that the nervous system also functions on the basis of units (neurons) which appear in many respects to be two-state.)

Program writing would seem to take up so much time that the high speed of the computer which operates at several thousand times the speed of a human mathematician, would be largely wasted because of the amount of time spent on programing. The reason why this is not the case is that once a program involving some complicated piece of mathematics has been written, it is stored and used again when the same piece of mathematics comes up — even though, of course, the actual numerical data may be different — and this means that the programs can be stored in libraries and used when needed.

These stored programs are actually called sub-routines or macros. Thus a great deal of standard programing of the computer is the organising of the sub-routines into the main program, and switching these sub-routines out again when they have been used. Thus it may be that we can easily specify, by editing, the steps in a lengthy and complex program by reference to portions or whole programs already well documented and sorted in the sub-routine library.

It is a natural devlopment from sub-routines to computer languages and we must now consider this approach to simplified computer programing.

8.2   COMPUTER LANGUAGES

Machine languages in computers are usually, though by no means always, in a binary form. As we have seen, the binary code depends on the use of only two primitive symbols, and since computers are concerned to a great extent with mathematical problems, it is first important to realise that our ordinary mathematical notation, the so-called decimal code, which has ten primitive symbols, can easily be mapped onto a language with only two primitive symbols, but not on one. It should be made clear that by primitive symbols we are here meaning only the actual numbers, or symbols, used for digits. There are, besides these symbols, other symbols for operations such as addition, subtraction, etc.

The translation from binary code is simple and straight forward:

$$
\begin{aligned}
0 &= 0 \\
1 &= 1 \\
2 &= 10 \\
3 &= 11 \\
4 &= 100 \\
5 &= 101 \\
6 &= 110 \\
7 &= 111 \\
8 &= 1000 \\
9 &= 1001 \quad \text{etc.}
\end{aligned}
$$

For the reader who is unfamiliar with binary code, a certain amount of practice is necessary before the full simplicity of the translation is readily recognised. The easiest way of regarding the matter is to realise that with only two symbols we must "move to the left" more quickly than we do if we have ten symbols available to us. Thus, in binary counting, starting with 0 and going on to 1 we cannot go on to 2 as a separate symbol, because there is no symbol which is designed to designate 2 alone. We therefore combine 0 and 1 in the same way as we do in the decimal code when we get to 10 so that 10 here stands for 2 and all subsequent binary numbers are combinations of the only two available symbols 0 and 1.

In much the same way, for the decimal code, the combination of symbols 0 to 9 inclusive, in fact, are the only numbers utilised after 9 has been reached. It is just a question of combining the available symbols and the fewer the symbols used in the original set the more quickly we will have to "move to the left", because of course all mathematical has a positional value — a 1 three places to the left of the decimal point in decimal code will represent 100 — five places to the left will represent 10,000, seven places 1,000,000 and so on. In the same way for binary code two places to the left represents 2, three places represents 4, four places 8, five places 16, six places 32, seven places 64 and so on. We are, in the binary code, going up in multiples of 2 rather than multiples of 10.

Another way of looking at the matter is to think of a decimal number like 378 as being shorthand for $(3 \times 10^2) + (7 \times 10) + (8 \times 1)$. Similarly a binary number 11011 is shorthand for $(1 \times 2^4) + (1 \times 2^3) + (1 \times 2^2) + (1 \times 2) + (1 \times 1)$. By the same argument an octal number 362 for example is shorthand for $(3 \times 8^2) + (6 \times 8) + (2 \times 1)$ i.e. 242 in decimal.

So much then for the internal organisation of computer codes. What we have said is extremely brief and elementary, but enough to show the reader that there is a problem of internal linguistic organisation for a computer and, what is much more important, that since the human programer can be assumed to speak a combination of ordinary English and decimal arithmentic, there is a problem of translation from one sort of language to another.

This problem of translation, of encoding and decoding is characteristic of machine-man relationships, through language. The main difference here, between ordinary linguistic communication and communication between the machine and the computer, is that the machine and the human being are in fact speaking different languages. The resemblance, therefore, is to a situation where an Englishman and a Frenchman or a Persian and a Japanese speak to each other, having to translate unit by unit — whether the unit be a word and the translation be word by word, phrase by phrase, or sentence by sentence — from one language to the other and vice versa. Where two people speaking the same language talk to each other, then there is still a translation of symbols into concepts, and we might ask ourselves whether there is any parallel to this in the human being "talking" to the computer. The answer is that the operations performed by the computer could be regarded as being the equivalent of concepts as represented by the language of the human being, and it should be perfectly possible for the computer to have two different languages, as it were; one for the internal binary code which is the equivalent, say, of human concepts, and the other any other language whatever which refers to that set of concepts. We shall be discussing this matter again in Chapter 15.

For purely practical reasons such a language as we have described has been found necessary. To explain why this is so, it has to be made clear that the programing of the computer to perform either organisational or computational operation is fairly complicated and requires a certain amount of skill and practice. Now it is also quite clear that we may expect many people to want to use the computer for some quite special purpose — and this is even more likely to be the case in the future — and yet not have the time or find it worthwhile to have to learn the fairly complicated computer language. Thus it is that he can learn a simplified language, such as a rather carefully stated version of ordinary English which can be translated by the machine itself into the programing language. This indeed is the basis of automatic programing.

There are in existence about four different kinds of what are usually called *autocodes*. The first one is called an "interpreter" and works by having some symbol which represents a computer operation, so that the whole set of computer programing operations can be represented by simple symbols. You then simply write down the instructions in the order you want them performed, or you write down the simple symbols that refer to the operations and the machine will either translate the simple symbols or interpret them directly — they must obviously be more simple than the original symbols used in the machine language — one by one, by the use of a translator in the actual storage of the computer.

An "assembler" code provides a similar sort of computer language apparatus as the interpreter, except that an assembler always requires translation but does not depend on the translator being built into the storage of the computer in such a way that the whole operation or translation and programing occurs together. With an assembler, the result of the translation is to produce a program as an output, which is subsequently fed into the computer again where it is in fact a program.

The third type of computer language is called a "compiler language" and this differs from the first two types of autocode in that the number of words used in the compiler language is very much less than the number of orders that will come out in the programing language. The basic idea here is that we shall be able to use one word to summarise a whole set of operations. For example, one may say "find the square root of some number", where the phase "find the square root of" represents or may represent, a whole set of some 20, 30 or 40 or more instructions. So the compiler code in general is very much more efficient and useful than the assemblers and interpreters. We must be clear that a compiler involves the process of translating from an autocode language (a source program) into a machine code program.

The fourth kind of programing language is a "generator". This has so far been little used, at least in its more sophisticated forms, and is closely connected with the learning and self-modification of the machine, and is therefore very close to cybernetic interests. With a generator the programmer needs only to specify the ends he wishes to have achieved, and the computer will itself derive the necessary program by which these ends are achieved. This differs of course from the first three types of autocoding procedures in that it makes no reference to the means whatever, only to the ends. It is therefore closely involved with what we would call *learning programs.*

One difficulty that is encountered in practice is that each computer model must have its own separate forms of autocode. An autocode for the *Atlas* computer, for example, will not be useful for an I.C.T. 1900 computer. To offset this difficulty, a great deal of work has been done to produce universal autocoding languages like ALGOL which is capable of translating any of the particular autocoding languages into a program language for any existing computer. COBOL is another such universal autocoding language; FORTRAN, too, has a degree of universality. More recently PL1 has been developed as a successor to FORTRAN.

The implications of this work on digital computers is of special interest to linguists, because it throws heavy emphasis on the need for precision in translation and in the rules of formation, or construction, of the particular languages. Any failure to be wholly precise would vitiate a program language and would lead to the computer not performing the desired ends.

One special aspect of computer languages should be mentioned once more in this context, and that is the attempts to produce "nearly natural" languages such as English for the programming of computers. There exists a number of attempts, that vary in detail and sophistication, to create computer languages in ordinary English. The first and immediate point that arises as soon as you try to use such a language as a compiler language or generator is the realisation that it is absolutely necessary to eliminate vagueness. Furthermore, although private usages are acceptable, they are only acceptable provided a translation of that private usage is given at the same time that it is used. This same condition, of course, holds with any language; no objection can be held against private usage provided that private usage is sufficiently explained.

We should mention here that George (1966, 1968), Napper (1966, 1967), Sarkar (1967) and others have been working on languages for communication between man and computers and computers with each other. Napper's is the nearest to everyday English and is styled the "compiler − compiler − compiler" or third order compiler language. But this will be discussed in some detail in Chapter 15.

8.3   LIST PROCESSING

One difficulty encountered in writing programs which deal with natural language is the relative inflexibility of such programs. One wants to be able to get at storage locations more easily and on a different basis than is normally possible with ordinary programming languages, hence the devlopment of list processing (Newell, 1961).

We construct our lists from cells such as the following:

where the first half is called the CAR and the second is CDR (called "cudder"), and by this division of a cell into two parts we can "marry up" different items which may be widely dispersed in the physical store of the computer. Both CAR and CDR can take symbols or addresses, so $X + Y$ can be represented, say, as:

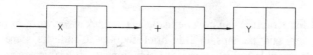

and $A + (B + C) \times D$ as:

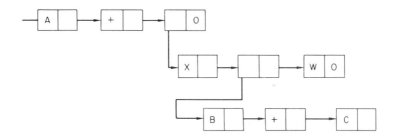

Here we call A the base register and use two sublists, and we use 0 to indicate the end of a list or sublist. We refer to such lists as one-way lists since we can only move here from left to right. By implication, in a two-way list we can, of course, move both ways.

One further illustration of the flexibility that list-processing makes possible is that of introducing a new symbol into a set of symbols. Suppose we had a list as follows:

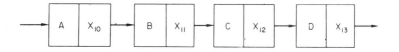

and we wished to introduce J between X_{11} and X_{12}. We use a spare box as follows:

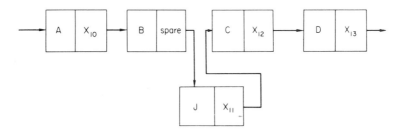

This whole list structure can now be made as complex as we wish, or need, it. Enough has been said perhaps in this brief section to indicate some of the flexibility made possible by list processing, which makes it a language especially suitable for classifying and re-classifying items and allows associations and cross-associations to occur. This facility is very necessary for the simulation of concepts and languages in the human brain.

8.4   LEARNING PROGRAMS

One further aspect of language in computers should now be mentioned: It is perfectly possible for computers to learn from experience. This, indeed, underlies the idea of a generator. If one computer operates in an environment which is unknown to it and there are some definite goals to achieve, or if one computer is playing another computer at some game where the game is well defined and the game is to be won or lost, then one computer can learn from the other.

The simplest situation to envisage is one where one computer plays a game perfectly and the other computer playing against it does not understand the tactical rules of that game (George, 1962). The second computer, by imitating the tactics of the first computer, and by generalising on those tactics, can achieve a game at least as efficient and perhaps in certain circumstances more efficient than the first computer. We say that it has learned from experience.

In a series of experiments carried out in Bristol, of the kind mentioned above, and in which one computer learned to play a game as a result of playing against another computer, it was clear that the computer playing the ideal game was playing from one set of rules, whereas the computer that had been doing the learning was playing from another set.

It was felt that the computer that had learned to play as efficiently as the one that had started efficiently should in fact play in exactly the same way and it is of interest to notice why it did not. The first computer played by a simple set of rules of generalisation which were translated into the computer machine language, and the second computer collected information and played by going through that collected information to see when the same sort of situations recurred. This meant that the second computer took rather longer (only fractionally longer by human standards) to make decisions as to what move was to be made in the game as compared with the first computer. It was not until generalisations about the various "winning" situations were made that the second computer could be said to have played from certain rules, as opposed to information collected into tables. However, there could be no guarantee whatever that the same set of rules was used by the second computer as the first, in that although at best they may represent the same tactical move, they certainly would not, in general, be represented in the same way inside the computer itself. Only if we had something like a compiler code in which the first set of rules was stated, and the second computer had access to these compiler rules, could the second computer represent his rules in anything like the same way. But even here it should be made clear that the only way that any sort of autocoded language could be known to refer to the same set of computer operations in the machine language is where someone has access to both storage systems. Thus if the second computer was taught the language only by observing some correlation between the symbols used and the external behaviour of the other computer and itself, then it may well find itself using words of the autocoding language to represent different sets of operations of the machine language.

This process of descriptions of rules in games is a rather complicated matter which we shall not go into fully here but it does form an interesting parallel with the human situation where languages are necessarily learned publicly and it is only by continued comparison between people's usage that we can have any hope (never a certainty) that we use words, phrases, etc. that have the same referents as our interlocutor.

We have talked so far about ideal game-playing situations with two-person games and one person playing optimally. The point should be made that much the same set of principles hold even when neither player plays optimally, provided the game is still relatively simple. Although regardless of the complexity of the game, provided the player who is learning can represent both his opponent and himself, there is still no difficulty.

In "non-ideal" games where information is incomplete or where a random element occurs, such as a deal in card games, the same principles hold, but the results can be somewhat different.

With a deterministic game an algorithm can be learned by virtue of experience. In practise this depends on the game being relatively simple. Noughts and crosses for example is such a game, whereas chess is not. The complexity of chess is such that an algorithm would take far too long to discover, or indeed to use had we discovered it. There are yet other cases and these especially apply where information is incomplete where algorithms cannot occur. In such cases we must use *heuristics*.

A heuristic is a rough rule of thumb or a short cut. It is general and needs to be interpreted for each occurrence. Thus "control the centre of the board" is one heuristic for chess which is not specific in what it implies.

Heuristic programming is a new branch of computing. It is so completely bound up with artificial intelligence that we shall postpone a major discussion of it until Chapter 13, when artificial intelligence is discussed.

From simple learning programs which are equivalent to the simple neural net we described in Chapter 7, and which was capable of maze running, we go on to consider the more complicated heuristic computer programming methods that are, as we have said, designed to provide short cuts to precise solutions, or provide rough and ready methods to help with problems which have no precise solutions. (Newell, Shaw and Simon, 1963; Gelerntner, 1963; Samuel, 1963, 1969; George 1966, 1967).

This sort of programming has a practical pay off but also helps to shed some light on possible mechanisms for intelligent behaviour.

8.5   HEURISTIC PROGRAMMING

We have already led up to this subject from the use of adaptive or learning programs.

Conventional computer methods cannot always be used where information is incomplete or where it is completely uneconomic to use such methods. This applies to decision taking, planning and problem solving all the way from the most abstract to the most concrete examples.

Simple heuristics, in the form of mathematical models, have been used now for several years in such fields as sales estimating, but the heuristics that have recently been developed are especially applicable to non-numerical or non-mathematical problems, as well as to numerical ones (Burstall, 1963; Tonge, 1963; Clarkson, 1963).

Machine loading illustrates the practical application of such methods. Suppose we have to plan to put raw materials or components, or both, on to various sets of machines which carry out the necessary processing such as turning components into products. We may have to replan our schedules every week for the next week, or even every day for the next day, and if the system is sufficiently complicated the planning could not be done by conventional means in the necessary time; a perfect plan that comes too late to use is obviously useless. In the past, the thought has been that such plans could not, as a result, be computerised, and must necessarily be done by people who must also — since they are far slower in such computational matters than computers — use slow *ad hoc* methods.

To generate such short cuts (heuristic) methods on the computer is of great value and this is what heuristic programming is concerned with.

We suggest next a rough plan which is nearly correct as far as we can tell, and then use this as a starting point. We can usually take over from the human planners their heuristics and make them explicit. It is not always easy, of course, to get every planner to say exactly what it is that he does, and it is precisely because of this that the processes of planning are not made explicit and not therefore liable to systematic improvement as a result of experience. We must try to illustrate the point by an example.

A manager of an industry who is responsible for producing some commodity is concerned with trying to ensure the "pipeline" is free from "bottlenecks". He tells different people to attend to this rather than that, as "this" is more urgent than "that". The problem is for him that he does not know whether he really has solved his problem in the best possible way or has even solved it at all. It he could write down the method he uses and discover the results, he could, of course, make the necessary comparisons and systematically learn; more than this, he could write a computer program to do the job for him and this is easier to improve than his own implicit planning and decision making processes. At this point he has entered the field of heuristic programming.

Here we have a link with natural language since we tend to think and make decisions, and certainly state those decisions, in ordinary English. If it is wished to generate better decisions than have been used so far, then we have to reformulate the original decisions in ordinary English. Instead of saying "put all the punching machines in Factory 3" we may say "put half the punching machines in Factory 3 and the other half in Factory 5". This suggests that our computing system should have the capability for making verbal generalisations. It is also obviously an advantage if it can make logical inferences; both things are possible, as we shall see in Chapter 14.

Suppose we have a message such as "Put all reaming machines into Factory 4", this can be encoded inside the computer into some logical form such as $(M_8 \in F_4)$ with a suitable prefix $(01...0)$ which indicates the tense of the verb and its imperative mood, among other things, and where $M_8 \equiv$ reaming machines and $F_4 \equiv$ Factory 4. The program can now look up its record of where each of the set (M_8) is located and make, by inference, such arrangements as are necessary to send all of them to F_4. This may also entail the organisation of transport and other detail. What we presuppose in our computer program is that all the logical entailments − part of the semantic rules − are in store. This means that if a reaming machine in the set (M_8) was located several miles from F_4, then appropriate transport would have to be obtained.

A natural language facility on the computer is not the same as a heuristic facility, but the two certainly go conveniently together (Chapter 15). This is because so much of human planning is still, necessarily, couched in non-numerical terms.

We can summarise current experimentation in the following terms. We recognise that certain applications such as payroll, certain allocation problems, accounts, inventory control and the like are capable of systematic and precise programming on to the computer. At the same time it *was* thought that when human beings made plans that were contingent or vague (ill-defined), these could not be programmed onto a computer. Current experiments are attempting to show that this latter class of problems is sensible in computer terms; we know they can be carried out on a computer; what it is necessary to show is that they can be done more efficiently this way than by human beings.

Heuristic programming is a complicated subject and we shall be returning to it more than once in the remainder of the book.

8.6   COMPUTERS AND AUTOMATA THEORY

We have said already that digital computers represent one hardware realisation of automata theory so it will repay a little consideration to see whether any useful results have yet emerged from this association.

We have already mentioned the Universal Turing Machine (Turing, 1936) for its resemblance to the general purpose digital computer. Its imitation of any Turing machine was based on a process very similar to that of programming a digital computer.

It is possible to be precise in our statement of the relation of any Turing machine to a digital computer. At this point we introduce the notion of a Program Machine M which is a digital computer with a finite store with infinite-sized registers. The programming unit can only tell whether a register is empty or not.

In terms of this program machine we can assert that every Turing machine T has an equivalent program machine. This is in fact the precursor to the more general result that any Turing machine T has an equivalent digital computer (with program) provided the programming tape is, like the Turing tape, potentially infinite.

One other similar approach to automata and computers was carried through by Wang (1957). He defines a B-machine which has an internal program and is thus like a digital computer, and yet operates with a tape very much like a Turing machine tape. The B-machine can mark the tape with only one kind of symbol and cannot erase at all. The B-machine accepts four kinds of instruction, move left, move right, mark scanned square, or conditionally jump as in a computer. The mark is used to designate a jump, whereas an unmarked square implies that the scanning should proceed in natural sequence.

A number of results have been shown with respect to a B-machine and they show more light on automata than computers. A few samples follow:

1) A universal Turing is still possible even if it cannot erase a symbol from the tape.

2) Shepherdson and Sturgis (1960) showed that there were other equally effective ways of producing the jump instructions, e.g. "jump if blank" is effectively the same as "jump if marked".

3) C. Y. Lee has shown that the absence of a "move left" instruction reduces the B-machine to a finite automaton. Another type of comparison, this time between finite automata and computers, suggests that a full adder in the digital computer is a finite automaton. This itself leads to some curious results which impose some limitation on a finite automaton, and a computer which has the possibility of adding indefinite amounts of peripheral storage becomes more like a growing automaton and less like a finite automaton.

Finally we should say that the program machine described earlier in this section can be shown to be equivalent to the set of generally recursive functions.

8.7   COMPUTER PROGRAMMING AND MATHEMATICAL LOGIC

A great deal has been written on the resemblance between program languages and logical languages (Brafford and Hirschberg, 1963) and this ranges from mechanical mathematics (Wang, 1960) to context-free language analysis (Chomsky and Schultzenberger, 1963). This is a field which has been relatively recently explored seriously for the first time, and raises questions as to which mathematical logical forms are most convenient for computer use. The use, for example of Herbrand's form in logic for computers is analogous to the older developments of numerical methods for use in presenting mathematical problems to the computer.

We shall not discuss current research in computer science because it is a vast subject most of which is irrelevant to cybernetics. Thos parts which are relevant are discussed in other chapters of this book.

At this point we shall conclude this chapter and move on in the next chapter to a brief discussion of information theory; this is another facet of cybernetics.

8.8   SUMMARY

This chapter has attempted to outline the basic principles on which digital computers work.

The programming of computers can be carried out in various ways, and therefore, apart from the basic machine code of the computer, we have different levels of language in which the computer can be programmed. These languages include interpreters, assemblers, compilers and generators.

The use of generators is a reminder that we can write computer languages that provide especially for the flexible learning type of programs which are so important to cybernetics.

We have carefully eschewed more modern talk in terms of central processors and the like since the aim, as far as computing was concerned, was simply to outline the basic operations in the simplest terms for cyberneticians.

CHAPTER 9

Information theory

Argument

Information theory is a branch of probability theory. Although information theory had its origins in the field of telecommunications and engineering it was soon found to have a much wider range of application. It is natural that cybernetics should be interested in what is an important part of the description of a control and communication situation.

We have discussed logic and logical nets, and seen in them a means of constructing automata, especially automata which are similar to the structure of the human being. Information theory is closely linked to such automata, and apart from supplying a model of information flow, tells us how to measure that information flow. In the same way it can be applied to describing automata, so obviously it can be applied to describing digital computers.

We shall at the end of this chapter describe a model of perception which combines logical nets and information theory. In the meantime, we shall simply describe information theory.

Information theory, or communication theory which is a slightly more general title, is a mathematical theory which measures information, its flow, size of communication channel, etc. especially as it applies to radio, telegraphy, television or indeed any other medium of communication whatever. The theory was originally concerned with a communication channel which was specified by a wavelength and frequency and involved vibrations of the air or electro-magnetic radiation; the process was usually continuous, but could be discrete, wherein information was encoded and subsequently decoded. This field of information theory is like that of automata theory in that it is abstract and can be used, like a formal language, to describe any empirical systems that have the same structure and properties.

Consider a simple example of information theory. A war is on and a H.Q. wishes to send a message to one of its generals some fifty miles away. It wants to send it quickly and it uses a morse buzzer and codes its message into morse and it is picked up by a teleprinter at the other end and translated back into ordinary English. But since there is a war on at the time, then H. Q. carries on a further coding into a cipher such that the original ideas are really doubly encoded and therefore need to be decoded three times. They start as ideas with the H. Q. and they encode them as sentences in English and then into cipher and then into morse code. They are transmitted as dots and dashes over a landline and decoded at the other end. A cipher clerk further decodes them and H. Q. further decodes them again into ideas or concepts.

Figure 1 depicts, by way of a simple diagram, the communication situation in which there is a source and a destination. The encoding procedure and a decoding procedure may, of course, be repeated any number of times, and this involves a translation at each stage.

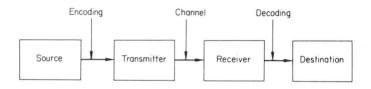

Figure 1   The noiseless communication channel between the source and destination of a message. The encoding and decoding procedures may be repeated any number of times.

In the general situation so far depicted, no mention has been made of a "noisy channel" although noisy channels do frequently occur in a communication situation. Noise is well known to communication, since it occurs as atmospherics in radio or in some form of technical interference that makes it impossible to pick up all of what has been communicated. Noise occurs literally in everyday conversation so that you miss a certain amount of information. Whatever the reason information is lost when communication takes place, we can be sure that in general some will be lost, and we shall call this loss the result of communication on a noisy channel.

Mistakes in encoding or decoding also account for loss of information when a message is sent from A to B. The people involved in carrying out the communication are fallible; both the people actually tapping out the message, and the people taking it down with paper and pencil are liable to make mistakes. Even if there were no other factors involved, this would in itself make communication very much a probabilistic matter; a matter of chance.

One of the best known measure of information so far suggested is that due to Shannon (see Shannon and Weaver, 1949), who has suggested the H be the name given to amount of information, or entropy as it may be called, and that H be defined by the following simple formula:

$$H = - \Sigma p_i \log_2 p_i$$

and we shall now try to show what this formula means.

It must be made clear that this is in some ways an arbitrary way of measuring information since, for example, the minus sign and logarithm to base 2 are just conveniences to the measuring process, while the p_i's are probabilities. They are the probabilities associated with choosing a single message from a whole set of possible messages each of which has a probability associated with it. The whole process is akin to that of formalising the word "information".

The method is easily illustrated. Suppose there are four horses running a race and let us suppose that they all have the same chance of winning — a very unlikely occurrence in practice — and therefore since one horse must win the chance of any one of them winning will be ¼ for each. If we label the horses A, B, C, and D, then the following table shows the odds for each:

	A	B	C	D
Probability of winning	3 to 1	3 to 1	3 to 1	3 to 1

Now we can say that the *average* amount of information passed by the system is given by our formula above. It is the sum of the log of each probability also multiplied by the same probability and added up. Now we can see the point of the logs and the minus sign. There is a theorem in logarithms which says Log X/Y = Log X - Log Y so, when we take the log base 2 which means log 1 is 0 (very convenient), the result is simply the positive sum of the log of all the denominators, i.e.

$$¼ \log 4 + ¼ \log 4 + ¼ \log 4 + ¼ \log 4$$

or adding up

$$½ + ½ + ½ + ½ = 2$$

i.e. simply log 4 which is 2, when the log is taken to base 2. Thus we say the information is worth 2 (or since we need a name for the unit of measurement) we say 2 bits. The word "bits" is a contraction of the words "binary digit".

Now arithmetic normally uses a *decimal system*. We use ten different symbols, 0 to 9 inclusive and then repeat these symbols in combinations of the form 10, 11, 12, ..., 20, ..., 30, ..., 100, ... etc. to get as many decimal numbers as we like. The *binary* system, which we have already discussed in the last chapter, makes use of two symbols 0 and 1 — a language especially well suited to a computer, and thus we have 0, 1, 10, 11, 100, 101, 111, 1000, and so on. The numbers just listed are the decimal number 0 to 8, written in binary form, and it should be easy to see how one can go on constructing number systems using binary code or

other codes involving any number of symbols. A ternary code for example would
be 0, 1, 2, 10, 11, 12, 20, 21, 22, 100, etc.

The following table shows the conversion from decimal to binary code,
following on from where we started it in the last chapter:

Decimal	Binary
10	01010
11	01011
12	1100
13	1101
14	1110
15	1111
16	10000
17	10001
18	10010
19	10011
20	10100
21	10101
22	10110
23	10111

The word "code" used above is quite appropriate in that it certainly is a
system of symbols for representing numbers, and for that matter any words in
English can also be put into binary code. In morse code, we can send ordinary
English sentences, and there we use a ternary code involving dot, dash and pause.
If we used just a dot (or dash) and a pause we should have a binary code for
language.

The measurement of information flow requires a further comment in the light
of what we have said about codes. The advantage of having 2 bits (or binary
digits) as our measure of information in the above example was that if you sent a
message saying that any one of the horses had won the race (not knowing in
advance which would win the race) you would need four distinguishable
messages to represent A, B, C and D. This requires just 2 binary digits, i.e. 00,
01, 10 and 11, therefore we say the average flow of information in the channel
will be 2 bits. 3 bits would be used to represent a race with 8 horses and so on.

We can thus measure information or at least the average rate of information
flow from a particular possible source. Similarly we can say that when a message
is passed, we can give a measure of what information that message contains. If A
wins the race the message contains log 4 or 2 bits. If the probabilities had not all
been the same in the last example we should see that the average amount of
single message, which is simply $\log_2 p_i$, where the particular p_i implied is the
probability of that particular horse (in the example) winning. Thus if the horse
were given probabilities 1/8, 1/8, 1/4 and 1/2 respectively for A, B, C and D, then

the message telling us D had won would be worth 1 bit. In other words our measure takes account of what we regard as unlikely, so that if we are told something that we did not expect we should receive more information than if we were told something we did expect. The limiting case in this matter of information is when you tell us something we know, or is certain — if such things ever occur empirically — and then you give us something with probability 1 and therefore having no bits of information at all. Quite clearly the greater the odds against an event the more information you give us if you tell us it has happened or correctly tell us it will happen. Similarly the maximum possible information for the system as a whole must occur with the maximum uncertainty and this is when the probabilities are equal.

We can go on from this starting point to measure the channel capacity of the system, and there is a very simple measure for this in the simplest case where all the probabilities are equal. If we have an alphabet A, B, ..., etc., of 16 symbols — these symbols could be names of horses if you like but they could also literally be letters as in the English alphabet — then if each symbol is of the same duration and thus carrying 4 bits of information, the capacity of the channel is $4n$ bits per second, where the channel is capable of transmitting n symbols per second. A more complicated measure applies when the symbols are all of the same duration and where the probabilities are unequal.

The duration of the symbol in the above discussion deserves some further mention. If you are transmitting any message whatever in code you have to face the fact that you need punctuation. If you do not have some form of punctuation then symbols — in our method of construction — get confused with each other. It is perhaps easiest to think of the morse code as an example here. If you sent three successive dots and could not use a pause which is really a sort of punctuation mark then you would not know whether there were three *Es*, and *I* and an *E* or an *E* and an *I* or a single *S*. Thanks however to the pause, we can tell which is being communicated. Similarly if all the words in an English message were run together, it might be difficult to disentangle individual words, and finally if we did not order our activities sensibly they would cease to be possible. For example you cannot pick up a telephone that is already picked up, and cannot go through a door-space without first opening the door. The order is a vital factor. It is punctuation that deals with order in language, and one possible solution, often used in computers which generally use binary code, is to have fixed word-lengths, so that every 32 binary symbols, say, make up a word and if your word happens to be simply "10" (just the two symbols) then it is still preceded by 30 0's. The mathematical theory of information now goes on from these simple beginnings to develop theorems about information flow showing the minimum size of channel necessary to communicate certain messages at a certain rate, and the most economical way of coding messages to maximise speed or accuracy or some other such variable.

9.1   LANGUAGE ANALYSIS

Let us now consider everyday language in terms of information theory. In the first place it is clear that in language we have constructed a system of symbols, in the form of words, and pauses, that can have its information content measured. This is also difficult, since if we wish to use Shannon's definition of information, we have to consider the whole set of possible words or sentences that *might* be used to assess the probability that any particular set should be used. However, although this seems difficult, it is in fact clear that a certain choice is involved in language and that the use of one word in a sentence, or the use of a sentence in a paragraph, limits the choice of further words or sentences.

An example of these constraints operating on the choice involved in language is simple; it is only necessary to consider the present sentence. Having started with "An", I would be unlikely to follow it with "An" but likely to follow it with a noun, and having said "An example" it is almost certain that I shall use next either a proposition or a conjunction. Indeed, a second's consideration will persuade the reader that with each successive word the rest of a sentence becomes increasingly inevitable.

It is the characteristic of repetition that is called *redundancy* and allows us to miss many words in a talk, or be unable to read a number of words in a friend's letter, but still allows us to decipher the sense of the letter; the property of statistical homogeneity is a very vital one. We know that a series of sentences are likely to have a definite relation to each other, and that a book that is dealing with fish, birds or cricket is likely to stick to that subject and this gives us a limited domain over which we have to guess the missing details.

These properties of redundancy and homogeneity are what allow us to "break codes". Without them it would be extremely difficult and the only consolation is that it would be difficult also to send messages where the destruction of any one symbol destroys the whole of the meaning. The idea that any one symbol could destroy the whole meaning of any actual message is clearly not a practical possibility, since no language ever goes in for such wholesale coding, and every symbol must have some relation to the next ... this is what is meant by the *context of a discussion*, and must occur with any communication.

Redundancy is a concept that can be given a precise measure, since if we say that the relative entropy of a system is the degree of actual information passed as a fraction of the amount of information that could have been passed, the complement of this is called the redundancy. In other words the extent to which the relative entropy is small, the redundancy is large. In practice, basic English has an enormous redundancy since the vocabulary is small and things take a great deal of saying and this lengthens, and is supposed to clarify, and does so by virtue of considerable redundancy. On the other hand *Finnegan's 'Wake* or *Ulysses*, the celebrated novels of James Joyce, have little redundancy because they use new words to stand for whole phrases in basic English, and they cut down the length of the description at the expense of greatly enlarging the vocabulary, and thus making glossaries of terms necessary.

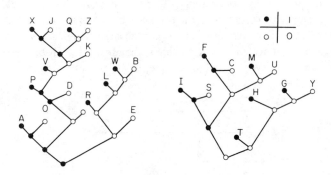

Figure 2   This shows the alphabet weighted according to their letter frequency in English. If each node is two-state switch then *R* would be reached by 1001 and *F* by 01011.

9.2 STOCHASTIC PROCESSES

One very important field of cybernetic interest that has arisen out of studies of information flow is the statistical one of "stochastic processes". A stochastic process is really a random series of symbols, let us use A, B, C ... which occurs in a purely random way, and for which a definite probability can be associated with the occurrence of each symbol. Thus for the following table:

Table 1

A	$\frac{1}{3}$
B	$\frac{1}{6}$
C	$\frac{1}{2}$

a series such as:

$$\text{A B C A B C A C C B A C C C}$$
$$\text{A A C C C B B C A C A C A C A C}$$

(1)

might be regarded as typical. Although quite obviously the longer the series the more likely it is to conform to the probabilities shown in the table. The process can be carried out in either direction. If the series leads to the table we often refer to the fractions in the table as "conditional probabilities", and say that the fraction, or probability, associated with each letter of the alphabet gives the ratio of occurence of the letter to the total number of letters occuring.

We can obviously generate more complicated cases from these simple beginnings, so that we may have a table of conditional probabilities extending over two successive events. As an example, using the same alphabet of A, B and C alone, consider:

Table 2

	A	B	C
A	$\frac{1}{4}$	$\frac{1}{4}$	$\frac{1}{2}$
B	7/8	1/8	0
C	0	3/8	5/8

which may generate a series such as:

A C C C B A C C C B B A A B A B A C C C C C B A A B A A C C C   (2)

we can have a conditional probability table of length 3. e.g.

Table 3

	AA	AB	AC	BA	BB	BC	CA	CB	CC
A	0	0	1/9	0	0	2/9	1/3	0	1/3
B	0	0	1/5	0	0	1/5	3/5	0	0
C	1/14	1/14	5/14	1/14	·1/14	0	1/14	1/7	1/7

Such a table applies to the same series as (1), above. Note that we only count 9 occurrences of A, since the last occurrence of A is followed by *one* symbol. The same argument applies to C.

It will be clear that the fact that O occurs in two places in table 2 ensures that B can never be followed by C, and C can never be followed by A. If, on the other hand, the table represents the series (in which case anything may happen) and what was, at any instant O, may become a positive fraction.

We can, with such stochastic tables, reconstruct English or any other language, so that if you consider conditional probabilities or as many as seven consecutive letters of the English language, including one letter for a space betweeen words or for any other punctuation mark, then a fair approximation to English can be achieved. One may guess that in the table for English he will expect to find the column headed U, in the row for Q, for two successive letters, being very nearly 1, since Q is nearly always followed by U in English.

Similarly all the rules of English can be reassembled in such a table. Of course words can be used, and probabilities can be associated with the words, and this more quickly will lead to the production of English sentences, although for sensible English a further weighting will have to be given to the context of the discussion. Thus matters in a particular context will take on special probabilities relative to that context. For example in a book on football the letters *ba* with two spaces to follow is likely to have a heavy probability towards 11, whereas in a book on "pubs" it is more likely to be *r*, followed by a pause.

This property of *statistical homogeneity* can be utilised in a special way. Different authors tend to build up slightly different vocabularies and as a result it is possible to carry out statistical tests to establish the authors of anonymous works by finding out the frequency with which certain words occur. Such a test of vocabulary tends to be as critical for each author as a test of fingerprints.

It is possible at this point to see the important significance of the stochastic process, because the discussion of conditioning and signs and the behaviouristic theory of language, which came earlier, was a theory about certain events following each other in specified orders. A stochastic process is precisely a way of specifying that order.

An ordering of symbols that tends to repeat itself with some regularity is called "ergodic". In fact an ergodic source is one that has precisely this property of being statistically homogeneous.

The whole field of stochastic processes and the special case of Markov nets have a rather special significance for cybernetics. Bush and Mosteller (1955) used it to describe the behaviour of statistical rats (starats) and their ability to learn from the documentation of experience.

There have been many attempts made to show that behaviour is appropriately described by stochastic processes of one kind or another. We saw the appropriateness of this in looking at neural nets and investigating the simple case of a neural net model that can learn by positive and negative reinforcement in the actual process of maze-running.

If we consider again a 3-choice maze whose solution is, say, $b_1 c_2 b_3 d_4 c_5 b_6 c_7$ then we know we can construct a neural (or logical) net which can perform the necessary learning. We can describe the structure in detail either by a net, by a logical formula, or by a reduced net (see Chapter 7) or by a reduced formula, or if we reduce the formula by a stochastic process. The reduced net for the above maze solution is constructed as follows:

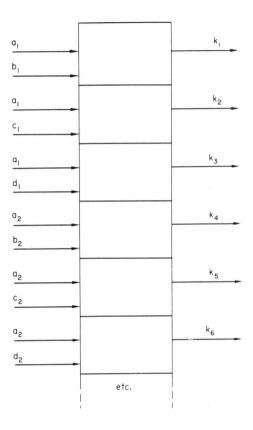

Figure 3   An abstract or reduced B-net, showing only input and output fibres.

The correct associations are clearly illustrated by the following table:

	b_1	b_2	b_3	b_4	b_5	b_6	b_7
a_1	$c_1;a_2$	$c_2;a_3$	$c_3;a_4$	$c_4;a_5$	$c_5;a_6$	$c_6;a_7$	c_7
	d_1	d_2	d_3	d_4	d_5	d_6	d_7

The complete B-net is hopelessly complicated. The reduced structural matrix is:

	A	B	C	D
A				
B		L		
C				
D				

Where only the submatrix L is non-zero, and L in detail is:

$$b_1 b_2 b_3 b_4 b_5 b_6 b_7 c_1 c_2 c_3 c_4 c_5 c_6 c_7 d_1 d_2 d_3 d_4 d_5 d_6 d_7$$

$L \equiv$ a_1 1 0 0 0 0 0 0 0 0 0 0 0 0 0 0 0 0 0 0 0 0

a_2 0 0 0 0 0 0 0 1 0 0 0 0 0 0 0 0 0 0 0 0 0

a_3 0 0 1 0 0 0 0 0 0 0 0 0 0 0 0 0 0 0 0 0 0

a_4 0 0 0 0 0 0 0 0 0 0 0 0 0 0 0 0 1 0 0 0 0

a_5 0 0 0 0 0 0 0 0 0 0 1 0 0 0 0 0 0 0 0 0 0

a_6 0 0 0 0 0 1 0 0 0 0 0 0 0 0 0 0 0 0 0 0 0

a_7 0 0 0 0 0 0 0 0 0 0 0 0 0 1 0 0 0 0 0 0 0

The reduced functional matrices could have 1's only where 1's occur in L, and this will depend on whether learning has or has not actually taken place.

We should mention here some recent work on stochastic automata by Fu (1967). Such stochastic automata are in reality a special case of probabilistic automata discussed earlier, but they do represent a rather special case.

We can follow Fu in defining a stochastic automaton as a quintuple (Y, Q, U, F, G) where Y is a finite set of inputs, where $Y = (y_1, y_2, ..., y_r)$, Q is a finite set of states $Q = (q_1, q_2, ..., q_s)$, U is a finite set of outputs $U = (u_1, u_2, ..., u_m)$, F is the next state function, so that

$$Q(n + 1) = F(y(n), q(n)).$$

This is obviously a version of the general form discussed in Chapter 5:

$$Q(t + 1) = G(Q(t), S(t))$$

except here we may expect F to be stochastic and G may be either deterministic or stochastic.

For each input y_k, the function F will generally be represented by a state transition probability matrix $M_k(n)$. The (i, j)th element $p_n{}^k(i, j)$ of $M_k(n)$ is defined by

$$p_n{}^k(i, j) = P(q(n + 1) = q, 1q(n) = q_i, y(n) = y_k)$$

and

$$P_n{}^k(i, j) = 1$$

the probability distribution of $q(n)$ and $y(n)$ determine the probability distribution of $q(n + 1)$.

We can now think of a set of state transition probability matrices $M_1, M_2 \ldots$ for inputs $y_1, y_2, \ldots$. If the automaton has a Markov sequence of inputs then the automaton is appropriately interpreted as a Markov chain.

Since our aim in this book is not to develop mathematical methods but merely use mathematics descriptively, we shall now show a few typical Markov chain matrices (Kemeny and Snell, 1960). They are chains for what is sometimes called a "random walk". A particle moves in unit steps and in a straight line. If the probability p is that it will move right and q that it will move left. If we take s_1 and s_5 as boundary states (cf. input — output elements) and s_2 s_3 and s_4 as interior states (cf. inner elements) then we will assume s_1 and s_5 are terminal. This gives a matrix with rows and columns both s_1 s_2 s_3 s_4 s_5.

$$\begin{pmatrix} 1 & 0 & 0 & 0 & 0 \\ q & 0 & p & 0 & 0 \\ 0 & q & 0 & p & 0 \\ 0 & 0 & q & 0 & p \\ 0 & 0 & 0 & 0 & 1 \end{pmatrix}$$

If, however, it rebounds rather than terminates we get the matrix

$$\begin{pmatrix} 0 & 1 & 0 & 0 & 0 \\ q & 0 & p & 0 & 0 \\ 0 & q & 0 & p & 0 \\ 0 & 0 & q & 0 & p \\ 0 & 0 & 0 & 1 & 0 \end{pmatrix}$$

If the boundary states on being reached have probability ½ of staying there, we get

$$\begin{pmatrix} ½ & 0 & 0 & 0 & ½ \\ q & 0 & p & 0 & 0 \\ 0 & q & 0 & p & 0 \\ 0 & 0 & q & 0 & p \\ ½ & 0 & 0 & 0 & ½ \end{pmatrix}$$

It will be easy for the reader to see that the role of the transition matrix is to define in probabilistic terms the behaviour of any particle, automaton, neuron, or person — any item whatever — that shows some sort of tree like structure in its movements. This is particularly appropriate for maze running but can also be applied at any level of sophistication.

Fu (1967) has added a reinforcement algorithm to his automaton. The performance has a weighting factor

$$\lambda_j^i = k,$$

where $k = 0$ if $i < j$, $k = 1$ if $i \geqslant j$, and where 0 is reinforcing and 1 is non-reinforcing. This weighting when superimposed on the random environment of an automaton gives "direction" and "purposiveness" to its activity. We shall be returning to this matter in a later chapter. Suffice it at the moment that stochastic automata are very much a subject of cybernetic interest.

9.3   INFORMATION THEORY MODELS IN CYBERNETICS

One example of information theory models must suffice, and this is due to Rapoport (1955). He suggested that the retina of the eye was linked to the visual part of the brain and that information was pumped down the fibres connecting the two.

Rapoport drew up some logical nets which provided a model of this total process. Rapoport assumed that the retina was a source of visual information patterns and the visual cortex at the back of the brain was the destination. Rapoport's model assumed that the number of photo-receptors (visual cells) was 10^8 and that the average refractory periods of these photo-receptors were taken out to be independent in their operation, then the following information model can be derived:

$$H = p_i \log p_i + q_i \log q_i$$

is the information content of the source, where p_i is the probability of firing the rth receptor in the ith instant.

$$q_i = 1 - p_i$$

and then if $p_i = \frac{1}{2}$ for all i, $H = n$ bits pen message. Then for $n = 10^8$, with refractory period 10^{-3} we have production of information at retina equal to 10" bits per second. This figure is in fact known to be far too large and implies the non-independence of the photo-receptors. Indeed we already know that they are highly redundant in their operation, and thus the information flow can be reduced to more natural proportions. The following two nets show the significant features of Rapoport's model, which is based on the necessary flows of information to perform vital operations — such as visual recognition.

Rapoport, and also Culbertson (1950), considered the problem of firing through a bottleneck, and this bottleneck implies both loss of information and the selection of information. Polyak has suggested that 10^8 photo-receptors map on to 10^8 ganglion cells, on the average and this represents a 100 to 1 ratio, which varies from 1 to 1 at the fovea to several hundreds to 1 at the periphery of the retina.

Rapoport has tackled the modelling procedure in terms of selecting appropriate codes, but Culbertson has regarded the same problem in terms of appropriate network structure.

Figure 4 shows a logical net model of one of the cells that make up the retina, where the element is an on—off element, which fires only when the retina is first stimulated or when it ceases to be stimulated.

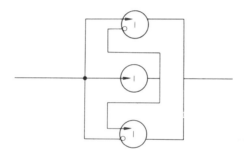

Figure 5 shows the manner of connecting the retinal input elements a, b, c and d with output elements a, b, c and d, where the number of fibres connecting the four input elements to the four output elements are less than four. This simulates a situation which actually occurs in the human visual system.

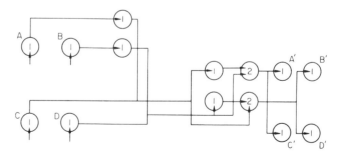

9.4   SEMANTIC INFORMATION

Carnap and Bar-Hillel (1952) initiated a form of measure of language which they called semantic information.

The origin of the semantic theory depended upon the point made by Shannon (Shannon and Weaver, 1949) that the meaning of the messages had no relevance to this theory of the information. The probability measure he suggested applies to the selection of a single message, with an associated probability, from a finite set of messages each with associated probabilities. It is of no consequence what the probabilities refer to.

Carnap and Bar-Hillel specified definitions of amount of meaning in a sentence s.

They defined cont(s) (the semantic content of the sentence s) as

$$\text{cont}(s) = p(\sim s)$$
$$= 1 - p(s)$$

where $p(s)$ is the logical probability of the sentence s being true. Hintikka and Pietarinen (1966) also define a similar function.

$$\text{inf}(s) = - \log_2 p(s)$$

or

$$\text{inf}(s) = \log_2 \frac{1}{1 - \text{cont}(s)}$$

and compare the two definitions. Both are similarly constrained:

1)   If $s_1 > s_2$ is logically true, then
$$I(s_1 \geqslant I(s_2)$$
for two sentences s_1 and s_2.

2) $I(s) \geqslant 0$

3)   If s is logically true, then $I(s) = 0$.

The function cont(s) now satisfies the following additive theorem

$$I(s_1 - s_2) = I(s_1) + I(s_2)$$

if and only if $(s_1 \text{ v } s_2)$ is logically true. inf(s) on the other hand satisfies the following:

$$I(s_1 . s_2) = I(s_1) + I(s_2)$$

if and only if $p(s_1 . s_2) = p(s_1) p(s_2)$.

These are attempts to define the absolute information content of a sentence in terms of its truth, and it can be seen that the information content of a sentence is greater the more possibilities it excludes.

This approach has been used by Hintikka and Pietarinen as a basis for induction and especially for the confirmation of theories. For us, since confirmation will play a vital part in the artificially intelligent automata, we may assume some such equivalent mechanisms will be available. In any event, it is a branch of information theory and therefore most relevant to cybernetic interests.

9.5   INFORMATION THEORY AND AUTOMATA

We conclude this chapter with a brief note on the relation of information theory to automata. We mentioned earlier that some writers (McNaughton, 1961) feel that the statistical type of information theoretic system characterises cybernetics, just as discrete mathematical and logic systems characterise automata theory. This is, as we have already said, too limited a basis for comparison, but it is true that this represents one aspect, indeed one central aspect, of the comparison. Wiener (1961, page 60) develops in detail the notion of time series and its relation to information. The argument is quite complicated mathematically and not particularly easy to follow. We shall not pursue the details here, but merely refer the interested reader to the appropriate reference. Much of the same argument is also available in Shannon and Weaver (1949).

We should add there exist other definitions of information besides that of Shannon, and here the interested reader should see Fisher (1958), MacKay (1950), Wilson (1966) and Brillouin (1956, 1964). These works take the reader away from the central themes of cybernetics to a discussion of related matters of entropy and the fields of statistical mechanics. We shall not pursue these matters further here.

9.6   SUMMARY

Since, as in the case of computers, information theory is something of a "service science" to cybernetics, we shall not attempt to discuss recent developments. In fact in this case very little recent development has occured.

Information theory provides measures of the flow of information, the channel capacity etc., which occurs in any communication between a source and a destination.

Information theory provides an alternative language to that of conventional mathematical and ordinary language to give a precise description to a communication system. Such a precise language which has been explained also offers a model-making procedure for cognitive functions such as perception; we have given one illustration of this.

CHAPTER 10

Human and animal behaviour

Argument

Human and animal behaviour can be considered at various levels both of experimentation and description; this chapter deals with the psychological level.

Psychology is the scientific study of human, and to some extent, animal behaviour, in both individuals and groups. Theories of perception, learning, memory, motivation, thinking, problem solving, etc., have all been put forward to explain behaviour.

Cybernetics overlaps psychology in that one of its roles is to supply precise simulations of certain behavioural functions. The cybernetician therefore should know something of psychological development.

In a sense cybernetics owes its origins to the belief that animals and men are "complicated machines" or, more guardedly, because the distinction between physico-chemical (non-living) and biological (living) systems was not clear cut.

10.1 PSYCHOLOGY AS A SCIENCE

Up to now we have dealt with various aspects of cybernetics, but have not clearly discussed its relation to other scientific disciplines such as psychology. We are, it should be added, thinking here of mathematics and logic not so much as sciences but as meta-sciences. In one sense, we could categorise psychology as the common ground of cybernetics and biology. However, this is rather broad and will hardly be sufficient to make clear the rather complicated relations that actually exist between the various parts of the biological and social sciences. It is true so far, however, to say that psychology overlaps cybernetics mainly in the field of cognition; that field which is concerned with learning, perception, thinking and language.

Psychology as a science has been the source of much misunderstanding, and some of these misunderstandings will be mentioned straight away. In the first place, psychology is not to be identified with psychiatry or abnormal psychology. The primary problem of the science of behaviour — and this is what psychology is — is to give a predictive account of what we call "normal" behaviour. Added to this is the admittedly very important problem of accounting for abnormal variations of the theme of "normal" behaviour. Such an analysis is designed primarily to explain and help the understanding of normal behaviour.

Another important point that needs to be emphasised in this context is that problems of science, or problems of knowledge in general, and problems of behaviour in particular, can be solved, understood, or explained at many different levels. If one asks an apparently simple question about an ordinary electric light switch − "Why does the throwing of this switch light the light?" − the answer could be couched in a variety of different ways, using complex electronic explanations or merely giving an answer couched in everyday terms. In other words, we again return to the fact that science is concerned with questions and their answers in a specific context.

The science of psychology is in much the same situation as any other science in that behaviour, like electronics or chemistry, can be investigated at many different levels of complexity. We can ask why Mr. Jones behaves the way he does, and we can explain his motives in terms of his observable behaviour and his, as well as our, over-all experience, or we can explain his observable behaviour in terms of his motives. We can also investigate the underlying physiological changes accompanying the observable behavioural changes. Indeed, these very physiological changes can themselves be investigated at the level of chemical or physical change. It is not suggested that each level of explanation is complete in itself, but that each offers a different aspect of the behaviour of the organiam-as-a-whole. It has become almost impossible to make any valid distinctions between these different levels and the different forms of explanation they entail. In particular, it makes little sense to try to draw any serious distinction between physiology and psychology. However, we may say, in broad terms, that psychology is concerned with the organism's behaviour-as-a-whole, when couched in terms of what we can publicly observe. This then means that the depth of detail in which the answer should be dressed as a function of the explanations that are to be used.

Psychology can be divided rather arbitrarily into two principal parts, the *pure* and the *applied*. If we concentrate on pure psychology, we have two large cognitive problems, which are very broad in their scope; they have been called the "problem of perception" and "problem of learning" respectively. Perception is concerned with the way human beings gather information about the outside world, the way they see, hear, feel, etc. It is the process of interpreting sensory, or incoming signals. Learning is concerned with a question not wholly separable from perception. It is concerned, of course, with how organisms are able to modify themselves according to their experience. A simple illustration of what we mean by learning can be given directly. Yerkes trained an earthwork to run along a T-shaped maze, which had dried leaves at one end of one of the short arms of the cross-piece of the T, and had an electrified grille in the other arm. The worm was shocked if he turned right and received dried leaves if he turned left. The directions of the turns, it should be noted, can be interchanged without affecting the experiment. Then, after some hundreds of trials, the earthworm always learned to turn away from the shock and toward the leaves. This is one of the simplest examples of what the psychologist means by learning. The fact is that some form of modification has been introduced into the earthworm which changes his behaviour. That there is also a neurological change taking place is fairly clear when one sees that the earthworm still retains his skill after his primitive brain — two small ganglia at the head end — is extirpated, and more important still that when the nervous tissue regenerates and grows new ganglia, the skill is lost. This example is not only of interest in demonstrating what we mean by the word "learning", it also suggests the sort of role the nervous system might — in a very general way — be expected to play in learning.

That thinking and linguistic behaviour are superimposed on such simple learning is assumed. The most general question asked of learning theory is simply: what changes occur in the organism when it learns? Or, to put it more in psychological and less in physiological terms, how can we describe changes in behaviour in terms of observables alone? Let us take an example of this.

If there are two men who have behaved in different ways in the past, we shall not be surprised if they behave in different ways from each other again in the future when faced with the same circumstances as they have been faced with in the past. Mr. X has always been brave and Mr. Y a coward. The very fact of classifying them as "brave" and "cowardly" springs from observations and descriptions which are made by other people and which are sometimes true and sometimes false. When there is the need to perform some brave act in the community and Mr. X and Mr. Y are both faced with this situation, then we shall predict that Mr. X will probably succeed and Mr. Y will probably fail. Most predictions are more complicated than this, since most people are not so easily classified as *brave* or *cowardly*.

This example is typical of how we commonly think in predicting behaviour, and we describe such predictions as common sense. We simply make *inductions*. This is, to some extent, a successful process, especially if we know the people and the circumstances well; but it is not enough for a science; it is in fact a part — albeit a vital part — of science.

If an inductive generalisation is justified it allows us to study learning in general terms, and we shall seek for more general rules governing learning which we shall then modify according to the characteristics of the particular species or individuals concerned. One of the difficulties is that many people have argued that the individual differences are greater than their common similarities. The answer is that one hopes that they are wrong, since otherwise a science will prove difficult. There is, happily, much evidence that they are wrong and that the similarity between people is greater than their differences, and so the methods adopted are justified. At the same time psychology lacks the degree of prediction achieved by the physical sciences, not only because it is involved in far more complicated systems, but also because of the far greater range of individual differences.

10.2   PSYCHOLOGICAL THEORIES

The beginnings of psychology were based on introspection, and the idea that there was something called a "mind" that operated and somehow controlled the body. It is true that some people still talk in these terms, which is harmless provided that by the word "mind" we are merely using a shorthand for the controlling aspects of behaviour, without implying that there is a mind that *is separate from* a body. Body and mind are as much one as a car and its engine. However, the fact remains that this historical dualism came into psychology and had a considerable influence for a very long time, although the "ghost in the machine" view, as Gilbert Ryle (1949) has called it, is now largely in disrepute.

For somewhat the same reasons that mental entities have been kept alive, there has been kept alive also a *vitalistic* view of behaviour, which uses descriptions in terms of operations that cannot be performed in a purely mechanistic way. Holders of vitalistic views are responsible for great emphasis being placed especially on instincts and insights because these seem to provide a block to mechanistic progress. In particular, work on animals higher up the evolutionary scale produced views that were dependent on notions such as insight, whereas those scientists working more at the level of the rat tended to emphasise the mechanical stimulus-response type of activity, more like a slot machine and less like an organism showing "free will". A famous example in the literature is that of Köhler's ape "Sultan" (1925) who was able to solve the problem of reaching a banana that was further away than either of his two sticks could reach. He fitted the two sticks together so that he then had one stick that was long enough. He was not shown how to do this, and it seemed to depend on his being able to see the situation-as-a-whole. The Gestalt school of psychology have made the most of such evidence for insisting on the importance of perception in learning, a fact that is now widely agreed upon.

However, at the time of these discoveries by the Gestalt theorists, the movement called "behaviourism" was well under way under the leadership of J.B. Watson (1930). The Gestalt evidence seemed to be, indeed was, in conflict with Watson's version of behaviourism. But behaviourism as a method of investigation and a philosphy-of-science was not ruled our on that account. Many early behaviourists insisted on the relative unimportance of instinct, and of inherited characteristics in general, believing that environment was all-important and that the process of conditioning was fundamental to it and was the key to our understanding of all behaviour.

There is in fact no critical dispute here between behaviourists and their opponents, although there appeared to be at the time. Thus it is unnecessary for the behaviourist to deny that complex behavioural characteristics can be inherited from one generation to the next, as long as we do not insist on this account that the mechanism of genetics which is directly responsible for this transmission, is itself non-mechanistic. Many people, unfortunately, have used the word "instinct" like "mind" as a word that is supposed in itself to have explanatory power, whereas it is merely a name for a classification that needs to be explained.

Early learning theorists disagreed with each other (Watson, 1930; Köhler, 1925) particularly over generalisations that were based upon limited observations of a limited number of species; such samples led to inadequate generalisations. In this regard it is still an unfortunate fact that nearly eighty per cent of all animal experiments in psychology have been done on the Norwegian rat. This loses for psychology much that is essential to what the biologists call "the comparative viewpoint".

The basic experiments on learning theory were those of Pavlov, and are called experiments in conditioning; or rather, the behaviour so illustrated is sometimes called "conditioned reflex" behaviour. The experiments can be illustrated quite quickly by first taking a characteristic example. Imagine a dog harnessed in a sound-proof room and subjected to the following stimulation. Some food is presented to him, at the sight of which he salivates. Then, after a while, a bell is rung whenever the food is presented. Then, after many trials in which the bell and the food are presented together, the ringing of the bell on its own is sufficient to elicit the salivation. It goes without saying that the dog would not salivate to the sound of the bell before the experiment started, so we say that he has been conditioned to salivate to the sound of the bell. It is as if the bell were a *sign* to him that food was about to be presented.

This experiment can be regarded as the prototype on which conditioning theory was built. It was found that the dog would not go on salivating indefinitely to the sound of the bell alone, unless it was at least reinforced from time to time by the food. There were also other complications. For example, suppose the tone of the bell was changed. How much could one change it before the animal failed to respond to a note for which he was already conditioned? How much did it matter if there was a considerable delay between the sound of the bell and the presentation of food when the situation was being reinforced by feeding? But these complications apart, what was important was that it was shown to be possible to condition, in much the same way, every conceivable kind of species from earthworm to man, and under a wide variety of different circumstances. An especially interesting fact of conditioning was that one could carry on second-order, third-order or even higher orders of conditioning, such that when the bell was rung in the above-mentioned experiment, another different stimulus took place, such as a flash of light. Then, in the future, the flash of light would be sufficient to lead to the response of salivation, and so on.

The assumption of the early and extreme behaviourists was that all behaviour was essentially of the same form as that described above, and that all seemingly complicated activity was more or less complex conditioning. From one point of view this is still the belief of behaviourists, although many would now take a somewhat broader view of a "reflex" than that implied by the above experiment. Part of the evolution of learning theory, and indeed, of science in general, has been to change terminology from time to time. It is not so much that the ideas or concepts that the words stand for are necessarily different, but that certain words get over-worked; they get emotional overtones attached to them; they become "loaded", and then they are dropped for a while. Sometimes, as in the case of the word "instinct", such terms return to fashion when the original battle has died down. This is also the case with conditional response or conditional reflex terminology. Most of modern learning theory has dealt with the same development, in different terms.

We can now use neural nets to show how conditioning operates. In the following net (figure 1) we are using the elements *to represent whole collections* of neurons and not single neurons, but the principle is still clearly exhibited by the network technique.

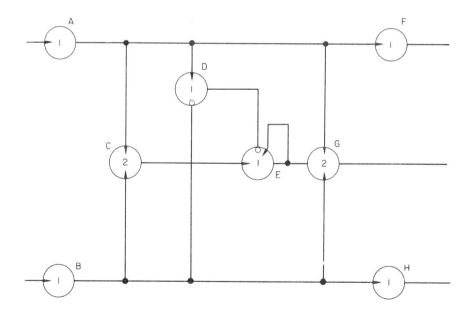

Figure 1   A simple associations net that could be interpreted as simple conditioning.

10.3   AUTOMATA AND PSYCHOLOGY

We have, in our behavioural theory, a black box (the organism) which, let us say, we cannot open, and we have to guess at what changes happen inside whenever there is a change in external conditions. It is now necessary to construct some sort of imaginary mechanisms that are supposed to operate inside the box. It is a sort of imaginary physiology which is sufficient to give a consistent account of the external behaviour. Freud (1938) introduced theoretical terms into psychological theory when he used the words "ego", "superego", "id" and others, which suggest a similar "imaginary mechanism". One advantage of using these so-called *theoretical terms* is that it does not commit the user to a possible misuse of physiological terminology.

We now generalise the original classical conditioning experiments, by extending the terms of conditioned-response theory to more general kinds of behaviour. There is what is called type II conditioning (Konorski, 1948) which incorporates four types of training; reward training, escape training, avoidance training, and secondary reward (or symbol) training. We shall give brief examples of these four types of behaviour.

A simple reward-training experiment is one where a rat runs a maze to be rewarded at the end of it. The rat has to move to get his reward and he does not, as in classical conditioning, have to be strapped in a sound-proof room. We will describe the escape and avoidance situation in a single experiment. If a rat is running a rotating wheel, part of which is electrifiable, and then we shock the rat when he is on the electrifiable part, he will escape from the situation by running until he is away from this electified part. If now we sound a bell before the shock starts, then the rat will be conditioned to run as soon as he hears the bell, and so avoid the shock. It is much the same as in the classical conditioning situation; the bell acts as a *sign* to the rat (Hilgard and Marquis, 1938).

Secondary reward is illustrated by apes, who could be trained to perform simple tasks, if they were suitably rewarded. The rewards took the form of red, blue and brass poker chips (Wolfe, 1936). The red chips were worth two grapes, the blue worth one grape, and the brass worth none. The apes would work and then pick out the red chips from a mixed pile as their reward, and when these had all gone, they picked the blue and left the brass untouched. They had, of course, initially to be conditioned to the relative values of the chips.

We next state briefly a general theory of learning as it might appear today. The theory will start with *stimulus* and *response* as undefined notions, the idea being that a stimulus is roughly what activates behaviour, and the set of responses that it elicits is the behaviour observed. The organism has to be motivated before it will respond at all, but motivations are plentiful. The basic ones are probably survival, food and sex, and the like, while all the means that get associated with these basic motivations become secondary motivators. If motivated then, the organism will respond to stimulation. The nature of his response will depend on his previous experience of the situation, or of similar situations. There will be a general tendency to retain whatever habits contribute towards a state of affairs satisfying to the organism — the state of *homeostasis* — and not to reproduce habits which are unsatisfying to the organism.

Intelligent interaction with its environment depends upon a memory store that allows it to classify experiences, so that some process of comparison can take place between the present situation and situations that have happened in the past. The cat that has narrowly escaped with his life in his meeting with a dog, say, will have learned very strongly that the situation, with a dog present, is dangerous, particularly if it involves the same dog which frightened him before, and to a decreasingly similar extent for all other dogs. Of course, some of these responses may be instinctive, innate or learned very early in life.

The ability to distinguish different situations, whether by touch, smell, vision or hearing is a matter that involves us in perception, so we shall consider that next. But before we do so, let us show a neural net model of a memory store and remind the reader of the similarity of our very general theory to the structure of computers.

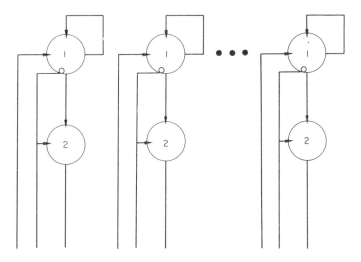

Figure 2   A storage system. The simple principle of storing binary digits by logical nets. All sorts of variations on the same theme are possible.

(Reproduced by courtesy of Pergamon Press.)

We must also demonstrate the generality of the simple neural net described in Figure 1. First of all let us redraw the net showing six looped elements instead of only one.

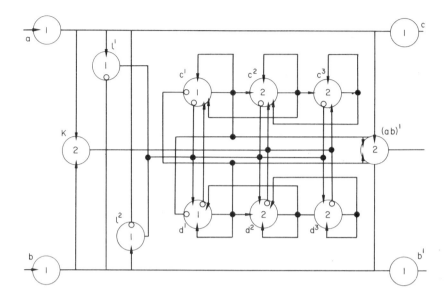

Figure 3   Belief network. We have referred to this network as a Belief-net or B-net. In general it associates any number of inputs and counts the degree of association to any extent.
(Reproduced by courtesy of Pergamon Press.)

We use these looped elements as memory stores and the result is that the so-called B-net (George, 1956, 1957, 1961) has the capacity to remember associations to any extent as a function of the order of the occurrence of the events and as a function of the number of counters, or looped elements, in the net. If the counters are in excess of the longest sequence of similar events $(a.b, \ .\sim a.b$ and $a \ .\sim b$ are the only events relevant to Figure 2) then the behaviour of the net is that of a simple Laplacian probability. i.e. If a fires then $(a.b)'$ fires if and only if $(a.b) \cdot > ((a \ .\sim b) \text{ v } (\sim a.b))$ for the total part of the system.

If this condition does not hold then the net gives a recency weighting to the probability and is concerned only with the last countable events. The generality of the system is also considerable.

10.4   PERCEPTION

As has been said, there is an important factor in learning that we find difficult to control, it is the process of perceiving. We cannot assume that because there actually is some object in the field of view of an organism, the organism will perceive it. He may, but he may not. It is there to be perceived, we can perceive it, and many others may perceive it too, so that it is almost certainly not an illusion, or an hallucination, but still any one person may not perceive it. If he fails to perceive a sign in the way we expect, then his behaviour will generally be different from what we will have expected.

It must be emphasised that we distinguish at the visual level between seeing and perceiving. The reason for this is to avoid confusion between the process of recording something outside ourselves and recognising what that something is. In other words, the process of perception seems to be an *interpretive* one. We have all had the experience of seeing something on the road ahead without being sure what that something is. If we are driving a car we shall be mainly interested in whether or not it will have the quality of "bumpiness", since there is a significant difference between a rock and a piece of paper in the context of the car driver, and the correctness of our perception may be important.

It is quite clear that our perceptual processes (inputs to the computer) contribute all the environmental factors to the organism's information. All he knows, other than anything he may have innately acquired, is learned by perception and therefore by use of the special senses. To use vision again as our example, the process can be likened to that of a camera which takes snapshots and leaves the brain to do the interpreting of what the snapshots are about. This is a reminder that if inputs in a computer are like the process of seeing itself, perception is a combination of this process with the use of the memory store (the interpreting). It is obvious that inputs are an essential part of learning, and if there is no memory of previous experience, no interpretation is possible, since interpretation means precisely the process of *classifying* in the light of what has happened to the organism previously.

We should mention that many people have denied that experience is essential to perception, but the argument has been greatly confused because the word "perception" has been used by the protagonists in at least two vitally different ways without either party being wholly aware of it (George, 1961). Perception is a subject that should be regarded from the point of view of all the senses, taken together, sounds over-simple when vision is considered alone. Ultimately, all the senses work together, and the process of perception is not wholly distinguishable from that of conceptualisation.

One example of work on visual perception will now be given. Psychologists have shown that what they call "set" directly influences perception, and makes clear how *active* a process behaviour is. Behaviour in general is seldom the mere passive reaction to stimuli, but is much more the searching, anticipating, and active interaction with the environment. Due to "set", we tend to see what we expect to see. If we go into the kitchen knowing there is likely to be a mouse there, we are apprehensive and start at even the smallest movement such as the shadow or a piece of paper on the floor. This matter of confusing people by leading them to expect one thing, and giving them another, is the basis of most tricks; the conjuror tries to get us to look where nothing is going on, although we should expect something to be there. It is fairly clear that such effects of "set", or one's expectations, will be closely related to illusions and hallucinations, and perhaps goes some way to account for many people's belief in matters of the occult and other curiosities. It is clear at any rate that suggestibility is something very similar to set.

10.5   PERCEPTUAL MODELS

We have a whole host of perceptual models in existence which have been built up over many years by various different workers in the field of cybernetics, psychology and physiology.

One convenient method of classifying these perceptual models is into *monotypic* and *genotypic* models (Rosenblatt, 1962). The monotypic model specifies a detailed anatomical or topological picture of the proposed "perceptual" model, whereas the genotypic model is satisfied with the same sort of functional description as in the form of mathematical operators. This distinction is, in some ways, similar to the distinction between *simulation* and *synthesis.* A simulation model aims to copy the original in both ends and means, whereas the synthetic model is only concerned with depicting the appropriate ends.

Cutting across the above distinction is that between *general purpose* and *special purpose* models of "perception". Hebb (1949) in his theory of phase sequences was describing a general purpose model, while Sutherland (1959) in describing "stimulus analysing mechanisms" is insisting on the importance of special purpose features in the sensory systems.

The above differences are probably differences of degree, since it is difficult to break down, into two phases only, the complex process of sensing a stimulus right through to the final identification of that stimulus (or stimulus complex). Insofar as our interests are peripheral, we would expect the emphasis to be on sensory models of the type suggested by Sutherland, insofar as they are central and relate more to the identification of the input and less to its recording, we would expect the emphasis to be on general purpose models. Uttley's classification and conditional probability models (1954, 1955, 1966), which we have already discussed, are general purpose models, and clearly can be thought of as either monotypic or genotypic.

A clearcut genotypic perceptual model is that due to Culbertson (1948, 1950, 1952, 1956). Culbertson gives the most detailed analysis in neural net form of layer after layer of the visual system, which allows it to act like a sorting system against a template. Images are rotated, expanded, dilated, etc., until a match is achieved.

Rapoport's (1955) model of vision is a combination of information theory and neural nets and, like Uttley's work, it lies somewhere along the continuum between a monotypic and genotypic theory.

There are also other examples of genotypic and special purpose theories connected with vision, and perhaps the best example is that due to Osgood and Heyer (1952) which assumes the "seen" contour lines of a figure are represented by statistical distributions of excitation in cortical area 17. The Osgood–Heyer model has been used for predicting such perceptual effects as the "figural after-effects" and "movement after-effects" and is primarily statistical in its form. We will now turn to a brief description of the perceptron.

10.6   PERCEPTRONS

One well-known class of pattern recognition models is that of Rosenblatt (1960a, 1960b, 1960c, 1962). These are so called genotypic models (as opposed to monotypic) in that they do not specify the detailed organisation of the structure of the system.

Let us now look at Rosenblatt's definition of a perceptron: A perceptron is a network composed of stimulus-unit, association-unit and response-unit with a variable interaction matrix V which depends ?on the sequence of past activity states of the network.

A stimulus (S) and response (R) unit generate "internal" and "external" signals, respectively. "Internal" means within the network, and "external" means within the environment. An association (A) unit receives signals *and* emits them.

Now a *simple perceptron* is defined as satisfying the following five conditions:

1) There is only one R-unit with a connection from every A-unit.

2) The perceptron is series-coupled, with connections only from from S-units to A-units, and from A-units to the R-unit.

3) The values of all sensory to A-unit connections are fixed.

4) The *transmission time* of every connection is either zero or equal to a fixed constant.

5) All signal generating functions of S, A and R-units are of the form $u_i^*(t) = f(a_i(t))$, where $a_i(t)$ is the algebraic sum of all input signals arriving

simultaneously at the unit μ_j.

Now we must define "transmission function", "value" and "interacting matrix".

A *transmission function* of connections in a perceptron depends on two parameters, the transmission time of the connection τ_{ij} and the *value* of the connection U_{ij}. Variable values are called *memory functions.*

The *interacting matrix* V for a perceptron is the matrix of coupling coefficient ij for pairs of units U_i and U_j. If U_i and U_j are unconnected then U_{ij} = 0.

An interacting matrix is what has been sometimes called a "structure matrix" George, 1956).

A perceptron can be represented as a logical net, so that any of the logical nets which have been described in this book would qualify for the name "perceptron". Rosenblatt has suggested other pictorial representation of perceptrons for different levels of precision. So far then, Rosenblatt has achieved only a slightly new notation. Let us look at his first "experimental" perceptron.

An "experimental system" can be called a simple perceptron coupled to reinforcement control system and in an environment (Figure 4). This again merely restates the simplest sort of cognitive situation.

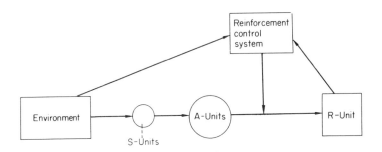

Figure 4

From these beginnings, Rosenblatt builds up a "universal perceptron" which can now be thought of as generalised nets, where the detailed topology is replaced by the general constraints previously mentioned.

A retinal set of S-units can now be constructed so that "differential" stimulation from different shapes can be achieved. If we now project two distinguishable shapes X_1 and X_2 on to the retina we have sets of A-units which simply fire or not according to whether the equivalent S-units fire.

Step by step, Rosenblatt constructs perceptrons or logical nets that can distinguish shapes, and shapes in connection with typical "shape-names" like "triangle", "circle", etc.

What distinguishes Rosenblatt's work from that of Culbertson, say, is precisely what Rosenblatt describes as the difference between monotypic and genotypic models. Culbertson specifies in logical detail the topology of his system, whereas Rosenblatt leaves open these topological considerations and replaces logically-defined detail by probabilistic functions. It seems that there is scope for both approaches to the modelling of biological systems. Indeed it seems to the present writer, as already hinted, that Rosenblatt had over-stated the difference between monotypic and genotypic systems and had obscured the fact that one can often quite easily be made into the other.

As far as pattern recognition is concerned, Rosenblatt has been able to show that discrimination of shapes in an environment can always be carried out by the analysis of the statistical distributions of impulses arriving from suitably connected S-units. The whole picture built up is a great deal more complicated than this. The great value of Rosenblatt's work, however, stems from the fact that it supplies a means of transition from well-defined (monotypic) logical nets of the kind that can be drawn from such models as those of Uttley and Culbertson to the more statistical theories of Rapoport and others.

What we have said, all too briefly, may be summarised as follows. Learning and perception together, with the associated factors of thinking, imagining, motivating and the like, are the subject of controlled experiment and observation, which is designed to allow us to state a general theory of behaviour that would be acceptable regardless of the organism concerned. It is certainly possible that the process of learning should be distinguished from that of retaining information. Upon the equations of this general theory we should want to compose an account of the individual differences applicable to whatever particular behavioural problem we are trying to solve, whether these individual constants are with reference to individuals, or to groups of people. The methods we would advocate would be cybernetic, and the job would be a *simulation*.

Many people think that it is self-evident that biological information of all kinds underlies the facts of overt human or animal behaviour. It is certain that the more that we learn about sciences such as psychology, biochemistry, biophysics and genetics, the more we can fill in the gaps in our knowledge of the organism. Furthermore, it is becoming clearer in principle, how the pieces of jigsaw – at various levels – fit together. It is certain that the theoretical terms of psychology have to be interpreted physiologically. The totality of facts about organisms, viewed from every point of view, will one day be the basis of what we shall no doubt think of as "human biology", and *a part of* cybernetics.

Let us now deal more explicitly with the link between psychology and our main theme of cybernetics. The overlap is quite clear, since both subjects are concerned with communication and control. It should be said, though, that there is no complete agreement about the relations of cybernetics to psychology. But we would propose that the matter should be thought of this way. Cybernetics tells us that all control and classification systems, all communication systems, have certain common characteristics which allow us to describe them in terms of their feedback and control mechanisms. This description fits in with the neo-behaviourist movement, in that cybernetics is prescribing a form of approach which allows us to state our theories of behaviour in a roughly known pattern of great generality. Cybernetics, of course, encourages the use of mathematical methods already employed in control engineering and in statistical thermodynamics, and other related disciplines from engineering to physics.

As a particular result of this viewpoint, we can see that a human being can be regarded as a machine with a certain kind of classification system working in a particular way, and its working throws up the problem that we call the problem of perception. And beyond the classification of the sensory inputs we have the control systems with their feedback loops and storage that give us the problem of learning. We should go on from these beginnings to consider both syntheses and simulations of problem-solving, thinking and decision-taking, and further discussion of this we postpone until Chapter 13.

Now we can say, in summary, that a cybernetic model of behaviour can be provided by a computer simulation, or by building neural nets or other automata, showing part or all of cognitive behaviour.

Inputs are associated with sensing (seeing, hearing, etc.), and this involves the memory store when perception occurs. Simple learning was achieved by the Grey Walter "tortoise" and the maze runners. Ashby showed something of purposiveness or goal-seeking with the homeostat, and as we graduate to more complex cognitive processes so we need increasingly to think of computer simulation.

Behaviour generally is a sort of deductive–inductive procedure and one for which a machine, however complex, can be an adequate model, or so cyberneticians think.

10.7 THINKING, PROBLEM SOLVING AND MEMORY

In this chapter on human behaviour it is important to make some mention of the higher cognitive faculties and this includes thinking and problem solving, and both in turn clearly depend on memory.

The most important developments in memory in recent years is the increased insistence on the distinction between long-term and short-term memory. This distinction applies to both the behavioural functions and the underlying neural structures subserving the two aspects of memory. We shall not attempt to discuss the evidence which bears on this matter, but merely refer to the main reference (Broadbent and Pribram, 1973).

Thinking we can think of as the process of symbolised learning; at least we would say that this is true in the main. In other words, we can think of the symbolisation of events through language and the process of manipulating those symbols as the essence of thinking.

Much recent work has been done on problem solving. This includes the use of State-space search methods and problem-reduction search methods (Nillson, 1971; Slagle, 1971), whereby we can represent problems in terms of their possible states and the operations which can manipulate the system from one state to another. The full range of possible states in the state space. Heuristics of course, arise in the search procedure by eliminating whole sets of states (whole branches of a search tree) at one fell swoop.

The notion of problem-reduction is well known to all mathematicians and simply involves the reduction of a problem to a series of sub-problems. If you wish to go from London to Oxford by road (and you shun motorways) then you have to first get from London to Beaconsfield (this is a sub-problem). If you can reduce a problem to a series of sub-problems – particulary ones you know how to solve – then of course the problem immediately becomes tractable.

The words of Bruner, Goodnow and Austin (1956) still remains a classic in the world of thinking and problem solving, and everyone should be familiar with the strategies they outline. They also emphasise the distinction between perception and conception and this is similar to the distinction we have made between the fuzziness of a perceived world and its translation into less fuzzy (or precise) concepts. This is the world of reality made into a conceptual world and providing the basis of human thought.

As the present author has said (George, 1970).

The vital processes of thinking explicitly discussed are:

1) Concept Formation.
2) Hypothesis Formation, which brings up the whole problem of induction.
3) Deduction.
4) Language.

Clearly we are envisaging a process here where, say, a problem and concepts and hypotheses are called up, and new concepts and hypotheses formulated if needed, and then the problem is solved or not as a mixture of induction and deductive processing interspersed with conversation and data retrieval.

So again we see that problem solving is a central part of what we call thinking although problem solving is probably the major part of thinking, it is not the only part, as is clear from the fact that we can "think" (allow associations to occur and recall memories of past events, etc.) about events without any way trying to solve any problem.

Since this is not a book which is primarily concerned with psychology we shall not discuss these higher cognitive activities any further here.

10.8   RECENT ADVANCES

As in the case of all subjects such as computer science and information theory, now experimental psychology and in the next chapter physiology, it is not easy to talk of recent advances which are directly relevant to cybernetics. Experimental psychologists are producing research papers at a great rate, but much of what is most relevant to cybernetics is subsumed under other chapters of this book such as pattern recognition. However, we accept the shadowy boundaries that exist between the various disciplines which make up the behavioural sciences and here draw attention to some recent work done in the field of thinking and reasoning.

First of all we draw attention of work done by Cornish and Wason (1970) which showed that a significantly greater number of affirmative (as opposed to negative) clues were remembered in a reasoning situation. This work followed up previous work done by Wason (1965) on the relationship between negative and positive statements. Along somewhat similar lines, Evans (1972) showed that positive rather than negative components predominated in reasoning situations.

Hodes (1971), in a more explicitly cybernetic context, applied the notions of formula manipulation to the solution of logical problems, but here we have arrived at that border country which overlaps logic, theorem proving, which will be the subject of a later chapter.

Perhaps the most important aspects of current behaviour model development lies in the empirical investigations of thinking — especially logical thinking — on one hand, and the attempt to develop more synthetic methods of problem solving — especially with respect to logical problems — on the other.

10.9   SUMMARY

This chapter has described some part of psychology, and particulary theories of learning and perception.

Cybernetics is concerned, through automata theory and computer programming, with simulating cognitive behaviour. So far we have simple models of adaptation, and more complex models of learning and perception. We are now beginning to develop yet more complex simulation models. But perhaps progress has been in synthesis rather than simulation, even though the two things are interdependent.

CHAPTER 11

Physiological models

Argument

Physiology, including neurophysiology, is concerned with the internal organisation of the human being. It constructs models from building bricks which may represent simple body cells. The cells of the nervous system are called neurons and have played a major part in such model construction methods.

The principle of *homeostasis* which is that of adjustment to external conditions to retain a balance inside the organism, is one direct link between cybernetics and physiology generally and neurophysiology in particular.

The field of self-adapting physiological models is sometimes called biocybernetics. Neural nets, which we discussed in Chapter 7, form a natural link between automata theory and neurophysiology. Just as cybernetics and psychology overlap, so does psychology and physiology, and cybernetics and physiology.

11.1   BIO-CYBERNETICS AND NEURO-CYBERNETICS

Physiology and anatomy deal with the function and structure of the organisms of the body. Human neurophysiology and human neuro-anatomy deal with the function and structure of the nervous system, and this is of special cybernetic interest. We shall concentrate here mainly on the human nervous system, for it is here that the problems of behaviour and cybernetics have come closest together so far.

Many psychological processes are clearly capable, in principle, of description in neurological terms. That is, we may observe and describe a simple response such as the patellar reflex ("knee-jerk") by reference to the nerves which travel to and from the knee. We must go further than this and say that it is desirable to reformulate, wherever possible, in a biological language, the observed behaviour already described directly. The theories of behaviour that attempt to explain behaviour in psychological terms, must also be translated into a language which refers to the internal functioning of the organism. At least this is so in contexts which demand the more detailed level of prediction.

It is not possible at the moment to put this programme fully into practice, but there are signs that we shall in the near future be thinking expressly in neurological terms when discussing behaviour. It is not *necessary* that we should do this, but it is desirable from the general point of view of integrating our scientific knowledge, and also because we seem not to be able to achieve the necessary degree of predictability by psychology unaided by biological data.

The problems of behaviour must be described first in neurological terms, and then, very much later, it may be possible to redescribe them in bio-chemical terms. The whole of this programme must in any case depend on the development of the rest of the biological sciences. Indeed, the present knowledge of the biochemical aspects of the nervous system does not permit of much immediate hope for quick development. At least this is so for the second stage of the plan; such a programme is sometimes called "reductionist".

The problem of describing behaviour in neural terms is very considerable. The difficulties of testing such hypotheses as may be forthcoming may be even more difficult. But this research is actually in progress now, and before we consider some of the suggestions that have been made, it is useful to reflect on our well-established knowledge of neurology and neurophysiology.

The central nervous system has often been likened to a complex telephone system, where the higher centres and synapses (the connecting points of neurons) are seen as similar to telephone exchanges. This analogy is useful up to a point, but only up to a point. There are certain adaptive features of nervous tissue that suggest differences as well as similarities.

All nervous tissues are elongations of the nerve cells that ramify throughout the body. The cells situated in the grey matter of the spinal tracts, and the brain itself, have a common origin with the other cells which make up the organism. But during evolution they have become specialised in their activity of communication. This, of course, is not to say that the properties of transmission are wholly excluded from other types of cell tissue, but certainly it is far less marked in other cells, due to the presence of special tissue, alleviating them of their burden.

Nerve cells have a cell body, many short-range off-shoots called dendrites, and usually a single long-range one called an axon. They can be categorised according to the number of off-shoots each nerve body has.

The brain itself (Figure l) is made up of tracts, connecting layers of grey cells; and the brain is a modified, highly specialised head-end of the spinal cord. The form the specialisation has taken is seen best in comparative terms. If an inspection is made of the nervous system of the earth-worm, the frog, the rat, and so on, in steps of increasing complexity, we can see the form that evolution has taken over very long periods of time. The simplest invertebrata have no specialised nerve cells, but in the earth-worm can be clearly seen the two principal nervous strands running throughout its length, with two more or less specialised nervous knots, or ganglia (collection of neurons) in the head-end, the leading end and also necessarily the end of maximum sensitivity.

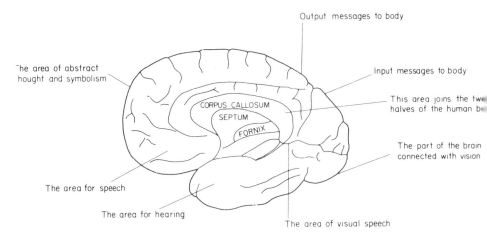

Figure 1   The diagram shows the main organs in a cross section of the human brain.

Man's central nervous system is made up of 10^{10} neurons, according to an estimate of Warren McCulloch. The complexities involved in possible combinations and recombinations of such a number defy the imagination. However, the human brain is conveniently, if rather arbitrarily, divided into sections – largely as a result of embryological evolution – and from the top of the spinal cord (going up) we have first the medulla oblongata, then the *midbrain*, and then the *pons varolii*. The *medulla* is probably a reflex mediating centre containing certain nuclei, or aggregations of neurons, and the same is probably true of both the midbrain and the pons; although the details, plotting of tracts, etc. is of considerable complexity. The cerebellum, a large motor organ attached behind the principal mass of the brain, is concerned with equilibrium and posture. The thalamus and hypothalamus, which are phylogenetically old, are concerned probably with the reflex mediation of "emotional" responses. It was probably at one time the controlling part of the brain; now it has become an end-station on the sensory system. It is reasonably certain that the thalamus and the hypothalamus, as well as the *basal ganglia* which are the last layer before the ultimate or top layer of the cerebral cortex, are all under cortical control. It is certain, in any event, that they work in close harmony with the controlling areas of the cerebral cortex, in the integrative behaviour of the organism. Discussion of these various controlling centres, particularly the lower reflex centres, and their relationship to the control of internal body-states (temperature, blood-pressure, etc.) would in itself fill volumes and still be incomplete. It is certain that to some extent the nervous system works as-a-whole in the organism, and so the above divisions should be regarded as fairly arbitrary.

The *cerebral cortex* is thought to represent the controlling centre of all behavioural activities in man and it is this complex layer of neural cells that has been the seat of most recent psychological and physiological investigation. The basal ganglia are the other large organs which merit mention, since they, too, work closely with the cortex. They once functioned in a controlling capacity, before the present degree of cortical development, and they still control, in part at any rate, laughing and yawning and many other involuntary activities.

Initially, in our discussion, we saw that the problem of understanding behaviour could be solved by filling in the gap between stimulus and response; whatever else happens between stimulus and response, it is certain that the cerebral cortex plays a vital part in "intelligent" human behaviour. Let us consider some of the evidence. The evidence coming from destruction of various parts of the cerebral cortex is of special interest, and, to describe this briefly, a simple map will help. The cortex is divided into four areas: the frontal areas that constitute most of the front half of the top of the brain; the temporal areas around the ear, and slightly above it; the parietal areas on top of the head and top sides, roughly in the centre of the head; and the occipital areas, constituting roughly the area covered by placing the open hand over the back of the head (see Figure 1).

The brain itself looks something like a very large walnut and is symmetrical in two hemispheres joined by connecting fibres, or association tracts. Thus, each of the four areas are duplicated: one on each side, and the areas themselves are isolated from each other by some of the more obvious crevices, or fissures, which are clearly visible on the surface of the brain. It is of special interest to consider what happens when any of these areas are either damaged or electrically stimulated.

The occipital areas are at the back of the head and specifically concerned with vision. Both stimulation and destruction of these areas have an effect on visual function. Destruction of the cortex in the occipital leads to partial blindness, in the form of loss of vision in half of the binocular field. The occipital area is concerned with the primary and secondary visual areas. The areas of *visual elaboration,* or secondary areas, are forward of the primary areas. The eyes (where integration of the "snapshots" occurs) are the main source of sensory input; the vast bulk of information the human being receives is through the eyes. It is true, of course, that much of this information could be picked up through the ears, or the other senses, but these are not normally employed to their full extent if the visual apparatus is functioning, although, of course, the input at any instant will generally involve all the senses.

The optical nervous pathways, starting at the retina (which is a thin nerve layer, made up principally of rods and cones in the back of the eye), run back to the optic chiasma, where part of the fibre tracts cross over, and then, after having certain connections with the thalamus, run back to the occipital areas.

The crossing-over of nerve fibres is typical of much of the nervous system: The right leg being controlled from the left hemisphere of the cerebral cortex and the left leg by the right hemisphere. Indeed, the left side of the body generally is controlled by the right hemisphere and vice versa. Right-handed people are left-hemisphere dominants. The occipital lobe is, except for the speech areas of the brain, probably the most specific in function of the whole of the cortical regions.

The speech areas will be dealt with briefly now. Various forms of speech defect, known collectively as *aphasia,* occur with damage of the speech areas. Penfield and Rasmussen (1950), in a survey, placed the primary speech areas in the superior, or upper frontal area, and in both the temporal and parietal areas. Destruction very near these areas may be carried out with impunity as they are rather clearly demarcated. Destruction of the speech areas themselves may lead to many different sorts of disorders: loss of speech, loss of various uses of words, loss of association of word and object, and so on.

The temporal areas are closely connected with "memory" functions, as well as containing areas serving both audition and equilibrium. Penfield found that direct electrical stimulation of the temporal areas, in a locally anaesthetised patient, results in reports of visual scenes which constitute part of the memory patterns of the individual. It is of great interest that we discover as much as possible about the location of memory, since, as with the digital computer, it is the extent of and accessibility of the memory that determines to a great extent the abilities of the organism.

Illusions and hallucinations are closely connected with this area. Electrical stimulation of this area can bewilder the patient completely as to the present state of his surroundings. It is this sort of evidence that places "introspection", and the less adequate psychological methods, in doubt. The general inference is that more stable neural patterns exist in this part of the cortex than any other. The synaptic connections, if these are indeed the foundation of "learning", are probably of a relatively permanent fashion in this area. The parietal lobe (on top of the head and upper sides) is not very revealing, and like the frontal lobe, does not respond markedly to electrical stimulation. However, Penfield and Rasmussen removed most of the parietal cortex in the non-dominant hemisphere, and the arm on the opposite side was affected, from the motor point of view: when the patient dressed, he made no use of his opposite (left) arm and acted just as if he was unaware of its presence. The parietal areas are therefore probably connected with mental projection of the opposite limb.

It is probable that the whole cerebral cortex involves a mapping of all systems (muscular, vascular, etc.) of the organism, and subserves most of the organism's functions. The "relations", however, are complex: the areas overlap, and the interrelated threshold values change differentially with changes of movement by the individual. The notion of threshold deserves mention. If a nerve fibre is stimulated, then it will respond, if and only if, stimulation is sufficiently strong. It is thus possible to stimulate a fibre and get no "response". The threshold is the point where a fibre responds to the minimal stimulation; it is a measure of the sensitivity of any neuron or collection of neurons.

In the cortex, in which an overlap of representation takes place, stimulation of a single point will elicit one or other functions according to the relative thresholds of the functions served by the particular point. The frontal lobe, which is almost certainly related to self-awareness and imagination, has caused the greatest interest, because here a considerable amount of destruction can take place without apparently affecting the overt behaviour of the individual. In fact, the changes are changes in so-called "personality". The most recent evolutionary development involves the social activities of man, and these seem to be largely represented by development of the frontal areas. A typical example will show the usual response to removal of large parts of the frontal lobes. A man, previously shy, and extremely retiring, with a considerable "blockage" or series of "frustrating states", was operated on, and the frontal areas partially destroyed. His complete recovery did not, at first, exhibit any change from his original self. But soon his friends reported marked changes in habits: no more shyness, but a gay disregard for conventions and money. His "frustration" had gone, and with it, any sence of planning or social organisation and responsibility; the two had gone together. Another example is that of damage to visual elaboration areas, which will impair visual function, since, although the receptors are functioning, the organised meaning of the visual receptions will be unclear. In terms of our visual analogy, we may say the brain gets all the snap-shots, but cannot interpret them.

The basis of much neurological experiment and the foundation of the theory has come from investigations conducted from the point of view of the *reflex arc* theory. The experiments which have revealed so much information have been done by electrical stimulation of muscle—nerve preparations; a typical piece of muscle used is from a frog's leg, and with it are taken its attached nerve fibres. Sir Charles Sherrington (1908) is a name that will always be connected with experiments of the reflex-arc type. From them he developed a fairly complex theory of neural functioning in which he used certain theoretical terms such as "central excitatory state", "central inhibitory state", and demonstrated processes of both inhibition and facilitation of a nerve impulse. Indeed, he gave us a picture of impulses travelling down nerves rather in the same manner as trains travel along many different railway lines. If two trains are running along parallel lines that run together into one, it is obviously necessary to stop one train and let is through first, so inhibiting or stopping the passage of the other train. When the impulses are not antagonistic, since now both may carry on together reinforcing each other — one train gets hooked onto the other making a bigger train. Figure 2 illustrates this point.

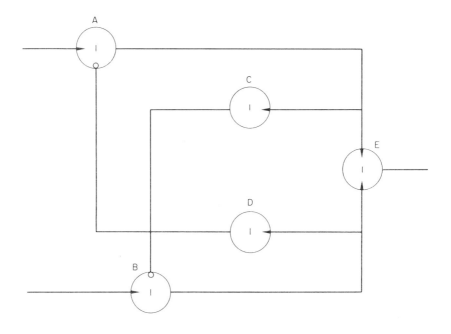

Figure 2   If a message $X = 1010$ comes in at A while $Y = 0101$ comes in at B
the output for E is 1111.

Sometimes circumstances arise when no train can pass at all, unless both the
component trains arrive together; in terms of our analogy, trains of five carriages
and no more must use the lines up to the junction, while all trains after the
junction must have at least ten carriages, so we must have two trains coming up
together. The central excitatory and inhibitory states refer to whether or not the
junction box is allowing trains through — "its signal is down" or not down,
which implies "signal up".

Of course, the picture is really more complex than this, but we shall use this
basic knowledge of the way nerve fibres behave when we construct our neural
networks. Figure 3 illustrates this point.

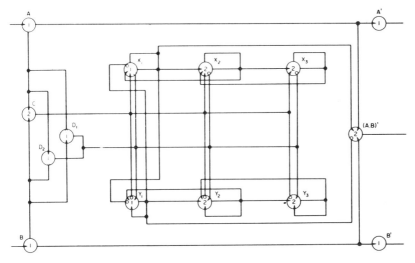

Figure 3   For just two inputs a and b, the net stores the ratio of the events $C = (a \cdot b)$ on one hand and either $B = D_1 \cdot D_2 = (\sim a \cdot b$ or $a \cdot \sim b)$ on the other. The element $(a \cdot b)'$ fires if there have been more C's than B's amongst the most recent recorded events.

The E.E.G. (or electro-encephalograph) is an instrument for measuring the electrical activity of the brain between any two points where the electrodes are placed. The best-known electrical characteristic is that of the alpha-rhythm, which occurs when a person at rest closes his eyes. It is of special interest because it is thought that this alpha-rhythm is associated with the steady scanning rhythm of the visual mechanism. This is what is used in television, and the resemblance between television and human vision is one that suggests the very development of cybernetics with which we are concerned.

The work that has been done recently on the E.E.G. has been on such a large scale that it would take too long a time to discuss. Perhaps the principal points of note are the facts that the electrical records so far collected indicate the strong interrelation existing between the electrical state of the organism and the chemical and other states. At the same time, the most general hypothesis derived from E.E.G. work is that there is a sort of homeostatic process which governs the electrical activity, in much the same way as there is a homeostatic principle that governs most, if not all, of behaviour. Perception is thus regarded as the process of scanning the visual field for sensory stimuli, and the analogy of television must, perforce, modify somewhat our picture of the nervous system. No longer is it just a telephone switchboard system, but a complex computer-like one involving the encoding and decoding of messages passing through it. This is not by any means inconsistent with the idea of a telephonic system, but somewhat more complex than the type of telephone system which might immediately occur to us.

11.2   CORTICAL LOCALISATION

Let us now briefly discuss cortical localisation. In rats, at least, cortical destruction, irrespective of the location in the cortex, seems to have the same effect on learning. Hebb (1949) found that the difficulty this implies for specific functioning is avoidable if it is seen that destruction of part of a neural network does not necessarily lead to loss of the associated function but is a short-circuiting which permits the associated function to be retained.

Hebb's theory of the cell assembly is closely connected with the long-held classical view that the nervous system must make new connections at the synapse when learning occurs. There now exists some comparative evidence for the presence of such synaptic knobs, which increase with age, at least during the period of early development. Hebb's own views have been built about a considerable body of experimental work on visual perception. He believes that a definite sequence of nerve stimulation takes place; He calls it a "phase-sequence", while the person is, say, scanning a simple geometrical shape. This ordered sequence permits, if suitable repetitions are made, the setting up of new networks, helped possibly by slight neural growth of a kind once suggested on a much larger scale by Arien Kappers (1936) and Lorente de Nó (1938a, 1938b, 1947). They have contributed the notion of "reverberatory circuits" — the existence of closed self-exciting neural circuits — and these they claim to have observed. Hebb (1949) uses this to allow the time for the necessary neural growth, which leads to the composition of the new network.

The notion of a reverberatory circuit was taken up by Hebb (1949) and made basic to his neuro-psychological theory of learning. Since Hebb's original work, Milner (1957, 1960) has suggested a modification which gives the original Hebb suggestions added neurophysiological plausibility. The facts are however, as outlined by Hebb, which depict a network of cells that grow and develop by specialised means such as fractionation and recruitment.

Clearly, for a cell assembly theory, we need to include concepts such as number of fibres firing on a cell at any one time, the sensitivity of the cell and neural fatigue, at the very least (George, 1961).

The most important point to mention now is that cell assemblies can easily be represented by neural nets. They could, of course, be constructed in hardware, and such efforts that have been made in this direction so far suggest that the original cell assembly at least was in need of reconsideration (Rochester, Holland, Haikt and Duda, 1956).

It is difficult, in a short section, to illustrate the depth and complexity of the subject, but the full import of the new theory is considerable: it means that the future possibility exists for description of behaviour in the necessary neural terms.

One possible misunderstanding should be avoided: the view put forward merely says that there is a need for a greater detailed analysis of the human organism, if a detailed predictive psychology is to be attained. However, it should not be thought that all the subject matter of psychology should be made up of propositions which are of a mathematical and neurological nature alone. Such propositions are indeed necessary to psychology, but they have to be transformed into psychologically descriptive propositions for most practical purposes. The whole point is that a descriptive psychology is inadequate without a detailed underlying model which may be used as a predictive check against all the details which we could not begin to answer by use of psychological theory alone.

The nature of these advances will be reviewed summarily. Between the stimulus and the response, a great deal happens. Life may be regarded as made up of complex, and continuous, patterns of external stimuli, to which the organism, in a continuous state of change, is reactable. Now we can build theoretical terms like "mind", "ego", etc. to come between the stimulus and the response, and the matter can be left there, or our theoretical terms can be drawn from neurology, and the biological sciences generally.

Both approaches are possible, and we believe that the first, on its own, is inadequate for some of the more serious purposes for which we need a science of psychology. But the difficulty has been to effect the link between behaviour and the biological "substratum". This has now become a possibility and should not only lead to the development of a rigorous science of behaviour but also allow the development of a descriptive theory, founded on a firm and testable basis, rather than on the present quicksand.

The importance of physiology to cybernetics, and vice versa, is much the same as it was for psychology. This is inevitable because, of course, we are thinking of physiology and psychology as being essentially the same subject, or at least two overlapping aspects of the same subject.

The importance of physiology is, of course, that it describes forms of control and communication systems. This allows us to understand human behaviour and so the human operator. There are a variety of ways in which we may use this information, but the most obvious way is in the simulation of human behaviour. But for synthesis too, our knowledge of possible physiological changes is of the utmost importance.

We are back with our "black box". We know what it does, and we can predict its behaviour with some accuracy by external observation alone. But for the more detailed prediction demanded by psychologists, the "internal" physiological details are necessary.

It is like looking at a car. Up to a point you can predict and understand without looking under the bonnet, but beyond that point it is hopeless, especially when the engine stops.

Cybernetics is as able to supply models at the detailed physiological level as at the broader psychological level. In doing so, it has mainly modelled the nervous system in a subject that is now called neurocybernetics.

11.3   RECENT ADVANCES

Conditioned reflexes have been the basis for much neurological investigation in the recent past. Doty (1965) for example showed that electrical stimulation of brains in macaques has systematic results of significance. He used 0.2–1.0 msec pulses as conditioned stimuli and these evoked lever pressing conditioned responses. He found that if a particular .point of the striatal cortex was stimulated, then the lever pressing started. He also found that this conditioned response could be elicited by stimulation of other points in the striatal cortex, even when stimulated from the contralateral area.

We should mention that Spinnelli and Pribram (1970) have shown that in all probability a functional connection is effected between the visual and motor cortex, where they used monkeys to make panel pressing discrimination responses. They studied the wave forms by electrodes planted in the visual and motor cortex and showed that after ablation the signs of functional connections were greatly diminished. Buchwald and Hull (1967) have shown that low-frequencey electric stimulation of the caudate, ventral, or ventral anterior nuclei of thalamus inhibits the performance of learned behaviour. A new afferent stimulus can disinhibit this effect: such a stimulus can either inhibit or disinhibit as (presumably) a function of the existing internal state of the nervous system.

Another experiment was carried out by Sharlock *et al.* (1965) and showed that cats could be trained to discriminate differences between sequences of tones. They then carried out bilateral ablation of the auditory cortex and followed it with a retention test. They worked out a map showing that certain areas of the cortex, when destroyed, not only destroyed the retention but stopped relearning. Semmes and Mishkin (1965) studied the effect of ablation of the sensori-motor region on monkeys. The monkeys were tested on a tactile discrimination test. When using the ipsilateral hand, they found their learning of difficult form discrimination was retarded; they were also less sensitive to rough surfaces, although not to different sizes of object.

Another recent development is that of Adey (1961) who implanted electrodes in the temporal lobes of cats and analysed records of their changes on a computer. He discovered certain characteristic wave patterns – one he called an "approach rhythm" which. he associated with learning. Adey has suggested that learning is associated with spatial pattern changes in neuronal currents, which is reminiscent of the models of Hebb and Milner.

The relation between the behavioural state of man, the state of awareness, and the electro-encephalographic record (Schadé and Ford 1965) is now known to some extent. For example, in a state of alert attentiveness, where the subject describes himself as concentrating, there is an associated E.E.G. record of characteristic partially synchronized low-amplitude waves. In deep sleep, on the other hand, where there is no consciousness, there is an E.E.G. record of large and very slow waves, with random irregular patterns. In a state of strong emotions, which can of course be artificially stimulated, there are variously described states of confusion, divided "attention", etc. with an associated E.E.G. record of desynchronised kind and of low to moderated amplitude. There are also fast mixed frequencies which accompany these highly emotional states.

Stellar (1960) views the concept of drive as that of lowering of thresholds for response patterns. But he also assumes that the degree of motivated behaviour varies directly with the activity of certain excitatory centres in the hypothalamus. Stellar assumes the interaction of inhibitory and excitatory hypothalamic centres. The external world can, of course, modify this hypothalamic state through sensory stimuli, and external states influence this hypothalamic state through the vascular system. It is also assumed that cortical and thalamic influences exert further excitatory and inhibitory influence on the hypothalamus.

Braitenberg (1967) has also described models derived from histological research, and has described them and other such models in cybernetic terms.

It is known that there are certain changes in neurophysiological states which are correlated with learning. Thinking too is related to neurological changes in the temporal, parietal and frontal areas. Furthermore, as Schade and Ford put it:

In general one can say that the speech mechanisms probably form a condition for certain kinds of thinking processes and provide a special way for handling of information.

Thinking and problem solving are known to be related to each other but perhaps it is not reasonable to expect that it is yet possible to distinguish one from the other at the neurological level.

11.4   A BRAIN MODEL

In this chapter it is being explicitly assumed that the brain is a data-processing system, with a very large store, or set of stores (such as fast and slower stores), which is working on coded information which travels along the pathways of the nervous system, as a function of certain complicated conditions.

The sensory pathways are primarily concerned with input, and this input activity is integrated into the complex selectivity reinforced processing of the brain. It seems clear that sensory inputs are independent classification systems and are partial and adaptive in their function. They act, in hierarchical fashion, as filters to a higher integrated partial classification system which is the central store.

All the information which is stored in the brain occurs at various levels of generality in the hierarchy, and it is reasonable to expect to be able to distinguish short-term from long-term memories: this is indeed connected with core as opposed to backing types of store. It is necessary to assume that much evidence derived from lower organisms is misleading when applied to the human brain which is far more complex and has far greater storage capacity, allowing the human being to be seen no longer as a passive receptor of, and reactor to, stimuli. What is called "free" (as opposed to "tied") thinking is a reminder that activity is often initiated by the human brain as a result of its conceptual activities.

More evidence is now available which suggests that cortical locations are the seat of the higher level memory stores where the conceptual processes of handling data, performing logical inferences, and the like occur. The notion of cortical localisation is renewed, but viewed as a dynamic rather than a static one. It seems certain that the cortical areas overlap and play very many different roles, according to whether an organism is learning, utilising information already learned, hypothesising or whatever.

The information is stored in an overlapping manner and detailed information, like data placed in computer registers, may vary from person to person and from time to time in the same person. The comparison with list-processing is an obvious one and suggests that the human brain has, in fact, compromised on localisation in the interests of flexibility. The reticular formation seems to be associated with motivation and drive. These features themselves though are complicated and concerned with selection, activation, priorities, emergencies, etc., all within the compass of a homeostatic principle which serves the organic needs of the body for survival: they are though obviously interconnected with the higher cortical (conceptual) activities in the hierarchy. The limbic system is almost certainly connected with motivational activity and is, as Pribram suggested, probably the regulator of the dispositions of organisms, this function being performed by use of neural homeostats.

There are still S-R activities of a reflex kind occurring (Spinelli and Pribram, 1970) in the brain, but they become something of an artefact as far as the human brain is concerned, if they are thought of as the basis of the total neural activity. Dotey (1965) has shown, while still using conditioning terminology, the greater detail of the workings of associations and classifications in store, which also suggests the very close association between equivalent areas in different hemispheres. It also though suggests that the growth of store has changed the reflex notion from a dominant to a recessive one.

Visual information is initially processed in the occipital areas of the cortex, auditory information in the tempoparietal areas, and so on. The regions which process language are probably the so-called "speech areas". Here, however, there is a problem since speech for the brain is complex. Human beings "vocalise" as a motor activity of a relatively simple kind, while they symbolise as a very high level conceptual activity. Sounds can be formalised as words and sentences and their utterance leads to an auditory response, which leads to translation into symbols. Language is itself motivated but does itself motivate. Words may remind us of, or initiate, needs and drives. Language is also closely associated with imagery, so that when humans "image" or "imagine" something, somehow some subset of the total set of sensory inputs which are involved in the actual sensory experience is stimulated.

Humans, it seems, learn to associate noises, such as those that represent words, with objects, relations and other conceptual factors, so that it must be assumed that the human brain stores language and data separately. Although separately stored, they are ultimately associated by something like a list-process or a complex cross-referencing system. Human beings can "image" an event from the past and can make statements about that event, such as giving a verbal description of it. In fact, humans tend to speak events as they "image" them, and can hardly speak about something without "imaging" it. Conceptualising is a process which is intimately bound up with language, and is thought to be a function closely associated with the frontal areas of the brain: there is some considerable neurophysiological evidence for this belief. The hierarchical nature of the brain suggests that the generation of new principles, recursion formulae, meta-rules, etc., which allow the solution of new problems is primarily a frontal lobe activity.

Research in cybernetics, particularly from the domains of computer synthesis and simulation, suggests that the brain is, and has been said, a complex hierarchical store with the ability to make inferences, both deductive and inductive, and perform computations, where the computational activity of mathematics has to be previously learned and conceptualised: it is readily available already in a digital computer, because of the programmer. One question of importance is why is there not a higher correlation between cortical damage and impairment of function. Search for memory traces of a dynamic character suggested by Lashley and others have been largely abandoned, so that it would seem to be necessary to accept instead the fact that the detailed information contained in any one cortical area varies according to the order in which it has occurred in the history of the owner, or at least partly by this and partly by his cross-reference system. In other words, information is contained in the detailed structures of the nervous system in a way which allows complicated overlapping of both functions and detail.

One way of fitting in the detail and testing the essential rightness of the views expressed is for a large team of scientists to build a large and detailed simulation of the brain on a computer, filling in all the detail that is known with some measure of confidence and adding on "plausible" detail until the model is fully connected and effective: this is a sort of empirical axiomatic system. The main test is that of seeing whether it, as a brain, can successfully program its environment, and to see if it can do so in the same way that human brains do.

In this discussion of the general organisation of the human brain, we have intentionally skirted around the neurological detail. Thus, it would be desirable to be able to assert exactly what function the amygdaloid bodies of the Brodman area 27 performs, but this is not possible. It is a picture rather like that of the organisation of a "fourth generation" multi-processing computer and it has dynamic properties.

The brain is currently seen as a hierarchically organised, highly adaptive, partial classification system, which has a high degree of specialisation which merges with a high degree of integrated function which is both anatomically and physiologically overlapping.

The basic units are Pribram's "graded function" homeostats, and it is possible to locate principal, statistically speaking, areas of importance in the cortex — for example, for integrated conceptual behaviour involving memory of the interpretation of the special senses. The "vertical" system, including the thalamus and limbic systems, are primarily emotional representations which are concerned with drive and reinforcement and are integrated closely with the cortex. Then the cerebellum and the associated tracts and closely connected areas are part of the motor control system which is so necessary to organised overt body movements.

The cortex is the primary representational centre for all the cognitive activities and must contain "models" of the "world outside" and the people in it as well as a "model" of the person himself. This last function is essential to consciousness and seems to be connected also with the function of the reticular formation: here, however, the world of existing evidence is left and the world of speculation entered.

Various paradoxes and uncertainties (not to say downright lack of knowledge) are also seen to play a major part in our still limited picture of brain models as of this time. But there is little doubt that Pribram's contribution to our understanding of brain activity is considerable. As a cybernetician, one might however feel that not enough attention is given to the methodological and logical analysis: this is where cybernetics can really contribute to brain modelling.

The original work of Pribram has been given a new impetus by his writings in his recent book "Languages of the Brain" (1971). This most recent account is entirely in keeping with his earlier writing but emphasises certain additional features.

He emphasises that neurons *and* neuronal junctions play an important part in brain modelling. This two-process mechanism accounts, in effect, for short-term and long-term changes in nervous tissue. Long-term memory therefore is seen as a function of junctional structure and short-term neural changes are a function of neuronal behaviour. Recoding is emphasised as being a powerful instrument in features of adaptation and internal changes relevant to changes of external states.

As before, TOTES are seen as adaptive mechanisms for feedback and feedforward operations. The TEST part of TOTE is associated with the junctional structures and the OPERATE part of the TOTE with the nervous impulse portion of the two process mechanism of brain function.

Perception and memory come in for especially detailed analysis. Both are considered to be non-specific and the leaning towards holistic views (not strictly holistic but anti-mechanistic) of such writers as Lashley, Goldstein and Köhler is marked.

The recent work on holograms also comes in for detailed discussion, emphasising that the need for special-purpose mechanisms over and above some mere translation or classification systems seems necessary to explain the neural mechanisms underlying perception.

11.5   SUMMARY †

Physiology enters the problem of predicting behaviour, since sometimes the black box approach of experimental psychology is insufficiently detailed to make precise prediction. In effect, this means opening the black box and replacing the abstract concept by a series of less abstract mechanisms.

Alternatively, we can think of physiology as supplying *molecular* black boxes to replace a *molar* black box. Physiology then attempts to interpret the sub-boxes in terms of neurons, fibres, brains and the like.

Neuro-cybernetics is a branch of cybernetics in its own right and aims to provide models of the various functions of the nervous system and special senses. There is a bridge here betweeen neural networks and idealised nervous systems and "actual" nervous systems whose properties we try to observe experimentally.

Physiology provides, as do most sciences, continual interplay of models and experimental observations.

---

† A recent book by G. Sommerhoff "Logic of the Living Brain", John Wiley (1975), deals with many factors central to this chapter.

CHAPTER 12

Programmed learning and cybernetics

Argument

Programmed learning is the process of supplying information in closed loop form, it is automated teaching in its main sense.

Teaching machines form a principal part of programmed learning and programmed learning can be thought of as a part of cybernetics. Here we are concerned with effectively transmitting information from source to destination — a typical example of a process coming within the purview of information theory and this is essentially the process of teaching. At least teaching is one of the main purposes to which such methods can be put.

Teaching is in an obvious sense the opposite of learning and is a feedback process, in which the material used as input is a function of the output of the system; it is thus characteristically cybernetic.

When we come to teach our computers what we think they should know we shall, as we must with human beings, use programmed instruction to achieve the desired end.

C.A.I. is the name given to computer assisted instruction which is concerned with the process of simulating the teacher on a digital computer. C.M.I. and C.O.I. are sometimes used to refer to computer managed instruction and computer organised instruction respectively.

Cybernetics has, as we have tried to show throughout the course of this book, many different facets and many different applications. No attempt has been made to discuss in detail applications of cybernetics in the field of automation, although clearly from one point of view automation could be regarded as merely the application of scientific ideas to industrial, commercial and similar situations. However, one of the most important applications or offshoots of cybernetics which will be discussed in this chapter is that of *programmed instruction*.

Programmed instruction, or programmed learning as it is sometimes called, is the general name for the field involving teaching machines, programmed books and group teaching whether under computer control (computer assisted instruction or C.A.I., and C.M.I. and C.O.I.) or by more formal methods, such as one meets in the language laboratory situation. Some of these aspects will be discussed in the remainder of this chapter.

Programmed instruction differs from other forms of instruction in that it involves the characteristic close-loop and negative feed-back type of situation.

There is, as is the case with the best possible teachers, particularly those working with small classes or individuals, a maximum interaction between the person being taught and the teacher. It is the closed-loop situation with the use of adaptive methods, that places programmed instruction within the domain of cybernetics. The idea that programmed instruction is a part of cybernetics is historically justified since many people who have devoted a great deal of their time to cybernetic research have also been involved in the field of programmed instruction. In this respect we might mention the names of Pask (1960, 1961), Gallanter (1959) and the present author (George 1966a, 1967). Also teaching is manifestly a control and communication process, and therefore is central to cybernetics.

12.1   TEACHING MACHINES

There are a variety of different kinds of *individual* teaching machines in existence as well as a few *group* teaching machines. Let us first of all consider the individual teaching machines.

Individual teaching machines tend to fall into two categories:

1) those that teach by description, and
2) those that teach by acquaintance.

Of those that teach by description, there is a further sub-division that can be made between machines that teach on the *branching* method and machines that teach on the *linear* method, and those that use both. The names of Crowder (1960) and Skinner (1958) are associated respectively with the origin of the branching and linear techniques when used in the domain of programmed instruction.

We shall first of all briefly mention the branching machine and the branching method of teaching. First of all a branching method of teaching is one where you have the possibility of alternative answers to a single question and where the student himself has to select the correct answer from a set of possible answers. Figure 1 shows simple branching:

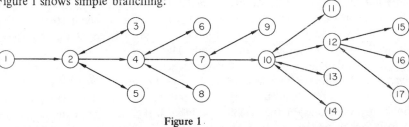

Figure 1

It is clear that the wrong answer frames such as numbers 3, 5, 6 and 8 above give additional information, hints or *prompts*, which will help the student to get the right answer before returning him to the original question frame, where he reads the original information again and then makes a further choice. He goes on until such a time as he selects the right answer. It is clear that this simple branching process has limited application in teaching by description, even though it may not be so limited when used, as was originally intended, in the field of *fault finding* for electronic equipment. To add to the flexibility of simple branching, we have to consider complex branching. The next figure, Figure 2, shows a simple state diagram for a complex branch:

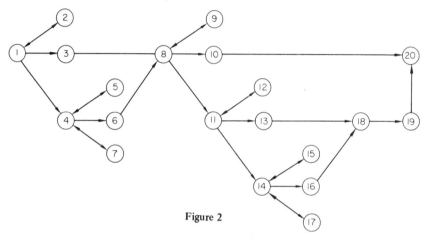

Figure 2

Here it will be seen that where the wrong answer is got on Frames 4, 11 and 14, the student is not asked to go back to re-read the original question, but has the principle restated on the frame where he has made the wrong choice; he is then subjected to a fresh set of alternative questions. This is known as a *remedial sub-route,* and as a result of it the student will not normally return to the original frame where he made his mistake.

It is clear from the above discussion of branching that at each branch point we can have *any* number of questions, and at each branch point we can follow up a remedial sub-route by another remedial sub-route and so on indefinitely. In practice, and for economic reasons, there is no point in these individual teaching machines providing too many sub-routes even when assuring that the most difficult principle is being understood. The reason for this is that every programme that goes on any individual teaching machine must be carefully *specified*. This means that an attempt is made to ensure that all the "assumed knowledge" is actually acquired by the student prior to reading the programmed book or programme for the machine, and thus it should never be the case that a person fails to understand some principle after, at most, three different kinds of explanation and a series of testing questions to follow. If the student does so fail, then he almost certainly fails to achieve the standard set by the specification.

This whole teaching procedure is encompassed in a testing framework. Tests of prior or assumed knowledge are used, as are tests of knowledge achieved as a result of having been through the programme, and from these tests an assessment can be made as to the effectiveness of the programme as a whole, and its effectivess for each individual student. There is of course no limit to the degree of precision that can be put into the specification.

The linear type of descriptive teaching machine is a simplified version of the branching machine, in the sense that it involves no branches at all, but merely provides frames with information and question and the answer to the previous question.

The following figure, Figure 3, show the simple "page-turning" format of a linear programme..

Figure 3

Here you have the same process of breaking information down into relatively small steps, and a question-and-answer technique being provided to link each step of information to the next.

There is much evidence to suggest that it is literally the breaking down of information into the steps and linking them by questions which is important to the reinforcement and retention of information. This is supported by detailed questioning, and in the case of linear programmes the need to answer (possibly writing the answer) the question before you turn to the next frame to see what the correct answer is.

The type of simple linear format, depicted in Figure 3, can be given some of the flexibility of the branching method by skips or jumps forward or back. These skips are usually when a "key question" or test is failed, or where a preliminary test showing knowledge of what is to come is passed.

Figure 4 depicts the linear format with skips.

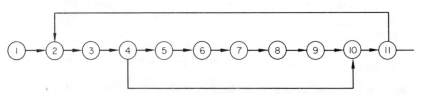

Figure 4

Simulation machines (machines that teach by acquaintance) teach manual skills, such as touch-typing, wiring apparatus, or any manual skill whatever. These sort of teaching machines tend to provide a physical performance or skill, or provide the basis of a physical performance or skill to the student who performs it. He has his performance recorded and as a result of his performance the input to him is modified as a function of his success or failure. Thus in the face of touch-typing, the more successful the student is with certain letters the less he will be asked to type those letters, and the overall increase of speed which he shows as a result of practice will result in the new information of touch type being provided at a greater and yet greater speed. Speed alone indeed and the emphasis on particular letters are only the two initial variables in skill.

It is fair to say that so far individual teaching machines working on the principle of description which are those that we have referred to above as branching and linear (although of course they can be *mixed* together) have been the most successful and most widely used methods so far. This does not mean that there is not a great deal of scope for the development of other methods, and the simulation method in particular. As against the relative paucity of branching machines, which by their very nature are bound to be more complex and expensive than their linear equivalent, there are in existence hundreds of different linear machines, although as the years go by fewer and fewer of them are commercially available.

12.2   PROGRAMMED TEACHING MACHINES

The presence of teaching machines has thrown great emphasis on the need to programme these machines effectively. The reason why machines on the whole have yet to find a world wide market is precisely because of the lack of skilled teaching machine programmers.

The actual processing of information for the teaching machine is a complicated and highly skilled business. Not only does the programmer have to specify carefully the information and who it is intended for, he also has to plan the programme in great detail. The planning of the processing of information for a teaching machine programme is analogous to the planning of a computer program.

There are various stages involved in the characteristic plan for programming a teaching machine and they might be broken down into the following stages:

1) specification;
2) ordering of contents;
3) flow charting;
4) frame writing;
5) testing of programme.

The specification of a programme should include at least the following:

a) age range of students;
b) I.Q. range of students;
c) whether programme is intended for a (or a part of a) particular examination;
d) knowledge of presupposed (test needs);
e) knowledge not required (test needed to be sure student does not already

know contents of programme);

f) Post-test to discover how much learned from programme.

Clear specification is vital to the testing stage of a programe, to be sure that a programme is tested in the light of its intended purpose. The second state is in the preparation of contents of the programme and a consideration, in the light of the specification, of the optimum order of presentation. At this stage it is also vital to consider order of abstraction. A programme should give the general overall view of the subject and describe the purpose of the programme, and then draw attention to detail, relating the detail to the overall view.

The third stage is flow charting, and in this the process is much as it is in the computer program. Here the flow charts may be at any number of levels down to a frame-by-frame basis if desired. At this stage, the question of the use of branches, if any, and the details of gradient learning, prompts, rate of accumulation of information, the use of the method of discovery and the type of questions and their patterning all become important. The following Figure 5 shows a simple frame-by-frame flow chart for the first seven frames of a programme on probability (George, 1966b, 1967).

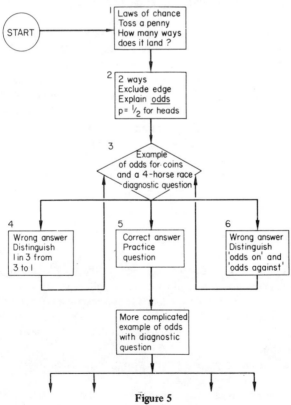

Figure 5

Frame writing comes at stage 4, and should be so constrained by the plan that it should not vary much with different writers.

12.3   THE DEVELOPMENT OF COMPUTER ASSISTED INSTRUCTION

Finally comes the testing which divides into several stages:

i)   routing tested;
ii)   layout (and diagrams) checked;
iii)   specialist reader;
iv)   validation copies printed and validation carried out (all tests used);
v)   if successful at validation programme is complete.

The most irksome and difficult process is that of validation, since the statistical analysis is difficult to assess. Suppose, for example, a particular frame k, is a source of almost universally wrong answers; should it then be re-written? The test here is to plant a similar question further on in the text and see if learning has or has not occurred.

We cannot attempt to reproduce all the necessary "tricks of the trade" and skills involved in writing programmes in this book, and other specialist texts and books should be read by the reader who is interested in learning how to programme a teaching machine for himself. We are here concerned more with saying that the range of application of such teaching machines is vast, and the process of communication from destination to a source is one that is capable of being described in terms of communication or information theory. Indeed from the information theoretic point of view, the very process of teaching is one that could be given the metric and the amount of information passed could be measured in terms of bits. It is of course hardly necessary to add that the process of teaching is in some sense the opposite side of the coin from that of learning.

12.4   GROUP TEACHING MACHINES

Many attempts have been made to provide group teaching by machine, and this can be done either by group stimuli with individual responses, individual stimuli with group responses, or group stimuli and group responses. Wherever the group responses are involved the problem is one of finding a procedure to decide what the group response is; it certainly involves the problems of leadership or decision taking in the group.

We shall be concerned primarily with computer assisted instruction (C.A.I.) for the remainder of this chapter. There are many so-called automated classrooms now in existence. They are all computer controlled and, although the bulk of them exist in the United States of America, there are also many in Europe. In particular the best known of computer assisted instruction units are at the Systems Development Corporation in Santa Monica, California, two at the University of Illinois at Urbana, at M.I.T. at Cambridge, Mass., and at Stanford University.

In every case the principles involved are the same; the computer control coupled with the storage system has input and output systems which are placed on each individual desk of the automated classroom. Each individual student sitting at his desk, and, of course, subject to group stimuli in the classroom as a whole is also subject to individual stimuli on the screen provided for that particular desk. He has a button control system on the desk which allows him to respond individually to either the group or the individual stimulus. The individual button control and the individual and the collective screens are all connected with the computer control and store. This means that the computer itself can control the nature of the input and output to the student, and can record the performance of each individual student separately and in such detail as is deemed necessary.

The advantage of the computer controlled classroom situation is that each individual student can ask a question independently without making public the nature of his enquiry, and the instructor can follow in detail the performance of the individual by consulting the computer store whenever he pleases. Some idea of the importance of this undertaking can be gleaned when it is said that several automated classroom units in America claim that they have the facilities for teaching more than a 1,000 students simultaneously working on some eight different programmes simultaneously.

12.5   COMPUTER ASSISTED INSTRUCTION (C.A.I.)

We shall concentrate now on some of the details of C.A.I.

The next phase of C.A.I., although not yet attained, is the complete decision making type of cybernetic control system. This means that a computer is given something like the full range of teacher flexibility. This requires the ability on the part of the computer to formulate generalisations in linguistic terms and to be capable of translating ordinary English. This means "I don't understand", or "Please explain it another way", etc., is translated by the computer and gives rise to an explanation which is not pre-programmed, but manufactured on line for the purpose, or at least is capable of such extemporisation.

Heuristic programming is now being developed (George, 1962; George, 1965; Levien and Maron, 1965) wherein inference making, data retrieval, use of natural language and all forms of hypothesis making and hypothesis testing, take place, and such matters are to be discussed in detail in later chapters. Such heuristic methods must be developed further before they can be utilised for teaching purposes, but computer assisted instruction (C.A.I.) does not wait on such development.

The short-term solution of C.A.I. lies in the control systems which are typified by Plato, Socrates and the Systems Development installation, as well as such programme writing methods as Coursewriter. Here we come to face immediate problems of input and output which will not be discussed in this book, since although a source of many practical problems it is not a central problem to the theory.

Our problem surrounds the organisation of the computer programme. We can easily allocate (George, 1966a) computer stores to keep a record of each individual's performance – in any necessary detail – and with respect to a particular teaching programme. Look at the following scheme for a teaching programme, where $A, B, ..., N$ are storage addresses, q_j^i are questions, where q_j is the jth question with i prescribed answers, a_l^k is the lth correct answer to question q_k, and b_n^m is the nth incorrect answer to question q_m. Herewith is our branching programme scheme.

$$A\ (q_1^1)$$
$$C\ (b_1^3)$$
$$E\ (a_2^3, q_3^2)$$
$$G\ (b_3^3, q_5^2)$$
$$I\ (b_4^5)$$
$$K\ (b_6^4)$$

$$B\ (a_1^1, q_2^3)$$
$$D\ (b_2^3)$$
$$F\ (a_3^3, q_4^3)$$
$$H\ (a_4^5, F)$$
$$J\ (b_5^4)$$
$$L\ (a_5^4, q_6^3)$$

... etc.

Such a branching scheme operates very simply provided the answers are multiple-choice and are stored in the computer and printed out as selected. The individual's record, for person S_1 can read simply as a list of choice points, omitting sincgle choice answers. So for the above programme we might have a record like:

r w r r w ... or r w (C) r r w ...,

which shows that he answered q_2 correctly first time, he failed at the q_3 and we could show his choice at C, then he was correct second time: he was correct first time with q_3 wrong with q_4 etc.

We can go on from these beginnings or even consider other methods for programmed instruction programming, but will leave the matter at this point, except for a short sample of part of a branching programme (George, unpublished).

From *i*

For the first example, we shall ask you to consider the following problems.

30 numbers are put in store representing 30 values of a variable, 1 to 30 inclusive. 30 further numbers are put in different stores and these further 30 are the weights (or frequencies) associated with the first 30 values.

Find the *arithmetic mean* of the numbers.

The arithmetic mean is defined at $\bar{x}$, where the formula for $\bar{x}$ is:

$$\bar{x} = \frac{\Sigma fx}{\Sigma f}$$

i.e. the arithmetic mean of a set of numbers is the sum of the product of the frequencies and the values divided by the sum of the frequencies.

So for the numbers 1, 1, 2, 2, 2, 3, 3, 4 the table is:

x	f	fx
1	2	2
2	3	6
3	2	6
4	1	4
	$\Sigma f = 8$	$\Sigma fx = 18$

For the numbers 2, 2, 3, 3, 3, 4 what is fx and f?

Go to 2.

From 1.

x	f	fx
2	2	4
3	3	9
4	1	4
	$\Sigma f = 6$	$\Sigma fx = 17$

$\Sigma f = 6$ and $\Sigma fx = 17$, where x's are the different numbers and f's are frequency of occurence of each.

If you like to think in numerical terms about our problem, take numbers $1 - 30$, and multiply them by any 30 numbers you like, say 1, 2, ..., 15, 15, 14, ..., 2, 1 and then divide by the sum of this second set.

What is the sum of the set of 30 numbers.

　　　　1, 2, ..., 15, 15, 14, ..., 2, 1.

3. 120

4. 240

5. 256

From 2.

Wrong

The set Σf is

$$1, 2, 3, 4, 5, 6, 7, 8, 9, 10, 11, 12, 13, 14, 15$$

twice over

and that is 240.

Return to 2.

From 2.

240 is correct.

Now what about the program?

Do not forget the aim of the program is to find

$$\Sigma fx/\!\!/ \Sigma f.$$

We think you ought to think carefully about this and try to write out the program for yourself before you carry on. The title of the program can be ARITHMETIC MEAN.

When you have made your attempt, go to 6.

From 2.

No.

The set Σf is

$$1, 2, 3, 4, 5, 6, 7, 8, 9, 10, 11, 12, 13, 14, 15,$$

twice over

and that is 240.

Return to 2.

From 4.

Have you actually written out your program for

$$\frac{\Sigma fx}{\Sigma f} \quad ?$$

If so, go to 7.

If not, do so now, before you go to 7.

Write out carefully, step by step, the autocode program for

$$\frac{\Sigma fx}{\Sigma f}$$

From 6.

Do you agree with this program?

```
SET 1 (i)
SET 4, 1
TITLE: ARITHMETIC MEAN
READ
VARY i = 1, 1, 30
READ a (i)
REPEAT i
E = 0
VARY i = 1, 1, 30
READ b (i)
E = B (i) + E
REPEAT i
VARY (i) = 1, 1, 30
C (i) = A (i) x B (i)
REPEAT i
D = 0
VARY i = 1, 1, 30
D = C (i) + D
REPEAT i
F = D/E
PRINT F
STOP.
```

If you agree with it, go to 8. If not, go to 9.

(If in doubt about the details you may need to refer back to Book 11, or your own note book.)

From 7.

Good.

The program is correct. So we can assume now that you find our autocode easy to use.

We have written PRINT F as the penultimate order.

If we had wanted four places to the right and three to the left of the decimal point, how would the order have read?

10.　PRINT F 3, 4

11.　PRINT F 3/4

12.　PRINT F 4, 3

From 7.

You are wrong if you think our program was wrong.

Our program would have done the job very nicely.

Go back to 7.

From 8.

No.

This would give you something different from what we demanded.

It would give us four places to the left and three to the right.

Return to 8.

From 8.

No.

This would give you something different, since 3/4 means "3 divided by 4".

Return to 8.

From 8.

You are quite correct.

Now we must undertake a more complicated compiler programming example. So first let us describe the details. We are going to calculate the batting averages of four batsmen whom we shall call Morgan, Smith, Jones and Green.

Batting averages are, of course, calculated by adding up all the runs made over some period of time, and then dividing by the number of *completed* innings in that time. So we have to cater for the fact that some innings were not completed — Smith, say, was 43 not out, and this adds 43 runs to his total but does not add anything to the number of completed innings.

Go to 13.

From 12.

The following are the scores made by Smith, Jones, Green and Morgan respectively:

Smith:	13, 27, 85, 142, 46*, 2, 45, 72, 12*
Jones:	96, 89, 12, 47, 13, 0, 78, 81, 64, 65*
Green:	33, 38, 47, 112, 101, 0, 2, 5, 1, 0*
Morgan:	61*, 2*, 49*, 8*, 21*, 46, 32, 72

where the * against a number means that the innings was *not* completed.

So the first thing you should do is to label these four batsmen b, c, d, and e.

Also you should write down the scores of each of them on a piece of paper and keep it ready at hand.

Go to 14.

From 13.

Now we actually start a program by setting out the input orders, and if we use 10 in front of a number to indicate "not out", then the following is the input data:

SMITH	JONES	GREEN	MORGAN
13	96	33	1061
27	89	38	1002
85	12	47	1049
142	47	112	1008
1046	13	101	1021
2	0	0	46
45	78	2	32
72	81	5	72
1012	64	1	
	1065	1000	

Note that Green scored 101 on one occasion and 0, not out, on another. If he had scored 1, not out, on the first occasion it would be written 1001, not 101.

Go to 15.

From 14.

Now our TITLE is "CRICKET BATTING AVERAGES" and we shall write our SET orders at the end, and then *place* them at the beginning of the program.

Now first of all let us face a problem. We have got to set up our program, so any one batsman has an innings recorded against him (say in $b(i)$) and has the innings where he is "not out" noted (say in $c(i)$) and also the c value must be subtracted from the b. Then the total number of runs will be in $d(i)$, the highest score in $e(i)$ and the average in $f(i)$.

So now we can start the first part of our problem by the following, or something like it. Is this correct or not?

(The arrow shows a cycle which is repeated.)

$$\text{VARY } i = 0; 1; 4$$
$$b(i) = 0$$
$$c(i) = 0$$
$$d(i) = 0$$
$$e(i) = 0$$
$$\text{REPEAT } i$$

16.   Incorrect

17.   Correct.

From 15.

You are wrong.

It will do quite well. Look again:

VARY $i = 0; 1; 4$ ——————┐
$b(i) = 0$
$c(i) = 0$
$d(i) = 0$
$e(i) = 0$
REPEAT i ——————————┘

We are not, of course, saying that the REPEAT order will come immediately after $e(i) = 0$; it will not.

Return to 15.

From 15.

Quite correct.

Look once more:

VARY $i = 0; 1; 4$ ——————┐
$b(i) = 0$
$c(i) = 0$
$d(i) = 0$
$e(i) = 0$
REPEAT i ——————————┘

Now remember that we have put 10 in front of scores that are "not out"; and also bear in mind that we must number orders if we need to transfer to them, otherwise you cannot fill in the n, in the order

TRANSFER $a = 0$ to n.

Go to 18.

12.6   SUMMARY

Programmed learning, or programmed instruction, is a part, a cybernetic part, of automated education. It has feedback loops and is capable of being made adaptive.

Programmes need to be very carefully planned, and such programmes are still at this stage fixed or pre-programmed. With the development of heuristic methods they may be made fully adaptive.

Linear, branching and mixed programmes are described, as are individual and group teaching machines.

Finally, computer assisted instruction (C.A.I.) is described with some sample of a branching programme.

CHAPTER 13

The problem of artificial intelligence

Argument

One of the central problems of cybernetics is that of simulating and synthesising
intelligence; this is the core of cybernetics.

We may simulate human intelligence or we may try and synthesise it, but in
the end there is the central problem of whether or not we can effectively
construct an organic system.

Even if in the end we could not construct a humanlike system or an actual
human being, then the fact remains that it is the aim: and in trying to fulfil this
aim we can achieve a great deal of vital importance to science.

This chapter is closely related to the next two which are concerned with two
principle features of artificial intelligence — reasoning and the use of (ordinary)
language, especially on computers.

Chapters 14 and 15 really go into detail on two central aspects of artificial
intelligence which is summarised in Chapter 13.

In this chapter we shall pinpoint what is regarded by many as the central
problem of cybernetics, that of artificial intelligence.

We have seen already that learning can occur in artificial systems; we have
also seen that perception and the analogs of other cognitive approaches can also
occur in artificial systems, or can — and this is equivalent — be simulated on the
computer. We have also seen how these various features can be studied from the
viewpoint of theory, by paper tape automata, computer programs or even as
hardware models. We now wish to dwell further on the general principles that
run throughout the field, and try to pinpoint the most important of the central
features.

The fact that learning can occur in suitably constructed machines as a result
of experience can hardly be doubted. Many examples have already been
discussed in this book. The learning envisaged, by and large, was *by acquaintance
with* the environment, and we need now to add the knowledge gained *by
description* of that environment. This distinction naturally arises as soon as
generalisations, or heuristics are considered. It is essential for digital computers
or automata which have pretensions to a fair amount of "intelligence", to have
the ability to manufacture generalisations, and to this end must have symbols
(words) to describe them.

What is being demanded is a language for a computer, and in doing so we are demanding no more than is available to human beings. The difficulty is of course that language represents one of the most complicated and sophisticated aspects of human behaviour.

A computer has a stock of autocodes, or high level programming languages as we have said, and these autocodes represent, in one sense, the equivalent of ordinary language. This is so in that they are used externally for the programmer to "talk" to the machine, or machines to "talk" to each other. The computer translates the information communicated in language into its own internal instructional language. Of course, it must be made clear that we have to add to this the fact that the computer must also show the ability to *learn* language as well as "learn facts" through experience, not merely *use* a language.

It is assumed now that simple adaptation and simple learning can be achieved by many different automata, including digital computers. This is achieved by negative feedback and selective reinforcement which also involves stored information, knowledge of results and ability to form generalisations.

The present problem is one of showing that more sophisticated learning demands the use of language, and that language can be computerised. Language is also relevant to the other aspects of cognition such as problem-solving and thinking, which can also be carried through on the computer, or so we are now claiming.

One can see the possibility of a computer being programmed to learn language in the ordinary way, and this is absolutely necessary to the *simulation* problem, if the standard of human intelligence is to be achieved. Such learning depends upon the ability to manufacture associations, which must be specifically between the symbols and the things symbolised, as well as between the sets of symbols. We shall not here discuss the relation between signs and symbols but merely remind the reader of discussions of semantics that have already occurred earlier.

A very important consideration immediately arises at this point; this is that we must have a "non-naive" model (or program) if it is going to be able to learn from experience and make important decisions. This is an essential requirement for an autonomous artificial intelligence used on matters such as decision making at a high level. This requires checking of the reliability of the validity of input information very carefully indeed. Learning by acquaintance, the computer will check the reliability of input information by virtue of its coherence with past information, by cross-checking and by other methods which are relatively straight forward in assessing the reliability of an input source (George, 1967, 1968). As soon as the input source becomes another person, or another "human-like" computer of the same kind as itself, the difficulty of the problem increases. In other words (to put it in ordinary human terms) if someone tells you something, you assess his reliability in general – how far this information he is giving you is consistent with that previously given, and whether *he* (it) *has any special motive in trying to deceive you*. An assessment of all these factors must be catered for in the processing of verbal information. This is absolutely essential if our model is not to be hoodwinked or bluffed as a result of its transactions (by description) with other models or any other source of information whatever. The essential feature to be detected is a motivational one. We have to assess the motives of our interlocuter and ask ourselves whether he has the motive to deceive us. If the answer is that he has got the necessary motive, then we have to consider reversing (or lowering) our assessment of the plausibility of his statements.

We shall now go on to consider the processing of verbal information in greater detail, and in doing so we bring in studies of a semantic and linguistic kind which have taken place over a long period of time. We shall also, by this means, pave the way for the more detailed discussion of the programming of language in Chapter 15.

13.1   THE PROCESSING OF VERBAL INFORMATION

What we need now to have is some clearer picture of the organism's method of processing language. We shall take our first illustration from linguistic philosophy. We know, for example, that the congruity of linguistic behaviour is not a guarantee of the identity of sensory experience. When two different people use the same word "green", for example, there is no guarantee that they are talking about the same thing. But we can assume, in general terms, that when two people use the same term, phrase or sentence, they are referring to *much the same* sort of thing; the differences are, in general, minor ones.

The model we have in mind is fairly crude in its functioning. It makes no demands of "absolute proof" or "certainty" as is normally done by philosophers. It accepts a high level of approximation and a fair measure of error, in attaining an approximately logical and coherent picture of its environment. This is made more difficult to fully appreciate because we use a form of logic in our description of the computer program which makes the system look quite precise, whereas this is really not the case. What we are trying to achieve is a precise description of an imprecise system. This entails that our description be probabilistic where the measure used for the probability (where this is attainable) must be quite precisely defined. We must be prepared to manufacture models which are both deterministic and probabilistic and work either on a precise or probabilistic basis. We shall now try to give a clearcut picture of the problem of artificial intelligence as tackled by programming a digital computer.

13.2   ARTIFICIAL INTELLIGENCE

One of the central problems of cybernetics is that of programming a computer to demonstrate various aspects of intelligence. We are concerned with both the synthesis and the simulation of intelligence by artificial means. The connection between synthesis and simulation is, as we have said, apparently inescapable, since any form of synthesis must, it seems, at least be suggestive of simulation; however the fact remains that synthesis as such is our primary object. We want to program a computer so that it can accept and understand questions in a natural language such as English, or possibly in a form of logic. It then searches through its own store to find the answer to these questions, and in general, it will state the answers if they are known to the computer.

We want also to program a computer so that it asks questions of any human-like source of information, person or computer in its environment. The reason for asking these questions will, in general, result from the need for information to complete some strategy, or act as a basis of information for some decision, whether or not this decision leads to action. It should be made clear that the computer is to be thought of as acting in an environment, which contains at least one human-like source of information and also contains events which occur, some of which may be under the control of the computer, and also capable of being described by it.

The computer's problem is to learn which aspects of the environment it can control, depending on information gained by direct experience of that environment on one hand, or by a question-and-answer interplay, through language, on the other. It should be said that apart from the ability to collect information and store that information, the computer must have the capacity to draw inferences (our subject for the next chapter, Chapter 14), of both an inductive and deductive kind, and take whatever steps are necessary to seek information which may be needed by some other source of information.

One of many such environments that cybernetics has been concerned with is that of a well-defined game, such as noughts-and-crosses (tic-tac-toe) or NIM. The game itself is obviously trivial, and it is only used because it is one which has a decision procedure, and is also one which illustrates the way in which either decision procedure can be discovered or heuristics supplied, without obscuring the process of that derivation because of the complexity of the game.

The position is that the computer both plays the game and makes inferences about it, based on the rules it has been told, at the same time. By the phrase "at the same time" we mean that the computer must go on-line then off-line, playing in what we have sometimes called a sequential manner, then arguing about or reasoning about or asking questions about the game, and then by playing the game again, and then making inferences again, the processes are gradually learned. This clearly implies the capacity in the computer to make inductive and deductive inferences, where the deductive process at least is one similar to that described by such writers as Newell, Shaw and Simon (1963), by Gelerntner (1963), Samuel (1963), and others.

The computer must be capable of describing what it is doing and answering questions it is asked with respect to what it is doing. The second stage of this operation is to show that the computer can be given a sufficiently general vocabulary and the formal rules of some further game, (e.g. draughts or checkers), so that without any more special programming technique being involved, the reasoning capacity derived from the first game, noughts-and-crosses, plus the actual playing of the game in an environment, is sufficient to allow it to improve its performance. Initially we shall expect this to be little more than definite improvement, without expecting it either to derive an algorithm (decision procedure), or without it necessarily being able to play a highly skilled game.

We can then generalise this technique and apply it to any games whatever, whether these games be well-defined such as noughts-and-crosses and draughts, or whether they will be ill-defined, requiring optimisation techniques, as well as the use of conditional probabilities and other techniques.

The computer must in the next stage of operation be able to generate new words *and* be able to understand new words which are supplied to it by the other computer or human-like source of information in its environment. We now would like, of course, also to generalise this and say there may be many human-like sources in its environment, and to this end, we shall have to have a model not only of the environment, in which the computer operates but also a model of all the features of that environment which are what we have called "human-like" sources. This means the computer must keep a model of each human-like source and must assess the likely reliability, in the light of experience (George, to be published), of that model and also the likely motivation that that human-like source may have in making the particular statement it has made.

The next stage in this programming undertaking is to write actual programs. Let us also make it absolutely clear that the main difficulties in trying to achieve these experimental requirements, surrounds the fact that we are not merely describing the process in general, but supplying either compiler codes or machine codes, which show precisely how the whole undertaking can actually be programmed.

It is clear from what has been said already that, although the aim is to provide a synthetic system of artificial intelligence, depending on the ability to learn to use language, and to develop and learn new languages, both from understanding external linguistic sources and from manufacturing new words internally, the over-all picture is one which comes near to being a simulation of the problem-solving, decision taking and planning activities of human beings.

It should be added that a large number of programs for a variety of different computers have already been written in pursuance of the plan laid out in this section, and we will explain a little more of the methods in the next section of this chapter.

13.3 METHODS USED IN PROGRAMMING FOR ARTIFICIAL INTELLIGENCE

In the last section of the chapter we gave an over-all glimpse of the plan on which the whole of our artificial intelligence undertaking is based. We gave a few clues as to previous work that fitted into this general picture, and we can remind ourselves again at this point of some of this source work:

1) Logic theorem proving and geometry theorem proving by Shaw, Simon and Newell on one hand and Gelerntner on the other (See Fiegenbaum and Feldman, 1963).

2) Pattern recognition problems, not primarily in the field of visual pattern recognition, but as the basis for inductive inference. Here the work of Minsky (1963) and Selfridge (1958), Minsky and Selfridge (1961) springs directly to mind; we discuss this matter in Chapter 16.

3) Problems in data retrieval, and the recovery of information from computer store, also discussed in Chapter 16.

4) Concept formation. The building up of heuristics and other forms of generalisation (Banerji, 1958; George, 1966, to be published).

5) The confirmation of hypotheses. This is a field which has so far impinged very little on artificial intelligence, and one thinks mainly in this context of the work of philosophers.

6) Risk analysis (Thrall, Coombs and Davis, 1954; Jeffreys, 1965), whereby it is possible (and certainly necessary) to assess the risk involved in the outcome of any action.

The above sample list of activities which are involved in the total process of artificial intelligence are more or less representative of the various stages through which the process must go.

The first stage of the incoming process from the computer point of view involves the ability to recognise the nature of the input. One decision the computer must make is as to whether the input is linguistic or non-linguistic, i.e. whether it is from a human-like source in a language form or whether it is from a non-human-like source and represents the occurence of events in the environment. As far as the computer is concerned, we have agreed that without the need for specific description of pattern recognition systems, a merely conventional distinction needs to be made between the linguistic and the non-linguistic inputs.

The recognition process (see Chapter 16) involves, among other things, comparison with existing information in store and, though there may be many stages in recognition, which associate it with recall and other forms of remembering, it also specifically associates it with the problem of data retrieval. It is at this stage of recognition that we have to specify the organisation of the storage system, the cross-indexing and cross-referencing, so that an input is appropriately associated with existing information in store. The second stage of the operation is the processing of the information once it has been suitably recognised. Information which is not recognised, of course, may be either discarded or treated by trial-and-error responses.

The internal processing of information at the simplest level is what we have sometimes called event-learning. Thus it is relatively easy to show that the computer can be programmed to collect information, and simulate a conditional probability computer, and learn to optimise output provided always that the game is either well-defined or reasonably well-defined, and there is a degree of periodicity (repetition) of events which allows some sort of predictibility to take place. This approach, which may be applied to simple games like noughts-and-crosses, leads to the discovery of a decision procedure without too much difficulty. The need, of course, is to show how to generalise over these simple games so that transfer can be made to more complicated games. The need is also to show that heuristics can be developed to deal with games where no decision procedure exists or where the games is far too complex for a decision procedure to be arrived at or even used in economical time. This required the ability to make inductive inferences which depends in turn on the ability to categorise events and situations in a theoretical way. This draws attention in turn to the fact that the ability to make generalisations depends on language, as well as repetition (or some such characteristic of fact), and draws attention further to the fact that the internal organisation of the computer must include relationships between the event occurrences which are stored and the verbal occurrences which are stored.

The relationship between these two sets of stored occurrences are what we might call the *semantic rules*. The semantic rules must themselves be capable of being learnt by the computer in the course of transacting with its environment. We might say at this stage that the computer has organised, in hierarchical fashion, sets of hypotheses or beliefs, ranging from more or less simple ones which require more or less simple responses to a stimulus, up to very much more complicated ones which are contingent on the occurrence or non-occurrence of various features in a very complex input. We can liken the process of confirming these hypotheses to those set down in the field of philosophy of science, and say that the next stage of proceedings which will interact between on-line and off-line learning by transaction with the environment, will be the process of confirming hypotheses. This is where the work on degree of factual support, credibility, inverse probability, Bayes Rule, and all the procedures of induction must be used to lend weight and credence, or the opposite, to the hypotheses stored inside the computer.

When dealing with simulation we *must* give some consideration to matters of priority and urgency. Thus, if our artificially intelligent system is to make decisions for us over a domain where urgency may be a prime factor, then some sort of recognition of the urgency, and this will occur right in the first stage of operations, must be brought into the picture.

The fact that language is critical to this whole undertaking is a reminder in the present context that natural language, such as English, will normally be transposed or translated into the logical form (the functional or relational calculi will be the general form of language used but with associated probabilities which give it the power of empirical description) and the ability to make deductive inferences on the part of the computer will result from the computer's ability to translate natural language statements, not, of course, only into machine code, which is necessary for manufacturing the necessary computer orders, but also into a logical language in order to allow it to make the necessary inferences with maximum convenience.

At the output end it must be remembered the computer is capable of performing acts, as well as making statements or asking questions. The difference between performing an act and asking a question or making a statement is critically important to the whole success of the undertaking. Wherever an act or a statement is required as the final output on the behalf of the computer, a prior analysis of *risk* must be undertaken (Chapter 17). The methods cannot be described here, but they are very closely associated with theory of games and so-called "games against nature" and they involve the important point of assessing the risk for any particular decision. It may be that the same odds, in probability terms, in one context will be a totally different risk from the same odds in another context. It is obvious that taking a risk over a game of cards in the family context is quite different from taking a risk over the use of a nuclear deterrent, even though the probabilities of success or failure may be the same for each.

We will now talk more generally about artificial intelligence.

13.4   IN GENERAL

Neural nets (Chapter 7), as well as computers, provide an effective structure into which artificially intelligent systems may be built. We can rest safe in the knowledge that we have thus provided a framework which is sufficiently close to the actual human nervous system. We cannot construct *plans* (another game that has been used for generalised procedures) and inferential processes and if necessary fit them into our neural nets.

We now have a machine that can formulate plans much as it can draw inferences and is in a state of searching to satisfy needs, and eliminating incongruences in its environment, or alternatively keeping itself in a state of homeostasis. But can such a system transact with our systems in the way that human beings can? It seems that many additional details need to be clarified and, at least one general principle added. The main one that needs to be added is one of language for description, and this we have already dealt with in general terms for computers. If a computer (or neural net) has to learn about its environment it must have the capacity to manufacture generalisations (make inductive inferences) *and* be able to understand an external description of its environment. This means we must have what has been called a "semantic machine".

13.5   RECENT ADVANCES

One type of recent development in artificial intelligence which is closely connected with language is due to Kiss (1969). He has developed an axiomatic system for the explanation of human linguistic behaviour. He is especially concerned with the existence of "word stores" in human beings and is especially concerned with the process of selecting appropriate words to utter in a particular statement. He introduces the familiar notion of a stochastic process which operates with the central processor in executing a search over the contents of the word store. The word store is viewed as a stochastic information system; this is something that has previously been suggested by Sarkar (1967). Such work is vital to the sorting out of the massive detail of linguistic behaviour, and bears directly on our linguistic work described in Chapter 15.

We should mention next a challenging piece of work by Sammet (1971). He suggests that more effort should be given to applying artificial intelligence to practical problems (as opposed to the more academic problems of games and logic). This is something with which we would absolutely agree and we have already seen considerable recent developments in the fields of critical path analysis, scheduling and the like. Sammet himself is primarily thinking of problems in programming itself and points out there are many problems such as the optimisation of programs, error correcting in programs and the translation of programs from one language to another that could be greatly improved. He suggests that artificial intelligence should be employed to solve such problems.

We should also mention here the work of Munson (1971) who believes that an intelligent robot must have knowledge of the effect of carrying out a plan in an incompletely described environment. He devises a formalism for comparing what is known of the universe at any particular time with the robot's model of it. It then considers the distinction between its own actions and the robot's description of those actions. Such research provides an important step towards the detailed planning of what all cyberneticians are concerned with — designing a universal robot (or automaton).

Finally we should merely mention an attempt by the present author (George, 1972) to provide the essential framework for an artificially intelligent system, or as we have described it above, a universal robot. This is an attempt to lay down the necessary, if not sufficient, conditions, that such a universal robot would have to satisfy.

We will conclude this chapter with a summary of the main general features of what is needed for artificial intelligence.

13.6   SUMMARY

The process of decision-making now involves the following at least.

1) Recognise input as linguistic or not.

2) If linguistic, translate and try to recognise whether question, statement, etc.

3) If not linguistic, interpret as symbolic of certain occurrences, and seek appropriate responses

4) If linguistic, identify source and compare with model of source.

5) Model of source gives statement of previous reliability, likely motives in making statements etc.

6) Whether linguistic or non-linguistic, we distinguish inputs to which appropriate responses (*plans*) are known from those to which appropriate responses are unknown.

7) If input represents unknown states, trial-and-error behaviour or hypothesess (*heuristics*) are necessary.

We cannot take this complicated implicit flow-chart any further here, but there are many more stages in data-processing involved and a great deal of flexibility to be introduced before we achieve the complete human or superhuman problem-solver or decision-taker. It is this continuing search which is aimed at the fundamental problem of cybernetics.

Inference making on computers

Argument

The processes of logic enter cybernetics in various ways. Logical descriptions are related to mathematical notions (Chapter 7) which are closely related to infinite automata in particular and automata theory in general. Logic, especially Boolean Algebra, describes networks, and especially the so-called logical circuitory which goes into the construction of digital computers (Chapter 8).

Now we see that logic, at another level, is something that can be used in a computer for inference making. Indeed it is closely related to the use of natural language in computing which we describe in the next chapter (Chapter 15).

Logic is also a central ingredient of the human cognitive process, whether that logic be deterministic or probabilistic, precise or fuzzy.

We introduced logic in Chapter four, and we laid emphasis on the syllogism as the beginnings of the emerging of formal logic, yet obviously based immediately on natural language usage. The syllogism in fact makes a good starting point for programming computers to draw inferences.

Now it is clear that any intelligent person can, by definition, draw inferences for himself. Thus any model, computer program or otherwise, which lays claim to showing humanlike intelligence must also be capable of making inferences. This chapter discusses the problem of machine inference-making entirely in terms of computer programming; at least it is this which we must always have in mind.

Our problem is to show how the computer draws simple logical inferences as in the case of the syllogism, this relates to the natural language programming we shall be discussing in the next·chapter. We must then indicate the form of more complex deductive, as well as inductive arguments.

14.1   DEDUCTIVE LOGIC

We shall start with deductive logic and leave induction until later. We must first attempt to repeat the distinction that logicians usually make between the notions of "formal" and "factual". We usually say that an argument is formal, if the conclusion follows from the premises regardless of the referents of ,the variables and constants in the relevant propositions. An example illustrates the point. "If I am in Cork and Cork is in Ireland, then I am in Ireland." This is a valid argument and the form is clearly sufficient for one to agree or disagree with it. The general form is:

$$X \subset Y . Y \subset Z \longrightarrow X \subset Z, \tag{1}$$

where $\subset$ means "is contained in", . means "and" and X, Y and Z are names of individuals or classes. If we replaced "Cork" and "Ireland" by "Glasgow" and "Scotland", we should still have a valid formal argument, and if we replaced "Cork" by "Glasgow" and left "Ireland" unchanged, the argument would still be *formal*, although now it would be invalid. "Cork", "Glasgow", etc. are the referents of Y, Z. etc., or we may choose to say that the city Cork is the referent to the word "Cork". These last matters are, of course, matters of semantics, and we have already said something about this in Chapter 4, and we shall be saying some more about this in the next chapter.

We test the validity of a formal argument by reference to facts where the referents are factual, and by the form alone if there are no factual referents.

Formal arguments are like fixed forms (Cohen and Nagel, 1934) to be filled in and which allows immediately of tests of validity. There are also, though, factual arguments in the sense that, say,

$$(NH_4)_2 \, SO_4 + Ba \, Cl_2 = Ba \, SO_4 + 2(NH_4)Cl. \tag{2}$$

We know the argument is valid because we know enough of the empirical facts of chemistry, but would not know otherwise. We would argue that (2) is a form and that we need empirical information to test the validity only, as in the case of (1), but it is more difficult to reproduce the equivalent formal structure of (3). Nevertheless we would not wish to over emphasise the formal factual distinction; it is only a matter of degree.

The relational argument

$$\text{if } Rxy \text{ and } Ryz \text{ then } Rxz \tag{3}$$

is formal for individuals x, y, z, and if R is "--- is taller than ..." then (3) is transitive, but if R is "--- is the father of ..." then (3) is non-transitive. But in either case facts are necessary to validate the argument. Indeed also the relationship of fact to formality is here made absolutely clear; whether a particular form is logically acceptable in a particular case depends upon the facts described. The fact that additional rules are needed to cover the formal versions of some argument forms, does not necessarily destroy their formal nature. But it can be seen clearly that their formality springs from the intended meanings of connectives or operators like, "--- is greater than ...", "--- is smaller than ...", etc.

To use a deductive argument in practise, necessarily involves a great deal of factual information as well as a great deal of information of what we call a semantic kind, and we shall return later to the relevance of this to artificial intelligence.

Since the syllogism is a special case of the functional calculus (F), or even the propositional calculus (P), it is plausible to assume that the formal logical systems, such as P or F or any other such axiomatic system, can also be programmed.

This matter has been looked at from two points of view:

1) to show deduction in computer program form;

2) to show that a well formed formula (wff) is, or is not, a theorem in some system such as P or F. This is theorem proving and we discuss it next.

14.2   THEOREM PROVING

We shall say something in this section about logic theorem proving both by heuristic and algorithmic computer techniques. We must be clear as to our aims. Our aim in artificial intelligence is both to demonstrate heuristics on one hand, and to supply an inference making facility to our artificially intelligent system (computer program). We will thus, in some circumstances, take advantage of all the algorithms that are available in formal calculi such as the propositional calculus, parts of the functional calculus, etc. and use truth-table methods, for example, whenever these are available to us.

In the use of truth-table methods, even apart from heuristics, there are difficulties (Dunham and North, 1963), which amount to the fact that a very large store is needed, and if a reasonable speed of operation is to be maintained, then a careful organisation of data in that store is also needed. This argument indeed applies to any complicated program, hence the need for list processing, (McCarthy 1960, Newell, 1961).

Newell, Shaw and Simon (1963) were amongst the first people to use heuristic methods for theorem-proving. They showed that a suitably programmed computer — called the Logic Theory Machine (L.T.) — was capable of proving theorems in the propositional calculus without the use of the decision procedure. The principle rules of inference they used were:

1) substitution;
2) replacement;
3) detachment.

By such rules of inference, new theorems can be generated from an axiom set. Substitution is in the traditional manner of substituting one wff for another wff, throughout some wff.

e.g. Substitute $p \supset q$ for p, and $q \supset p$ for q throughout $p \supset q \supset p$ gives:

$$p \supset q \supset : q \supset p \supset p \supset q. \qquad (4)$$

Replacement is the substitute of a definition for a corrective, e.g. $p \supset q \equiv \sim p \vee q$.

Detachment is the method which says that if A, and $A \supset B$ are theorems, then B is a theorem, where A and B are meta-variables of P. We mean of course by meta-variables, the variables used in the language which describes P and its rules. So we could, for example, refer to $p \supset . q \supset p$ or $p \supset p$ as A and B in meta-variable terms.

The heuristic methods used for generating theorems are:

1) the substitution method;
2) the detachment method;
3) the chaining method.

We can use these methods in any order and in any mixture we please.

The so-called executive routine organises the four methods (substitution, detachment, replacement and chaining) so that when a new problem is presented it tries *substitution* in all the axioms and theorems already known and stored in a theorem list. *Detachment* is tried next, which is the substitution of a new sub-problem for the original problem. So if the problem expression is C, then we search for some form $B \supset C$, and we now take B as the sub-problem. So if we can prove B, C follows.

By *chaining* we create a new sub-problem by using the transitivity of material implication. So, for example, a c, reduces to a b and b c, and so on. Usually we use substitution after each new sub-problem has been set up by either detachment or chaining.

An important part of the theorem proving process is called *matching*. This means that L.T. shows that the main connectives are placed in the same position and then that the left-hand side of the wff's are the same, etc.

To give a simple example:

$$\text{To prove: } p \supset . q \supset p \qquad (5)$$

Match (1) with $p \supset (q \vee p)$, which is already proved and is in our store. p to the left and the first $\supset$ are the same, so we need to transpose $q \supset p$ into $q \vee p$; but $q \supset p = \mathrm{df} \sim q \vee p$, so L.T. substitutes $\sim q$ for q, and the two statements match, and therefore (5) is a theorem.

Matching is also used with chaining and detachment, and is central to L.T.'s operation. It is extended by similarity tests which eliminate wff's which are so obviously dissimilar that to try to match them is a waste of time. This is a very brief description of the essence of L.T., but there are some examples available in more detailed descriptions of L.T. (Feigenbam and Feldman, 1963). We would add that the methods used are not, as they stand, fully adaptive in that new heuristics cannot be generated within L.T.

A pattern recognition method has been used by Hao Wang (1960) for theorem-proving, and this is different from the work of Newell, Shaw and Simon in that it is only concerned with the end product (the theorem itself) and is not concerned with simulating human-like methods.

14.3 LOGIC AND LANGUAGE

It must be emphasised that if our aim is to supply a logical capability for an artificially intelligent system, our aim is not necessarily to simulate human-like methods. This means that all algorithms are to be used where available, and this implies that Wang's methods are of obvious importance.

Indeed we shall in these circumstances use any and every method — the more convenient and time and effort saving the better — to allow our programs, or set of programs, to draw all the inferences they need.

The link is of course with English as a language of communication, hence the importance of translating English sentences into logical form and vice-versa. The reason that English (or some other natural language) is important is, because of the man-machine relationship which exists increasingly at all levels of science.

14.4 PROBABILISTIC LOGIC

We can take any of the logical systems P, F, etc. and map them on to the calculus of probability. This has been done by Kaplan and Schott (1957), and George (1961) among others, and also relates to the work of Woodgar (1951, 1952) and a whole host of approaches which relate to probabilistic methods some of which are discussed in Chapter 17.

To take a simple example, we can say:

C means certainly
N means almost certainly not
O means almost certainly not
Q means probably not
M means possibly
P means probably
D means almost certainly

and in terms of probability, where a measure is available, $C = 1$, $N = 0$, and the intervals for O, Q, M, P and D *could* be, say, $(0; 1/18)$, $(1/18, 7/18)$, $(7/18)$, $(11/18, 17/18)$.

An example will illustrate the point. Let us suppose that the starting question is:

Is Charles the brother of Ann?

(6)

We now have the base statements

Charles and Ann have the same surname   (7)

Charles and Ann look somewhat alike   (8)

Charles and Ann live in the same house   (9)

Given the truth of (7), (8), and (9), we might say $\vdash D$ (6) where $\vdash$ means "is an accepted statement" of the system.

We might however feel that (7), (8) and (9) imply D (10), where (10) is:

Charles and Ann are husband and wife.   (10)

Only (8) *tends* to support (6) and not (10), so if $\vdash$ (7), (8) then $\vdash D$ (10) and if $\vdash$ (7), (8) then $\vdash M$ (6) and so on. Those descriptions that fit best into such a probabilistic system, are those properties which are simply commutable e.g. $A/B = 9/10$, which A has followed B nine times out of ten. Such a commuting base makes the development of a probabilistic logic especially easy. It is, of course, also a basis for inductive inference.

14.5   INDUCTION

To make our underlying assumptions clearer, it should be said that we are explicitly assuming that we have in our model the apparatus of language (see Chapter 15) the equivalent of which is built up through experience like other learned skills. We assume that language, as people grow up, is increasingly used to refer to their experiences of the external world, or indeed to a description of the internal world, and operates together with certain "physiological" or "psychological" occurrences called "images".

Language is both a description of, and also part of, since it is self-referential, the internal conceptual model; we have an internal model of the world about us and of ourselves, and we as humans are assumed to be aware of words and images often in complex associations with each other. At this level the processes are to be thought of as fairly crude and depend on cross-associative principles, but underlying these *molar* processes are the molecular functions and structures which make the processes possible. These are assumed to be activities of the nervous system. We are certainly unaware of our neurons firing in their various complex patterns, but there is no reason to doubt that this is what is actually occurring. Since the effect of these complex firing patterns is to suggest a mechanism which worked *as if* it were a complex and sophisticated mathematical process, it seems reasonable to try to synthesise it. We can here use these same mathematical processes for both; they have become, in effect, descriptions of the nervous system. The nervous system at this stage could be called "conceptual" rather than real, although this is a difference that can only be one of degree.

We must next consider *belief formation* (George and Handlon, 1955, 1957) as, the process which is subserved by induction. We are thinking here of beliefs as being the same as hypotheses (some of which are heuristic, Samuel, 1963, 1969; George, 1966) and being in need of confirmation by empirical evidence. We write:

$$c \ (h,e)$$

to be read "the degree of confirmation of the hypothesis h by evidence e" and we will generally identify this with some value p such that $0 \ p \ 1$, so that

$$c \ (h,e) = p.$$

It is clear that evidence in the objective sense will not always apply to our personal beliefs, but will in general apply to rational beliefs, but we still need to try to state some satisfactory criteria for "rational". In doing so, we are moving into familiar territory. Some aspects of this territory are discussed in Chapter 17, and we shall devote the next section to a very brief summary of the differences and difficulties met so far in the fields of induction and inductive logic.

14.6   INDUCTIVE LOGIC

Inductive logic is a system for providing both evidence for and confirmation of inductive inferences. If we say:

"All cats are green"   (11)

then if I have seen 256 cats all of which are green, and no cat that is non-green, this constitutes evidence to support (11) above.

Difficulties occur in inductive logic for various reasons, one of them being concerned with the so-called contra-factual conditional, which says what might have happened had you done something that you in fact did not. Another difficulty is over evidence and confirmation which demands sets of relevant statements which are themselves capable of being confirmed. In the case above we have problems because we need a system capable of including all inductive logical statement forms which allow us to make generalisations, and those only, which are in keeping with common sense.

Let us look at our problem briefly in terms of a particular example. Let us write "All cats are green" as:

$$(Ax) (S(x) \supset W(x)) \qquad (12)$$

and for a particular cat a, we have

$$S(a) \supset W(a). \qquad (13)$$

But (11) is *logically equivalent* to (14), which is:

$$(Ax) (\sim S(x) \supset \sim W(x)), \qquad (14)$$

which for an instance b, we have

$$\sim S(b) \supset \sim W(b). \qquad (15)$$

But (13) confirms (12), and (15) appears not to, since (15) asserts that a non-cat (e.g. a motor car) is not green (e.g. red). So the question could be put: does a particular motor car being red in any way confirm that all cats are green.

We shall waste no time over the more technical points (Hempel, 1945; Carnap, 1962; Von Wright, 1966; Black, 1966; Suppes, 1966) of inductive logic, but say merely that a certain support, primarily for syntactical reasons, has been found for the view that such statements as (12) *are* confirmed by such statements as (15). We however will say, following the famous Nicod's condition, that (15) is irrelevant to (12), just as (13) is irrelevant to (14). But before we leave this matter, it should be mentioned that the problem of relevance as met above is involved with the use of material implication. Material implication has been defined as follows:

$$a \supset b = \text{df.} \sim a \vee b \qquad (16)$$

This was intended to be interpreted as "if ... then ---".

This use may be defensible in a syntactical theory, but it has the consequence that where a and   are interpreted as statements, one may imply the other even though they are not in any way empirically connected with each other, i.e. are irrelevant to each other. This is certainly contrary to traditional human usage and is of essentially the same nature as the defect, for our purposes, which we observe in universal confirmation.

We will now say then that a statement S, *is relevant to* another statement S_2 if it has a common subject or predicate or if it can be *linked* by a common subject or predicate (George, 1966).

Thus any statement *directly* relevant to (12) must be one of the following formulae:

$$(Ax)\,(S(x) \supset X(x)) \tag{17}$$

$$(Ax)\,(T(x) \supset X(x)) \tag{18}$$

and similar formulae prefixed by the existential operator, and where X and T are any functional variables other than W and S. Furthermore, any statement is *indirectly* relevant to (12) if it has a form which can be traced by the same associative principle such as in (17) and (18). For example $(Ax)\,(M(x) \supset N(x))$ is indirectly relevant to (12) if there exist a finite number of statements of a similar kind linked to it, one at least of which involves the functions W or S.

The other vital point about relevance is presumably about *causal* relations. If, for example, other species of cats, like some wild cats, are thought to be biologically related to domesticated cats, and if they are all green, then this might be thought to be confirmatory evidence for (12). So we must accept the fact that there may exist causal chains which are not necessarily descriptively or logically complete, although in principle they are capable of being completed. It is assumed, of course, that all statements such as (17) and (18) will not be on the same level of generality; this does not however affect the argument. What has been said so far is hardly likely to settle many problems in the field of confirmation, but at least it clarifies our starting position, and we shall, by virtue of extensive testing in computer programming be prepared to make changes as, when and if they become necessary, i.e. according to the pragmatic test of whether or not such programs work well enough or not.

We shall certainly want throughout these operations to be able to make use of all known statistical techniques and this implies that we need to include a measure wherever this is possible, and also use some further features such as weight of evidence or degrees of factual support. Without this we should be in principle incapable of using such statistical techniques as correlations, t-tests, etc. which are most necessary. We are not though concerned here with showing how frequency theory statistics relates to probability theory, any more than we are trying to show how mathematics follows from recursive function theory and set theory. We are merely concerned to remind the reader of the vital importance of linguistically based corporately developed methods. From the synthetic point of view, the introduction of statistical methods implies no more than having the appropriate standard computer programs avilable and having the capacity to recognise (pattern recognition) when they are needed, although the problem of recognition must necessarily be heuristic and is, of course, inductive.

Briefly, we shall now deal with some other related methods. We should separate *credibility* from *probability* (Russel, 1948). We will say that credibility includes probability, and that whenever a statement can be supported by (or confirmed by) an objective (relevant) probability then it comes within our concept of confirmation. It is clear, as a matter of human psychology, that human beings often regard statements as credible on non-objective bases (and still be correct) and indeed will support credible statements on objective probabilistic bases, even though they may be incorrect. This situation is in fact inevitable and follows as a direct consequence of what we are attempting, and we accept this as true of any system which is to perform systematically under conditions of uncertainty. We shall however use confirmation as a necessary condition for acceptance, and in general say that the extent of one is proportional to the extent of the other, subject to risk analysis with use.

Inductive generalisations, we shall say, are confirmed by specific techniques such as Bayes Rule, stimulus sampling (associated with Markov chains etc.) and these coupled with work on explanation, factual support etc. are all part and parcel of the justificatory process. We should say that there is some temptation to draw a distinction between confirming theories or hypotheses on one hand and providing a basis for decision-making on the other. This distinction though is in some ways similar to our main distinction between formal (normative) and factual (behaviouristic) accounts of decision-making. This is especially true if we follow Suppes (1966) and compare concept formation (Banerji, 1963; George, 1966) and Bayes decision taking (see Chapter 17) which presupposes a whole universe of possibilities from the start; they are like examples of growth and fixed automata respectively.

The above distinction is important though on grounds of utility, since it seems that in using heuristic computer methods, the stimulus sampling, Markov net type of approach, which easily allows for the addition of new concepts, is also more economic to use. This point has been well demonstrated by Suppes (1966).

Arguing either from a true (certain) or probabilistic datum, is another point worthy of mention. Clearly no empirical data are certain and although we could argue, as does Russell (1948) that a datum could be a proposition that

has some degree of rational credibility on its own account, independently of any argument derived from other propositions

this is not too easy an idea to use in practice, nor obviously useful. This anyway is hardly an important point for us since our own view is more nearly that of C.S. Peirce that we have a set of more or less coherent and more or less confirmed beliefs, which we regard in their totality, as our knowledge and use to provide a basis for inference making. We will accept therefore, probabilistic data as a basis for induction and as a result must knowingly expose ourselves to the danger of drawing false, or at least improbable, conclusions.

Our basic difficulty is that we are having to talk in terms of logical and factual bedrock, when in fact we are on a sort of quicksand, which may let us down at any time.

Cybernetics has a central problem that is the manufacturing of machine intelligence, and much of what has so far been missed is the need for making induction a "machine-like" activity.

Again we must remind ourselves that we are trying to find a starting point somewhere between mathematico-logical formalism and behaviouristic explanation. We are seeking starting conditions to form a basis for artificial intelligence, in its central capacity of searching for similarities among differences and differences among similarities. We want to derive evidence to confirm our beliefs and will use any method for which there is evidence (logical or empirical) of success, and we, at this point, must accept confirmation, even on a probabilistic data base, within the context of relevant information. We will also use any well-defined tool of statistic or mathematics that helps us to achieve these ends.

We shall now return to a further discussion of the manufacturing of generalisations.

14.7   METHODS OF GENERALISING

This is a field sometimes called heuristic generation,†especially in the field of artificial intelligence. It is, in more general terms the field of formulating *any* general principle at all, although the only additional feature that makes such a general principle a heuristic is its active use in decision-taking; this at least seems a reasonable distinction for us to make.

So far we have talked exclusively about confirming generalisations or beliefs. Learning is the use of collected information to improve performances whether of artefacts or humans, but we are mainly concerned here with the generalisations that are capable of being acquired from the learned data.

Generalisations can, of course, take many forms, so that from tabulated experience we can formulate a matrix for Bayesian or game-theoretic strategies. Alternatively we can supply mathematical formulae which show the general features of trends and variations, and this forms part of our subject matter of Chapter 16 on pattern recognition. Methods like those of differences, summation of series and all forms of curve-fitting are precisely forms of generalised pattern descriptions.

In discussing the generating of generalisations, we should not, of course, overlook the fact that the principle method for human beings is that of "being told". The bulk of heuristics and hypotheses, covering most work-a-day circumstances are passed by word-of-mouth. Even "old wive's tales" are examples of early hypotheses, or more often heuristics, badly confirmed in some cases. Thus with all artificially intelligent systems the ability to communicate with outside sources is vital.

Yet another important method of deriving generalisations is *by analogy*. Bobrow (1966) has illustrated the method which allows the computer, like the

†A very complex and sophisticated example called Heuristic Dendril has been produced by E.A. Feigenbaum.

human being, to argue from a structure to a similar structure. It is rather like saying, we shall assume, "a wolf" is much the same as "a dog", so we can make statements about wolves, etc., as a result of our experience of dogs. The need to check such analogical arguments carefully, and to be prepared to use only some aspects of an analogy in a particular context and for a particular purpose, is quite clear; the consequences of failing to see the limitations of the analogy would certainly in our example prove fatal. Our problem is to develop more flexible programs.

In talking of logic theorem proving we should certainly mention the work of Meltzer, (1974). He points out that the main single method has been syntactical and recent work has depended especially upon Robinson's resolution logic. This is so because a proof procedure depends upon two things: finding appropriate substitutions and then testing the clause instances for contradiction. Robinson's logic provides a framework for both tasks simultaneously by the use of a *single* rule of inference.

We can take Meltzer's example to illustrate what is entailed. We want, let us suppose, to show the contradictions of the sets of literals in the four clause instances:

$$\sim M(a) \text{ or } D[f(a) ,a] \text{ or } \sim N(a) \tag{1}$$

$$\sim D[f(a) ,a] \tag{2}$$

$$\sim M(a) \text{ or } N(a) \tag{3}$$

$$M(a) \tag{4}$$

We can carry our the test by use of truth-tables, but we can do it more simply since (2) contains the negation of one of the literals in (1). This means we can infer the clause

$$\sim M(a) \text{ or } \sim N(a) \tag{5}$$

from (1) and (2). Similarly from (5) and (3) we can infer

$$\sim M(a) \tag{6}$$

(6) and (4) now yield an immediate contradiction. We can, by analogy, infer from (6) and (4) the so-called empty clause: this concludes the proof. There are a series of steps in the process. Any two clauses are examined to see if one contains a literal which is a negation of a literal in the other. For example, in the above argument (3) and (4) clearly contain $\sim M(a)$ and $M(a)$. If they do, a new clause is formed which is the set of all the remaining literals. One merely writes the two clauses after eliminating the two complements and when the clause inferred is empty, the proof is complete.

Robinson's resolution logic though avoids the need to generate the set of instances. It operates more generally using clauses with variables. In the above example, it takes as input the four general clauses. In the following, primes are used to indicate that the different clauses have different variables:

$$\sim M(x) \text{ or } D[f(x),x] \text{ or } N(x) \tag{7}$$

$$\sim D(X^1,y^1) \tag{8}$$

$$\sim M(x^{11}) \text{ or } N(x^{11}) \tag{9}$$

$$M(a). \tag{10}$$

You now look for literals that might be made complementary by applying an appropriate substitution to the variables. Thus in (7) and (8) if we substitute $x^1 = f(x), y^1 = x$, we can infer:

$$\sim M(x) \text{ or } \sim N(x). \tag{11}$$

Then in (11) and (9) we make the substitution $x^{11} = x$ giving

$$\sim M(x). \tag{12}$$

Now (12) and (10) with substitution $x = a$ giving the empty clause and the proof.

The resolution procedure is permissive and says only what *can* be done. To convert this to a proof procedure, which says what shall be made, constraints need to be added which we shall not describe here. There are, of course, other limitations on these methods such as its clumsiness in handling equality, but nevertheless such methods hold out hope for future development in deductive logic.

We have also similar hopes for what is perhaps an even more important task, the development of inductive logic.

14.8   CURRENT RESEARCH

Much work has recently been done on logic theorem proving and we should draw attention to the work of Darlington (1969) on theorem proving and information retrieval. He makes the point that an information retrieval system should be able to perform logical inferences as well as merely retrieve data. He goes on to say that such inference making is similar to that performed in logic theorem proving and in question-answering programs. He provides a good deal of detail to support the development of such information retrieval systems.

Simmons and Bruce (1971) have worked on the relationship between a predicate calculus and a semantic net representation of discourse. They show that networks can be used to represent the syntactic trees of the semantic relationships holding between different words of a sentence. They present a method for converting a semantic network into predicate calculus formalism. A semantic network is defined as a system of unambiguous symbols interconnected by definable semantic relations.

The value of using such semantic networks is that rules can be supplied to cover vague or partially defined concepts. They provide an example:

prob. v. eat

"The old man ate some fish"
"Did the old man eat some fish?"
"Yes"

Such a dialogue does not presume a precise understanding, for example, of the word "some". Such semantic nets allow the use of simple matching procedures and seems nearer to natural language form than the predicate calculus.

Lee (1971) has furthered a type of logical thinking that has been in existence for some time. This is now referred to as "fuzzy logic" (the logic with fuzzy boundaries to replace the hard lines of Euler-Venn Diagrams). Lee has developed some theorems of fuzzy logic and has pointed out the importance of fuzzy logic (compare the use of heuristics) in problem solving.

Kling (1971) has also developed the use of heuristics for problem solving, and the special interest in his work lies in the use of analogical thinking in a manner reminiscent of Bobrow (1966). His work is designed to speed the problem solving search and to this end he has designed a system called ZORBA which helps the generating of analogies. The system uses a simple logical theory and demantic rules. The analogies are not formal, but they can be handled within the context of a formal theory which can be conveniently dovetailed to individual needs, furthermore it not only supplies relevant analogies but suggests the manner in which such analogies could be used.

Finally we should mention among our selection of recent contributions, the work of Koenig and Schultz (1972). They have made a mathematical analysis for a general logical discourse to enable the computer to communicate conveniently with a human being. The mathematical analysis is essentially set theoretic and deals in combinational mathematics in order to establish sets of primitives for what they call a "prerequisite graph" and a "sequence graph" for logical discourse. These represent methods for structuring logical discourse for the inter-action between man and machine and in some ways reminiscent of Amarel's work on the representation of problems and the effect this representation has on the simplicity with which such problems can be solved.

14.9 SUMMARY

This chapter has attempted to bring together various features which need to be included in an overall view of artificial intelligence. To some extent, the ingredients needed are precisely the subject matter for the rest of the book.

This chapter is thus an alternative way of looking at cybernetics, as opposed to the more formal breakdown of Chapter 1. Chapter 1 dealt in categories of problems and methods, whereas this last chapter brings many of these methods together again in an attempt to provide an integral model for a complete problem solver.

The categories which are vital are: (1) concept formation, (2) hypothesis formation, (3) learning, (4) thinking, (5) language, and as a result, (6) problem solving. Various methods such as heuristics and the need for references and relevancy are also vital ingredients of the complete problem solver.

CHAPTER 15

Natural language programming

Argument

Natural language programs represent an attempt to program computers by the use of ordinary English, as opposed to a machine language, or a compiled language such as COBOL or ALGOL.

Natural language programs also represent the possibility of a "conversation" between a person and the computer. Such natural language systems can be used for data retrieval, inference making or both together.

Many such languages already exist which permit of the use of English, even if in somewhat stylised form. Examples such as BASEBALL, SAD SAM, SYNTHEX and LIP, are among those discussed in this chapter. LIP is the author's own language, and is essentially an inference-based natural language for computers, hence the direct connection between the last chapter and this.

In this chapter an attempt will be made to say something about language, which links our earlier discussion of basic semantics and pragmatics with the programming of computers, whereby it is possible to use natural language. In these first sections the overall scene is being set. Two points are basic, if we may repeat the recipe for the whole scientific context of our analysis. They are:

1) Almost all scientific analysis should be directed towards a specific goal or purpose; either to achieve specific goals or answer particular questions.

2) All such analysis should be within a specific and sufficiently well-defined context.

A part of the point of our two basic statements of principle is to eliminate the classical philosophical arguments where we try to complete the sentence stems "meaning is—" or "truth is—", and deal with such issues as "how carefully need I define a particular term in order to clarify or explain a particular point of view".

This view does not mean that theories and models should not be created, they should and will. We must though consider the classical breakdown of a great deal of linguistic studies into (1) pragmatics, (2) semantics and (3) syntax, and these have all been subdivided into "pure" and "applied" (or descriptive).

15.1   PRAGMATICS

Pragmatics is concerned with the total behavioural context in which discussion takes place, and discussion can be thought to include all forms of communication such as a person reading a book, watching a television, or listening to a radio, or may involve a total behavioural interaction between many people or groups of people.

Pragmaticists are concerned with psychological consideration and will often assert that communication is seldom, if ever, purely linguistic. Gestures, speech inflection and the like all clearly change the meaning of a statement in the context of a discussion, and modify the effect the words alone would have on a listener. Korzybski (1933), Morris (1946) and other pragmaticists have thus tended to argue that a study of language (logic and mathematics, too) and meaning only makes sense in the total pragmatic context.

To some extent such an argument seems to cut across the view which states that language can be formalised and precise models can, as a result, be supplied; the interpretation of these models are the languages used in daily communication. The pragmaticist would argue that the total communication situation cannot be wholly formalised except within a metalinguistic system which includes a description of the psychological processes of the people having the discussion. Some people have tried to formalise this meta-linguistic description and called the result "pure pragmatics" (Sellars, 1949) where the model of pragmatic systems is itself the goal. We are concerned primarily with "descriptive pragmatics" for which the formalisation is what has been called pure pragmatics.

Let us now merely add that to some pragmaticists the title "pure pragmatics" is a contradiction in terms. The reason is that we cannot carry through the program completely; as Morris (1946) has said we must always in the end rely on the use of some unanalysed terms. It seems though that this objection is not valid, since we can always formalise a scientific theory and that is precisely what we mean by "pure pragmatics".

We should notice that it is natural for the pragmaticist to regard the complete sentence as the basic unit of meaning. His motive is to explain language and symbols in terms of behaviour.

We are left with the question of whether the pure pragmaticist has a subject matter. In fact a scientist who is formalising behaviour theory could be said to be in precisely the same position as the pure pragmaticist and there seem to be good reasons — analogous to those involved in Gödel's incompleteness theorem for doubting the possibility of his "complete" success. But this would not matter to those who believe in the context theory of analysis that is being proposed here. We shall move on now to semantics.

15.2   SEMANTICS

Although the word "semantics" is used rather loosely to describe the world of meaning, the more precise definition is one that deals with the relating of terms to their referents. We use words like "denotation" or "referent" to apply to whatever is referred to by a word.

It is abundantly clear that words are not the things they refer to, when we consider the case of physical object words (Korzybski, 1933) so that "Chicago" is not the same as Chicago. We are as usual using the quotes here to refer to the word (or name) and the word without quotes to refer to the object, in this case the city of Chicago. It is not always so easy to distinguish the word from its referent in the case of other sorts of words such as those which we sometimes say have connotation but not denotation.

"The Author of Waverly" refers to the same denotation as "Sir Walter Scott" but they have a different connotation. Indeed this is where the question of the context of our analysis rears its head, so that we can say that *for some purposes,* for example when asked about someone, I could identify him as easily by either one of the two labels. Since we usually ask for a person's name as the identifier, the latter label is probably the most acceptable.

In other cases, it may be vital to distinguish the two labels. We might then say (Woodger, 1951) that one is a "temporal subset" of the other. Of all the things Sir Walter Scott (S) did in his life

$$\sum_{i=1}^{m} S_{t_i} \, ,$$

a part of it was to be the author of Waverly.

$$(W) \sum_{j=1}^{m} W_{t_j}, \text{ where } \sum_{j=1}^{m} W_{t_j} \subset \sum_{i=1}^{n} S_{t_i}.$$

We could of course, if necessary, and in principle, actually set out the temporal partitions which indicate when he was actually being the author of Waverly, and when he was not.

Similarly we could make whatever distinctions (differences among similarities) or amalgamations (similarities among differences) in any way we chose or could achieve for some particular purpose.

A convenient form of analysis for some purposes is to say that denotation is the same as connotation, where by denotation we mean the *concepts* referred to. Since from the point of view of the language user the concepts may exist whether or not they refer to things which have existence or not.

If we now turn our attention to formalisation, we may ask whether we should now take a different view. To formalise a system we need to provide an axiom set, rules of inference, and look for properties such as completeness and consistency. Ordinary English has not yet been formalised although many current studies attempt to provide a basis for such formalisation.

It is natural that if, as we have, as separate the syntax (or grammar) from the semantics on one hand and from pragmatics on the other, we might expect that if we are looking for a formalisation of syntax, and we are, then we should also formalise the semantics which include the syntax.

This leads naturally to rules of designation (denotation or reference) e.g.

"Chicago" *desig.* Chicago

We are here carrying through a programme of formalising our terms, the price we pay is, to limit their meaning by destroying their contextual definitional character. They are now "context free". We could retain their ambiguity and partially formalise them and and they would remain "context sensitive".

We must now look at syntactical analyses.

15.3   SYNTAX

Syntax is concerned with the grammatical structure of sentences. We could say, for example, that the syntax of the propositional calculus is formalised since there are rules of formation which state recursively what are the well formed strings. These well formed strings are either true statements or not in the system.

We have not formalised the syntax of English as yet, but have a set of heuristics which guide the analysis of sentences into subject and predicate, and then into their syntactic categories and the role they play in the sentence.

We might ask that from the syntactic point of view the maximum amount of meaning may be placed in the syntactic analysis. Thus sentences such as

"the child is an adult"
or "the bachelor's wife is unwell"

are ruled out as illegitimate because of certain constraints placed on the statement blanks. This is something that we have already mentioned in the last chapter.

Syntactically we accept the statement blank "— is ..." but one constraint on this form is that the classes referred to in the space are not mutually exclusive. Another constraint is that the second space cannot be filled by an individual name of a member of a class, where that class name fills the first space.

Relational statements illustrate a similar set of constraints. For example if we have the form:

$$Rab. \ Rbc \rightarrow Rac$$

then there are constraints on a, b and c for any R. e.g. If "Alan is the father of John" (Rab) and "John is the father of Tony" (Rbc), then it is nonsense to say that "Alan is the father of Tony" (*Rac*). But if $R \equiv$ "to the left of", then such an argument for the same interpretation of a, b and c would be acceptable.

Now our problem is seen to be bound up with the model–theory relationship, or, to put it another way, the way we interpret our symbolic models. The constraints can, as it were, be built into the structural formats or statement blanks allowed. It is now a matter of convention whether one regards what has been done purely as syntactical analysis or whether it is purely semantic; the boundary between one and the other is clearly shadowy, or in current terminology, fuzzy. What determines the nature of our approach will be the purpose we have in mind.

For the formalisation of natural language such a statement of constraints on statement blanks seems wholly right and proper. But it must be remembered that the price paid for formalisation is the elimination of many phrases which are context-dependent and certainly capable of being *given* meaning by a listener. This giving of meaning particularly applies to linguistic usage in the poetic or fictional mode.

Furthermore, partly for the above reasons, we are wrong in general in looking at historically given language and asking about their grammatical structure. In much the same way we should not analyse words and phrases and ask what their meaning is. The reason in each case is that the system is not formalised and we shall find vagueness and context-dependent cloaking of both meaning and structure. It would thus seem better to state a clear purpose such as "I am analysing language with a view to facilitating language-translation or computer–man conversation" and then whatever analysis one carries out has the property of testability which is essential to a scientific undertaking.

Let us now turn our attention to the problem of syntax more specifically in the computer context.

15.4   GRAMMAR AND SYNTACTICAL ANALYSIS

One common feature of almost all natural language systems that have been used on the computer is that they have and involve a parsing process.

Some systems, such as SIR (Raphael, 1964) admittedly has fixed formats and thus demands no syntactic analysis, but the bulk of the rest have analysed grammatical structures.

Grammar is a set of rules which express grammatical relations between the parts of a sentence and will repay a brief survey. Indo-European languages such as English are subject-predicate languages, so that a sentence $S \equiv$ "Jack hit the ball" divides immediately into the subject "Jack" and the predicate "hit the ball"

We write: (Figure 1):

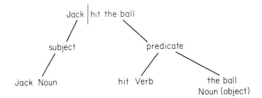

Figure 1

The word "the" in front of the ball is the definite article which is a member of the class of indexical symbols, and deals with "the", "a", "this", etc.

We shall use N, V, NP, VP, A, Adj, AP, Adj, P, etc. for "noun", "verb", "noun phrase", "verb phrase", "adverb", "adjective", "Adverb(ial) phrase" and "adjectival phrase", and add other abbreviations as we need them.

Consider next a more complicated sentence such as S_2 where S_2 = the large black dog fiercely chased the small boy away from the house.

We get a sort of breakdown as in Figure 2.

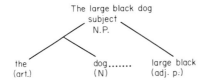

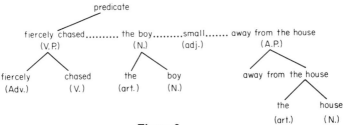

Figure 2

Alternatively we could draw our diagram as in Figure 3.

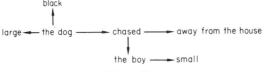

Figure 3

We say that the syntactic graph of Figure 3 shows the syntactic links between the main words "the dog", "chased" etc. and the dependent words "black", "large" and "chased" with respect to "the dog" and "away from the house", "the boy" with respect to "chased" and finally "small" with respect to the boy.

Figure 3 could be drawn as the abstract syntax form as in Figure 4.

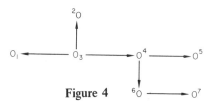

Figure 4

So that any other sentence with the same form as in Figure 4 is equivalent to it in structure. Thus S_3, where S_3 = the large foolish man kicked the large dog out of the house, has the same form as S_2 and can be depicted by the same graph.

One of the most important features of our semantic structures is that an interrogative word, and this is usually a pronoun, can be used to introduce a dependent element. So for example the links between the adjectives "black" and "large" can be related to "dog", by the interrogative phrase "What kind of —". We can always redraw Figure 3 or Figure 4 and write in the interrogative words for each link.

Let us take a more complicated example (Klir and Valach, 1965).

S_4 = "The fine silver veil fluttered from the shoulders of the dancer as if a summer breeze were blowing the shadow of clouds away from the white town, and came to rest on the dark ground."

Figure 5 shows the syntactic graph and Figure 6 shows the interrogative syntactic link graph.

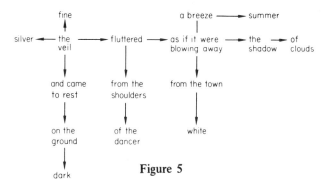

Figure 5

The graphs representing each interrogative element provide the subgraphs of the total graph. The interrogative terms and their relation to sentence structures is of the utmost importance from the point of view of question-answering on computers. This after all, is one of our main interests.

We should now mention briefly some particular types of syntactical analysis.

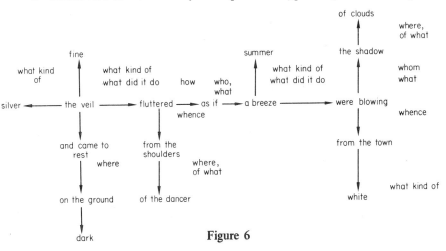

Figure 6

15.4.1 Dependency grammar

The work of Hays (1962), and Simmons, Klein and McConlogue (1964), has highlighted the particular use of what is called dependency grammars. These are hierarchial syntactical structures which have dependency relations among themselves.

For example the sentence "the man treats the boy and girl in the park" can lead to a whole range of search nodes and trees, one of which appears in Figure 7.

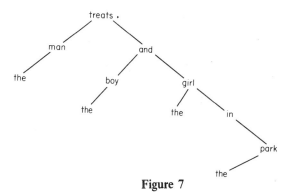

Figure 7

The syntactical class of the words determines the rules which apply to each sentence, subject to so-called agreement rules which determine some part of the syntactical dependencies.

Such dependency grammars are necessarily open to error and thus explicitly employ heuristics such as:

1) Closest linkages are given preference, in general, over more distant linkages. This means that the most frequently occuring links are always considered first.

2) Always consider the independent words first. Ambiguous nouns therefore always become subjects or objects in a sentence rather than modifiers such as adverbs, adjectives, etc.

3) Semantic analysis is always applied in the form of a test for statistical homogeneity to see if continuity of meaning is being established.

15.4.2 Immediate constituent grammars

Hiz (1965) and Chomsky (1957) are names that are especially associated with context-free phrase-structure grammars, and their work has been especially important in the field.

The immediate constituent grammar is a grammar whereby the sentence, such as "the girl loved the man" is placed in non-overlapping parentheses:

$$(((\text{the girl}) (\text{loved (the man)}))),$$

Where braces ( ) are used for the sentence, square brackets [ ] for the V.P., and ( ) for the N.P. † we get:

$$((\text{the girl}) [\text{loved (the man)}]$$

The phrase-structure diagram for this sentence is as show in Figure 8.

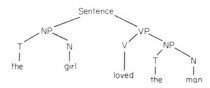

Figure 8

---

†For typographical reasons we use here ( ) for both the sentence and the N.P.

The nodal points of this diagram are the syntactic classes and not the words themselves as in the case of dependency grammars.

There are also various rules of form which allow the unravelling of complex sentence structures, but for greater detail regarding this or any other syntactical analysis reference should be made to the various specialised texts (Borko, 1967; Hays, 1967).

15.4.3 Transformational grammars

There are grammars where transformation rules (called re-write rules) are used to identify the syntactical structure of the sentence.

A typical re-write rule is of the form:

$$ZXW \rightarrow ZYW,$$

where Z and W are the context of X and where Y is a string of symbols. If we add the additional constraint that

$$Y = f(Z,W)$$

for some function f, then we say that the sentence is context sensitive (as opposed to context free).

Consider the simplest example such as "he walks" where the structure is:

$$S \longrightarrow PR \quad + \quad VI$$

he   walks

and where $PR \equiv$ pronoun and $VI \equiv$ intransitive Verb. Then if we re-write this we can derive two structures (single and plural) giving "they walk" as well as "he walks". The point about such transformations is to ensure that the range of possible transformations is utilised, and then the original sentence identified.

Phrase structure grammars through such transitive rules which, for example, transform a sentence in the active voice to a sentence in the passive voice. Then a comparison can be made with a sort of template, called here a kernel sentence, which again is with the motive of identification.

15.5   THE USE OF NATURAL LANGUAGE ON A DIGITAL COMPUTER

Natural language programming is something that follows very closely on the heels of inference making on computers. Inferences are made in language, whether formal or otherwise, and much of what is entailed in human thinking is a mixture of language and logic.

This section of the chapter is not meant as an overall summary of the work that has been done on natural language programming, since two surveys of this have been undertaken by Simmons (1965, 1969), and although a great deal more has since been done, the job of an overall summary is, partly for that very reason, the subject of a complete book of its own right, not just of one section of a single chapter.

The attempt will be made here to summarise the type of language translation or conversational systems, give an example of each, and finally summarise the similarities between all the methods, and the implications of such work for people interested in problems of artificial intelligence.

15.6   COMPILER LANGUAGES

As we stated in Chapter 8, compiler languages play a very vital part in computer programming. Such compiler languages as CLEO, AUTOCODER, or the universal ones such as FORTRAN, ALGOL, COBOL and PL1 all represent powerful means for simplifying programming and cutting down programming time. They translate from a language into machine code, and various code words and divide in the compiler language reserve store for suitable types of numbers, allocate addresses, etc. This is a sort of language with a built-in translation. It is the precursor of other more flexible languages with a two-way translation. But there is the clear possibility, as yet not achieved, of using ordinary English as a compiler language.

It is on this basis of compiler writing that one attempt at natural language usage has been built. First, it should be noticed that if a compiler is needed to ease the burden of writing machine-code programs, an obvious extension of this is to use a compiler-compiler (Brooker, Morris and Rohl, 1963; Napper, 1965) to help researchers write compiler programs. Napper (1965, 1966) has suggested that such methods could be extended, giving flexibility to the compiler language, and allowing it to grow and develop new formats and new terms as they are needed. The method is expected to be self-generating and bears some resemblance to some of the more "conventional" approaches to natural language programming. If the word "conventional" seems odd here it is simply because almost all the work done in this field has been since 1960.

15.7   LANGUAGE TRANSLATION

Conventional language translation bears a close similarity to our problem of natural language programming, but also differs from it in an important way. With language translation, the computer has an input in language L_1 and translates into another language L_2 which is the output.

In compiler writing we also generate another language, but the languages are completely formalised so the translation provides no special problem. With natural language the main problems are that of ambiguity of words, the use of colloquial phrases, and in general, that fact that natural languages are not formalised. This eliminates a whole world of potential precision.

The basic principles of language translation are:

1) The language is coded in numbers.
2) A dictionary must exist showing equivalent words in the two languages.

The second problem is very great because of verbs having different tenses, and such like syntactic problems. This requires a special dictionary which reduces all versions of a word to a standard form. But the dictionary has also got to help resolve ambiguities, which means that it is also necessary to have a Thesaurus on hand, and we must pay some attention to *syntax* and *context* on the other. One way is to have so-called "structure numbers" $SN1$, $SN2$, ..., SNK which give

1) the different translation of the basic form;
2) the syntax, part of speech, etc;
3) the subject matter being discussed;
4) special colloquial phrase and so on.

All of these problems enter into natural language programming, when the problem is different, since we now want the answer to a question, or the modification of an internal instruction and not the same phrase in a different language.

15.8   NATURAL LANGUAGE PROGRAMS

These are sometimes called "question-answering", or conversational", but the aim is to produce an intelligent conversation in natural language, with or without the associated inference-making.. Simmons (1965) has divided natural language programs into major groups as follows:

1) list structural data-based systems;
2) graphic data-based systems;
3) text-based systems;
4) logical inference systems.

We shall discuss one example of each of these types, but before doing so let us outline a system which was a precursor of these form types.

The first precursor language to be considered is the Conversation Machine (Green, Berkeley and Gotleib, 1959).

It was restricted in its range of conversation to discussions regarding the weather, and the general idea of the Conversation Machine stemmed from the Turing interrogation game in which a conversation was used as a way to try to distinguish man from machine. This is, of course, only a test *in principle* and the Conversation Machine is an attempt to supply the machine part of the test.

Meaning, environment and experience were the three factors making up the program. Experience involved previous information, derived from statements which had, of course, meaning. Both meaning and experience referred to this limited meteorological environment.

The words used in the sentence were *ordinary* such as "rain", "snow", etc., *operators* such as "stop", "change", etc. and *time* words such as "when", or more specifically dates or times. Sub-routines were written for each category and when a statement was fed in, a dictionary look-up table was referred to which listed attribute-pairs, such as (operation − stop).

The input sentence was used to elicit the output without the need for any syntactic analysis, so a statement such as "I like a hot June" would be replied to by some statement as "June is usually hot, so you will probably be lucky" or "June is usually hot provided you are in the Northern Hemisphere". From these simple beginnings our other languages develop, so we return now to our four types.

We start the *List-structural Data-Based Systems:*

1) We select SAD SAM as our example. This is a program concerned with answering questions about data based in store. SAD SAM is an acronym which stands for Sentence Appriser and Diagrammer and Semantic Analysing Machine (Lindsay, 1963). The program for SAD SAM was written in IPL V by Lindsay (1963) and divides naturally into two parts:

a) parsing;
b) semantics.

The system is something like basic English and is concerned with family tree relationships (the data-base).

When a sentence is read into the computer, it is parsed, and we discover that someone is someone else's brother, father, etc. This parsing system represents a separate program and provides an input to the semantic section which is a sentence whose parts are labelled respectively noun, verb, noun phrase, and the like, as well as a tree-structure showing the relationship among these grammatical features.

The semantic phase searches for subject-complement combinations which are associated with the verb "to be".

Let us give an example: John's father, Bill, is Mary's father. "John's father" is the complement "Mary's father". "Bill" is analysed so that we find:

Bill (father) Mary
Bill (father) John

and these relations are added to the family tree, so we find:

Attribute	Value
Husband	Bill
Wife	Unknown
Offspring	John, Mary
Husband's parents	Unknown
Wife's parents	Unknown
etc.	

We now know that John and Mary are brother and sister. If we learn that Bill's wife is called Carole, then we also know the name of the mother of John and Mary.

2) We now move to graphic data-based systems. As an example of this, we shall take PLM (Picture Language Maker) (Rankin, 1961; Cohen, 1962; Sillars, 1963 and Kirsch, 1964). The input is composed of pictures and sentences. It translates both into logical form and assesses the truth of what is asserted
PLM has three sub—systems:

1) a parser;
2) a formaliser;
3) a predicate evaluator.

The language is a part of English and the subject is three geometric figures. The parsing process substitutes symbols for words and continues to do so, until the top of the "parsing tree" is reached. The parsing procuces a tree structure and the formaliser translates this into a formal sentence (the first order functional calculus) which involves the usual primitive as well as the usual quantifiers.
Singular predicates are as follows:

Cir (a) $\equiv$ a is a circle
Top (a) $\equiv$ a is at the top
Whi (a) $\equiv$ a is white.

Binary predicates are as follows:

Smr (a,b) $\equiv$ a is smaller than b
Shp (a,b) $\equiv$ is the same shape as b, and so on.

The parsing produces the formalised sentence such as:

$$(AX_1)\ [CiR\ (X_1) \supset (EX_2)\ [(Cir\ (X_2).Whi\ (X_2).(X_1=X_2)]] \tag{1}$$

So to the question "are all circles white?" and that is what is asserted in (1). The answer, by (1), is "yes".

The information is scanned by SADIE and acts as input to the computer. The inputs are simple geometric figures. The problem of the input is the problem of pattern recognition various techniques being used to distinguish triangles from circles, and the like.

3) Text-based systems are best illustrated by the example of PROTO-SYNTHEX (Simmons, Klein and McConlogue, 1963).

The attempt is to answer questions in English from an encyclopoedia. Protosynthex indexes the text, uses a synonym dictionary, a complex intersection logic and a simple information scoring function to extract from the text those sentences that most resemble the question being processed. The question and the text which has been retrieved are both parsed and compared. We then accept the sentences which match most closely and before final acceptance we analyse the semantic content of the sentences.

VAPS numbers, so-called earmark the contents of the text on terms of volume, article, paragraph and sentence for the address of each occurrence of the indexed word. We now look up all the VAPS numbers and check the context. Look at the following example question:

$Qi \equiv$ "What animals live longer than men?"

VAPS words occur now such as:

Word	Related words
animals	mammals, reptiles, fish
live	age
longer	older, ancient
men	person, people, woman

We now find where the greatest number of these words intersect. Those VAPS numbers with the highest score retrieve the associated texts.

Dependency-logic (Hays, 1962) is now used to parse further with the question of the text. We show an example:

Question: "What do worms eat?"

worms

   eat

     what

Answer: "Worms eat grass".

worms

    eat

        grass

Second answer: "Worms eat their way through the ground".

        worms

        eat

    way   through

  their   ground

        the

The output would be:

worms	=	worms
eat	=	eat
what	=	grass
what	=	their way
what	=	through the ground

We need to score each of the words in phrases corresponding to "what". The system is a "look-up" dictionary and supplies answers as a function of its experience.

4) Finally, we have logical inference systems and one of the best known is SIR (Raphael, 1964). SIR stands for Semantic Information Retriever.

The input is made up of English statements. The model considers English words as objects having relations with other words (objects). The calculus of relations is the formalisation of the model and the program recognises fixed sentence formats and thus does not need syntax analysis. Information is structured hierarchially so "every boy is a person" inplies that "boy" is a subset of "person" and "person" is a superset of "boy", and of course "girl", "child", etc.

Let us give an example of the input "every boy is a person". We make appeal to the relation SETR (Boy, Person).
Similarly we get the following discourse:

Input Statement	Formalisation
Every boy is a person	SETR (Boy, Person)
John is a boy	SETR (John, Boy)
Any person has two hands	PARTRN (Hand, Person, 2)
A finger is a part of a hand	PARTR (Finger, Hand)

Question
How many fingers are on John?   PARTRNG (Finger, John)
Computer Response
How many fingers per hand?
Input Statement
Every hand has five fingers   PARTRN (Finger, Hand, 5)
Answer
The answer is 10.

All the question-answering systems have certain common features:

1) They all need large scale careful ordering of storage data.
2) All the systems require syntactical or semantic analysis, or both.
3) All the systems transpose the input into some sort of standard form, for matching or scoring purposes.
4) The text-based systems also include indexing methods.

The main problems are:

1) Ambiguity over meanings of words.
2) The enormous tree-searching problem in a realistic vocabulary.
3) The lack of sensory information accompanying the verbal inputs.

Let us conclude this section by reference to the language LIP (Language for Information Processing) (George, 1960).

In LIP, the attempt has been made to provide the full gamut of possibilities that are required by language even though they are not necessarily used.

The natural language statement is analysed first in syntactical terms. At the moment there is a limit on the number of noun phrases that can be accepted. There is also a limit on the number of verb phrases; only one principal VP can be accepted in each statement.

The analysis selects the principal VP, and then selects the subject NP, and then attaches modifiers (adverbs and adjectives) to the subject and verb. Then, according to the transitivity of the VP, an object NP is selected and modifiers for this if they occur. The order of the words is the basis for such identifications which may, of course, be wrong. The completed sentence (S_1) is then translated into symbolic form. If it cannot be so translated then the computer cannot know all the words involved. It then outputs its version of the statement, with the additional statement "is this what you meant?" "What does X mean?" where X is a word for which no translation exists.

If the human answers in terms that are suitable to the computer, it can add the word to its vocabulary, supply a code for it, and will know its referent. This requires though the use of a special format by the human being. The alternative is for the computer to guess at X's referent which will generally mean wrong results or further man-machine discussion.

When the translation into symbolic form is complete, it is also established whether a question is being asked or a statement made. In the case of the question, a search is then made to match the symbolic question form and to print out the required answer if it is available. If data-retrieval is insufficient then a search for relevant statements are made, where relevancy is interpreted as having some common variable in the symbolic form of the question or where the question refers to some coherent block of statements (a story) in computer store. An inference can then perhaps be made leading to an answer which is printed out.

A further facility for fomulating suitable (hopefully relevant) heuristics is now being worked on but is still as yet incomplete (George, to be published).

The language LIP can be most effectively used in a list-processing form and where the vocabulary is itself adaptively stored.

Gelt (1971) has developed a program called HAPPINESS which solves basic probability problems in English. The language analysis involves sentence transformation, what he calls keyword and semantic scanning and syntactic analysis based on a context-free grammar.

The keyword analysis uses heuristics and also recognises problem elements which contain semantic information. It is a system which is more general for example than STUDENT (Bobrow, 1964) and one which it would be easy to extend.

Other such systems have also been developed (e.g. Kaplan, 1971; Ramani, 1971; Goldsmith, 1972) which attempt to deal with different aspects of the complicated problem of computer language usage. Goldsmith, in his analysis, makes appeal to the traditional work of Ogden and Richards (1949) and Korzybski (1933) in his attempt to show that meaning is context dependent.

We can say finally that the field sometimes called "natural language programming" is a flourishing one and we may expect to see further large-scale advances in the near future that will take the researchers further into the field of pragmatics. This means, in effect, that in the list of words to be used, those used most often come at the top.

Among more recent attempts to provide conversational systems, we can list that of Ross Quillian (1968). He addressed himself to the problem of how semantic information is organised within a person's memory. As he puts it:

What sort of representational format can permit the "meanings" of words to be stored, so that human-like use of these meanings is possible?

Quillian suggests a model which is composed of a mass of nodes interconnected by suitable associative links. A node is related to the concept

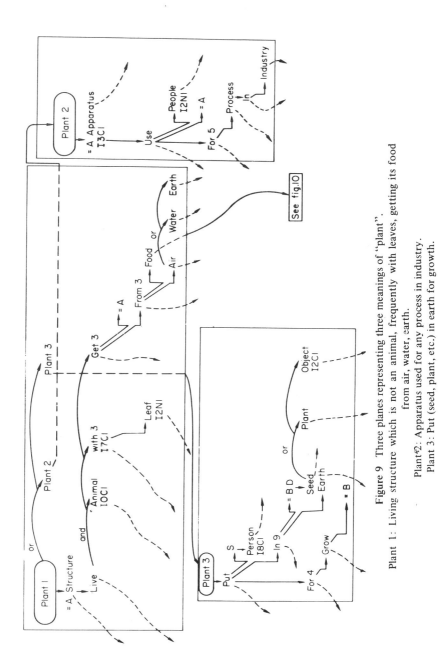

Figure 9 Three planes representing three meanings of "plant".

Plant 1: Living structure which is not an animal, frequently with leaves, getting its food from air, water, earth.

Plant [*]2: Apparatus used for any process in industry.

Plant 3: Put (seed, plant, etc.) in earth for growth.

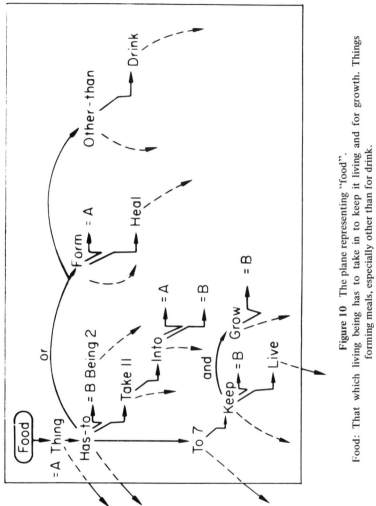

Figure 10 The plane representing "food".

Food: That which living being has to take in to keep it living and for growth. Things forming meals, especially other than for drink.

227

underlying a word in two ways – it relates directly to other nodes which represent the meaning of the word (a node that does so is a *type node*) a seccond association is with the concepts type node (this is a *token node*). This represents, of course, a familiar distinction made by Wittgensten and others. The token nodes make it possible for a word's meaning to be built up from other word meanings. An example will help. We will consider the semantics of the word "plant" (Figure 9).

To summarise Quillian's notion we say that a word's full concept is defined in the memory model to be all the nodes that can be reached by an exhaustive tracing process, originating at its initial, patriarchical type node, together with the total sum of relationships among these nodes specified by within-plane, token-to-token links.

Quillian's work is described in considerable detail and is the precursor of much work being currently done on semantic maps. We shall leave the reader at this point to explore the original literature on the subject and merely mention that vast linguistic data banks, composed of dictionaries and the like are, certain to be needed by any system aiming to reconstruct the full range of natural language.

15.9 SUMMARY

In this chapter we have discussed what is sometimes called "natural language programming", or "conversational programming". The main problem is one of reproducing ordinary conversation in English. The job of the computer is to have all the necessary information to answer questions or to ask questions in ordinary English, or indeed for that matter, in any other natural language. In fact all efforts so far have been with respect to English.

The biggest problem seems to be that of analysing what is said in terms of the syntax of the statements made and in terms of the meaning of the terms used. The sort of flexibility achieved by human beings is essentially context-dependent and of a heuristic form and also depends upon a great deal of redundancy.

Natural language programming which is a recent development is now well under way and will eventually lead to a machine – an appropriately programmed computer – being capable of intelligent conversation.

CHAPTER 16

Pattern recognition

Argument

Pattern recognition is involved at almost all stages of artificial intelligence and has been mentioned in various ways throughout the book.

Pattern recognition is involved in visual perception and indeed in all perception, and this is one place where psychology and cybernetics overlap (Chapter 10). But pattern recognition is also closely bound up with logic, in theorem proving and in making inductions (Chapter 14), so pattern recognition is itself a vast and central subject.

This chapter deals with pattern recognition from the limited point of view of artificial intelligence, and especially with both computer simulation and synthesis in mind.

16.1   IN GENERAL

The problem of pattern recognition is a central problem of cybernetics (Uhr, 1966) and takes many different forms. Many of these forms, under such diverse names as semantics, pragmatics, inference making, theorem proving and perception have been used throughout this book.

If we choose to tackle pattern recognition in relative isolation, we should talk primarily of experiment and theory in visual pattern recognition (e.g. Deutsch, 1955; Dodwell, 1961; Rapoport, 1953) of conceptual pattern recognition, and also of the various allied cognitive topics.

We should discuss hill-climbing and other types of learning which, while seeking specific solutions or optima, are dependent upon the very basic procedures of recognising patterns of one sort or another in the environment.

Let us start our discussion by saying a few words about a typical pattern recognition system, Pandemonium (Selfridge, 1959).

16.2   PANDEMONIUM

Pandemonium is a pattern recognition system which *learns to recognise* patterns. It has not therefore a fixed pre-processed range of patterns it can recognise but can develop its range as it experiences new patterns. Indeed Pandemonium can be taught the names of patterns, and can quite quickly be taught to say what the name of a pattern is before it is told; this is reminiscent of avoidance training within conditioning theory.

The method used in the first idealised version of Pandemonium is that of minimising the difference between a received message and a set of transmitted messages; in other words, ensuring the nearest thing possible to an exact match is obtained.

Figure 1 shows the idealised version of Pandemonium, whereas Figure 2 shows the amended version.

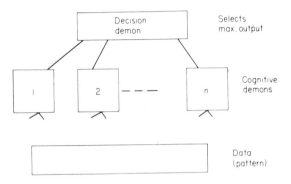

Figure 1   An idealised *pandemonium* as a classifying system

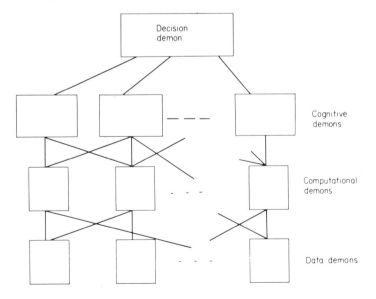

Figure 2   A realistic *pandemonium* extending to as many levels as are needed

The amendment is necessary because the demons are not always able to discriminate sufficiently to allow of a clearcut solution to the problem in hand.

The problem is that given a received message M_r^i and a range of transmitted messages, n

$$\sum_{t=1}^{m} M_t^i$$

then to choose an M_s^i such that the difference between M_r^i and M_s^i is minimal.

The difficulty is that the demons often need the support of the sub-demons, and it is now easy to see that the data demons are supplying information to the sub-demons, and they in turn are supplying it in partially classified form to the demons; this is a system which is essentially a classifying system.

We now consider the differential weighting or feedback. There is a need to score or weight the different features.

Given the output of a demon (a cognitive demon which has classified an input as:

$$d_i = \Sigma \lambda_j^i d_j$$

so that the set

$$\lambda = \lambda_1^1, \lambda_2^1, ..., \lambda_1^2, ..., \lambda_m^n$$

is a set of weights over all the demons. We now need to seek an optimum and this is once more a hill-climbing activity with all the attendant difficulties of dealing with local sub-optimal peaks and isolated optimal peaks.

We can, however, show an improvement in performance by changing our demons and sub-demons and "breeding" new ones. This all means that, like a heuristic modifying and heuristic generating system, Pandemonium can be made potentially fully-adaptive. Selfridge has developed a particular, or special purpose Pandemonium for translating morse code into the printed word.

16.3   OTHER PATTERN RECOGNITION MODELS

There are a whole host of pattern recognition models and we should mention that of Grimsdale, Sumner, Tunis and Kilburn (1959), where a flying-spot scanner is connected to a digital computer, which analyses a description of a pattern to compare it with a stored set of patterns. This is the digital computer equivalent of Culbertson's (1950) theory of visual perception which compares visual patterns, *via* their description, with a retinally stored set of patterns. It is, however, fixed in the range of patterns it recognises.

Another similar system of adaptive models for pattern recognition purposes is supplied by Roberts (1960). Roberts chose the problem of automatic recognition of different alphabetic symbols from English.

The method used was to make up a reinforcing system which also had the discrimination capacity based on a network of 2048 cells, a subset of which were associated with each characteristic pattern. As with Culbertson, such transformations as rotation, dilating and contracting made no difference to the effectiveness of the differential rewarding procedures.

Uttley's models (1954, 1955) and some of the other hardware models discussed in Chapter 3 are further examples of pattern recognition systems.

One feature (Uhr and Vossler, 1963) of most pattern recognition systems is that they are either pre-processed to differentiate one from a set of fixed patterns, or they learn to do so, after starting from scratch.

There are a whole range of such pattern recognition systems and at this point we shall simply refer the reader to further references (Rosenblatt, 1958, 1960; Baran and Estrin, 1960; Doyle, 1960; Unger, 1960; Bledsoe and Browning, 1959, 1961; Banerji, 1966, 1967, 1968).

To some extent, as has been said, these models and methods have been discussed already under other headings, so the remainder of this chapter deals with more particular problems of pattern recognition.

Let us now consider the problem of pattern recognition in terms of our universal computing system. We are thinking now of a computer C_1 with large store and to be programmed heuristically, as well as using algorithms, and designed primarily to make plans and play games.

16.4   RECOGNITION

This section deals primarily with the input to C_1. The problem of input is central to the problem of recognition, and of perception, recall and, in general, the total process of remembering. The problem is that of providing the basis for saying, in effect, such things as "I recognise X, X is ———." "That is a sort of elephant", "Yes, I can recall your cousin's name", and "I remember your cousin well", although in this last example "remember" could well be read as "recall". In fact the input of our system is closely connected with the store and central organisation, since what is recognised or perceived depends upon previous experience.

We shall not here be discussing *visual pattern recognition* in the sense of the ability of a "machine" to read and discriminate letters, or numbers, typed, printed or cursive, nor will we be primarily concerned with the ability of a machine to discriminate shapes or patterns. These admittedly interesting and important aspects of cybernetic ideas are not directly relevant to our own computer simulation of decision taking, where it is assumed that *all* events in the environment have now been transduced into a digital form and have been punched onto tape or cards.

Recognition here is the ability to classify digital messages with respect to relevancy, etc. We wish also to investigate the associated questions of *recall*. Can the computer be made to recall information relevant to certain events? Clearly both in recall (cf. data retrieval) and recognition, the ability to "recognise" both similarities among differences and differences among similarities are vital characteristics.

Let us start by what we shall call *initial classification*. This means that we must distinguish between on-line computing in real time and off-line computing. In on-line computing, we may expect to have to devote "attention" to all that occurs and can only reject information *after* it has been at least partially processed. If it is being used for off-line computing *routines* (linear programmes, statistical correlations and other formal computing activities) then some other form of filter may be used to decide what messages are allowed into the computer either at the same time, or indeed perhaps to stop temporarily the off-line computing. We shall therefore approach the problem of recognition first of all in the former terms, at which point the latter becomes a special case.

Our basic input category distinctions now will be:

1) language, and
2) events.

We shall use the word "event" for all occurrences other than those from human or human-like (intelligent) sources. This is, in many ways, similar to the difference between feeding a *compiler program* into C_1, as opposed to feeding in a *machine code program*. We simply need a conventional distinction at the central point of processing, e.g. two different input channels and we can represent these either in a different symbolism or following a different code word. e.g. everything in a statement *after* 1, the first digit of the statement, is linguistic and everything after 0, also a first digit, is an event.

In the limit, of course, we may not be able to readily distinguish a *language* input from an events input since, as in the case of humans, we may not know whether a light-flashing or a source of noise is a *message* from a human source or some "accident" of nature. Nevertheless, let us assume for the moment that we can distinguish language inputs from event inputs, and let us now consider what each will lead to.

Language inputs will go to a *translator,* which will decode the message with respect to stored information. They will be translated into machine code. The details of language translation processes have already been discussed in the last chapter, and they will be discussed again later, since they are central to the whole question of language for communication between computers. Let us look at a simple flow chart:

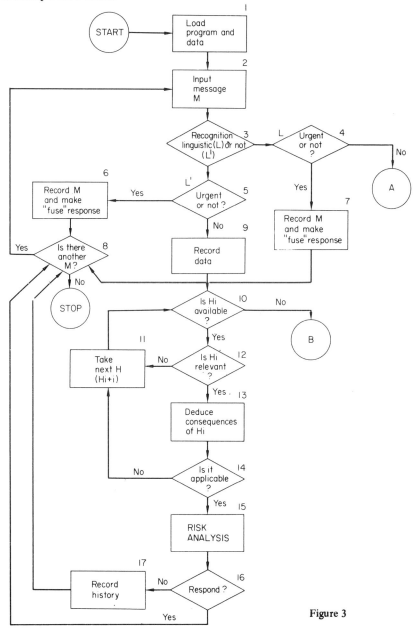

Figure 3

What we should mention next is that event inputs, which are conventionally distinguished from language inputs, will proceed straight through the stages of more detailed recognition. We must explain now in ordinary language what those stages are both for language and event inputs.

The first major stage of the problem for any "intelligent" automaton, as with a human being, is to *recognise* the input. This recognition of the input occurs *in stages* and is clearly a process which merges with the recognition of the appropriate output. We are now going to concentrate our attention primarily on the input end.

The first step in C_1's recognition process is, as we have said, to decide whether the input is linguistic or non-linguistic. In general, the effect on the internal state of the automaton will be as if both had occurred even though the input may in fact be only one of the two. With regard to the question of any input simulating both linguistic and non-linguistic features of the internal store, we should explain the following points. A word, or a statement made to someone, may precipitate an answer, or a statement, or even silence, perhaps accompanied by a change of attitude. An event which occurs may also change internal states or precipitate vocal responses, but we can still distinguish between verbal and non-verbal inputs.

The point that is important here is that, although we *can* distinguish verbal from non-verbal inputs, as inputs, their effect may be both; i.e. they may effect both verbal and non-verbal features of the store. We shall wish to say, for example, that a linguistic statement has the effect of producing new instructions, and new data has also the effect of producing new instructions.

Of course, we must remember in the above context, as always, that further distinctions and differences must be made according to whether we are trying to *simulate* growing or non-growing, human or non-human type intelligence systems, or whether our interest is only in *synthesis*. In fact, we must remember we are primarily pursuing the goal of an automaton which is intelligent, but not necessarily human-like; we are interested primarily in synthesis rather than simulation.

Because we are concerned primarily with non-human-like intelligence, we can to some extent separate linguistic inputs from non-linguistic inputs in a conventional way as already discussed. At any rate, C_1 must recognise, at least on a purely conventional basis, when an input is a language sign, or symbol, as opposed to a "direct sign" or an event. We do not particularly wish to get involved in defining *signs* and *symbols* at this stage, but we can say that a *sign* is something which has been associated with, and experienced with respect to, something else in such a way that when it occurs in the input it "reminds (C_1) of" the things with which it has been associated. If the association is purely an arbitrary one, such as say in algebra where we say "let 'x' stand for some domain of numbers", then we refer to the stimulus as a *symbol* rather than a *sign*.

Further distinctions can be made, of course, if it is deemed necessary, but we shall not wish to make them until, and if, the necessity arises.

If the input is linguistic then the object of the input will be to change the internal state of the automaton and possibly also to produce an overt (external) or correct (internal) response. A part of the internal organisation of C_1 has been previously outlined (George, 1962), and here we shall wish to build on the same stochastic tables generated there. A great deal more information in the form of linguistic statements will be stored in C_1 which will certainly be more than mere lists, in that they must suggest actual structures or models of the environment of C_1.

We will be thinking in terms of different automata, or computers, C_2, C_3, ..., C_n in different environments to test out the effectiveness of the methods we are hoping to describe, but it is absolutely necessary that C_1 has a model of other automata (or organisms) in its environment as well as the natural features of that environment. This distinction between other human-like sources and natural features is a vitally important one since when a linguistic input is recognised then it is known to come from other automata or organisms, and must be regarded as *purposive*. This means that the receiving automaton C_1 must have some sort of model or parameters or indices which refer to the source of information. To put it anthropomorphically, we might say of a person that he is a reliable sort of person, and the only thing is that under these circumstances he has rather a doubtful motive in telling us some particular piece of information. Therefore, bearing in mind the context, we ought to be very careful how we answer it.

It is fairly easy to see how simple instances of this assessment of a source of information can be carried through and this is part of the recognition process, but it is a part that grades over into the internal organisation of C_1 and the output process, since as soon as one asks oneself the question of what the *risk* entailed is in answering a question, or giving information to an external source, you are considering really the choice of output.

Recognition then, in synthetic models, establishes whether an input is linguistic or non-linguistic; if it is linguistic then something of the nature of the source of the information is essential. If the source is not actually known and some record kept of its reliability, then one must consider the likely motives involved and the probable reliability entailed in the light of all the available information. This we shall be describing in greater detail later. It is clear that some sort of *risk analysis* must be carried out however, since giving information in answer to one sort of question in one sort of context could be completely harmless, whereas giving the same sort of information to a similar questioner in another sort of context could be extremely dangerous.

As ever, if we want C_1 to be a surviving automaton and also purposive, it must always analyse the risk entailed and this risk refers not only to its own independent existence but to any society in which the automaton might exist. It may seem ridiculous at first sight to consider societies of automata, but in practice, of course, since most of language and most of intelligent behaviour in human beings comes from their social background, then it is increasingly obvious that we can only really think of intelligent decision making automata in a social situation.

The non-linguistic recognition process may involve a search through stochastic tables looking for appropriate responses to a stimulus. Recognition here means essentially that you have some record of a response previously made to a stimulus, and if by looking through the tables you could find some record of the stimulus by direct comparison with the input state, then of course you can recognise the appropriate response.

This problem of recognition is very much more complicated for human beings where pattern recognition problems occur through the special sensory equipment that human beings use, and this is a problem we do not meet if we are programming a computer with a view to synthesis. The computer C_1 simply represents symbols on punched tape or punched cards and it is easy enough for the computer to discover whether any symbols occurred previously or not or at least whether any record is kept of that symbol or set of symbols, so that the recognition problem of the computer, which is restricted to a punch tape or punch card input, is a simpler process that is involved for the human being using eyes, ears, etc.

No doubt, if special purpose equipment such as radar sets, etc., were attached to a computer, then the problem of recognition would become as complicated or may become as complicated as it is in the human being. We are not, however, considering that particular problem of *visual* pattern recognition in this chapter.

Whether the input is linguistic or non-linguistic, the appropriate processing involves a search through the storage for appropriate responses, which, if not found, lead to either trial-and-error activity or, on some basis of similarity, the assumption that although it is different from any previous recorded stimulus to C_1, it is sufficiently similar to warrant some sort of identification. It may be, of course, that some linguistic generalisation is appropriate to the stimulus, but if this is the case then some sort of class of stimuli to which the linguistic generalisation is appropriate should anyway be found by the search process. Recognition itself can be curtailed under the circumstances of *urgency*, and the computer must operate on the basis of the least risk, where a high degree of urgency occurs demanding some sort of response.

It is clear that an overt response is not always called for by stimuli, although always some internal change of state will evolve as a result of the stimulus. The recognition process itself leads on to the internal processing and reorganisation and updating of all information about the environment and about other automata or organisms in the environment. This is the process which grades over from *recognition* into what one might reasonably call *thinking* (cf. the relation of perception to conception). Much of thinking is undoubtedly done in linguistic terms alone, and quite apart from the translation of linguistic inputs if appropriately recognised into either internal machine code) or into further verbal generalisations, all sorts of complex processing must go on inside C_1. So complex may this process become in the case of a human being that in these experiments, insofar as they involve simulations, we can hope to do little more than simulate the simple instances of decision taking processes over relatively simple environments.

Let us now return to the flow chart (Figure 3). If L and L^1 are recognised *by convention* then the future of the linguistic input is that of translation, and the future of the event input is that of "processing". But we should notice that a part of our input information is that of the source.

We must now remember that *recognition* is not quite all of *perception,* and that *recall* (data retrieval) and remembering generally (which may be a mixture of recall and recognition) are all involved.

We can now begin to see the full size of our problem, and we cannot hope to give a clear picture of all these above-mentioned features of cognition in one chapter alone. We must instead start specifying the more precise details of our store (C_1's computer store and its coding) with a view to showing how much C_1's programs can simulate or synthesize these more elaborate aspects of recognition and memory. Let us now turn to the organisation of C_1's store.

16.5   STORE CONTENTS AND ARRANGEMENT

The computer store of C_1 can be thought of as "one-level", as opposed to being broken down into computer and backing store. The store is composed of a set of registers, with addresses for each register. Some registers contain numbers and some contain instructions.

For our "underspecified" programming, we need to regard all *events* as numbers, and they are stored (or not) according to existing instructions, or instructions manufactured for their storing, as in the process of recognition.

To take the easiest case, we have game being played on-line, and a board-state (set of digits) reaches C_1 and is placed in the registers already allocated to it. The board-state is then processed according to the rules already arrived at. It can, before any further move is made, operate to effect a new *generalisation* or *heuristic* which may in turn modify the orders which perform the processing.

This use of instructions, and the generating of new instructions, at many different levels involving instructions-about-instructions, etc., is to be thought of as being at the *linguistic* rather than at the *event* level. Thus for ordinary day-to-day computer programming, we shall say instructions are linguistic and data is non-linguistic, although we shall still make a second distinction between language and instructions. This means that our distinction between language and events (and language and instructions) is one to be carefully noted at the computer level:

$$TRA/A/B/C$$

or

$$05/200/201/202$$

represent sentences in programmer's language (P.L.) where a, b and c are events (data) in P.L., where the data, say a/b, c/d, e/f, etc. refers to some game where a, b, ..., f are numbers. When C_1 has a record of a board-state with board spaces named x_1, x_2, ..., x_n then the spaces themselves are events, and their names are:

$$"x_1", "x_2", ..., "x_n".$$

This distinction is the traditional distinction between *words* and their *referents*. We need to adhere to it in our underspecified programs because we need to distinguish an input that is linguistic (i.e. a message from a human or "intelligent" source) and one that is a direct observation. Since both linguistic and event inputs are punched onto tape or cards, it would be easy to overlook this distinction, which is vital, if we are to enact different processes on the box.

The recording of

$$x_1, x_2, ..., x_n$$

need involve no fear of being *bluffed,* etc. But the recording of "x_1", "x_2", ..., "x_n", carries the possibility of such deceits. Similarly, we shall distinguish words referring to events, from words referring to words. Thus the use of

$$"TRA"$$

or

$$"TRA/A/B/C"$$

or

$$"05/200/201/202"$$

means the linguistic statement about the words, in the same way as we use the word Chicago to refer to the city and the word "Chicago" to refer to the name of the city.

At any moment in time, the internal state of C_1 is characteristically composed of data in certain registers, instructions in others, linguistic descriptions at many levels of both words and events in yet others.

Let us next make some coding distinction, which will help to clarify this situation.

16.6   THE STORE OF C_1

If we suppose C_1 (a large store version of C_1) has storage capacity of 1,000,000 20 decimal digit words. The addresses will be:

> 000000
> 000001
> 000002
> ------------
> 999999

Each instruction word will be of the form:

$$I/A/B/C$$

$$ij/a_1 a_2 a_3 a_4 a_5 a_6/b_1 b_2 b_3 b_4 b_5 b_6/c_1 c_2 c_3 c_4 c_5 c_6.$$

We can now say let addresses:

> 000000
> 000001   300,000 registers
> -----------
> 299,999

be for instructions

> 300,000
> 300,001   300,000 registers
> --------------
> 599,999

be for data, and for language:

> 6000,000
> 600,001   300,000 registers
> -----------
> 899,999

leaving 900,000 to 999,999 for special purposes.

We now need to encode inputs and outputs so that C_1 can distinguish language inputs (outputs) from event inputs (outputs). We can let the extreme left digit of the 20-digit code word be 1 or 0 according to whether the following words are linguistic or not. This means that a code word such as:

$(111111 ---- 1)$

$(011111 ---- 1)$

must be used to indicate whether what follows is linguistic (words) or events (words).

We can set aside a further set of registers for the input into C_1^1. Let us always put inputs into registers with address in the D-block, i.e.

900,000

900,001

----

etc.

as defined, and then we can re-allocate these inputs to further storage resisters as necessary, after (at least, partial) recognition has taken place.

It is clear that we need to have a clearcut connection (as well as a distinction) between the linguistic words and their references.

The effect of the need for *semantic rules* is that the computer C_1 must contain a set of registers which allow it to translate symbols into symbols, and interpret symbols as referring to particular events, as recorded.

The simplest example of a semantic rule is to say:

$$I = \text{df. "implication"}$$
and if $\quad A = \text{df. "wives"}$
and if $\quad B = \text{df. "woman"}$

there is some sense in the analytic statement $(x)\,((x = A) \Rightarrow (x = B))$.

The very fact of making the above statement in the form of symbolic logic is a reminder that C_1 will be capable of handling and translating more than one type of language.

16.7   CLASSIFICATION

Chapman (1959), Uttley (1954, 1955), George (1961, 1962, 1966, 1967) and others have argued in favour of classification systems in the context of *simulation*, but even where *synthesis* is involved, we would expect to classify, and perhaps cross-classify information.

A simple classification system will distinguish, say, a "well-defined" from an "ill-defined" game. It will distinguish a "game against nature" from a "2-, 3- or n-person game". Indeed when an input arrives at C_1^1 (or C_1) its first stage in the processes of recognition must involve identification of input as either linguistic or otherwise, understood or not, answers to questions available or not, etc. After this C^1 has the problem of finding out if a game is mentioned, whether it is well-defined, etc. When the classification is sufficiently broken down, it will proceed to search for the particular title, such as OAX, CHECKERS, CHESS, BRIDGE, DECISIONS OF ONE KIND OR ANOTHER, etc.

This form of classification is easily arranged, and can be made flexible and changed, and herein lies the significance of cross-classification.

Suppose an event A occurs and event A has characteristics (properties)

$$a_1 \ b_3 \ c_2 \ d_5$$

then we may classify it (uncertainly or not) under various heads.
For example, we may say:

$$A \ \Sigma \ X_1, A \ \Sigma \ X_2, \ ... \ \text{etc.}$$

where $X_1 \quad = \quad a_1 \ b_2 \ a_3 \ a_4$

$X_2 \quad = \quad a_1 \ b_3 \ c_4 \ d_6 \qquad \text{etc.}$

It is easy to see that A *may* belong to a number of different classes (categories) according to the purpose of the classification.

Now with the principle of association we wish to say that "one thing makes us think of another", and this is vital to simulation, but also vital to synthesis. If we say let:

$$A \ \Sigma \ X_1 \ \text{and} \ X_1 \ \text{only}$$

and a repetition of A, where $A \ \Sigma \ X_2$, occurs, then we shall respond inappropriately.

In C_1^1 we can include in store a word with each stored event word or statement (set of linguistic words making a sentence title meaningful whole) a set of digits giving the address of other associated categories.

We shall refer to $C_1, C_2, ..., C_n$ or $C_1^1, C_2^1, ..., C_m$ which are all computers which may have stores of different sizes, but we shall always retain the categories of store as follows:

A — registers contain instructions
B — registers contain data
C — registers contain language
D — registers contain special functions, such as input etc.

So much for the input properties of our system (the set of possible computers). We shall all the time be aware of the fact that our inputs are never wholly isolated from the internal working of our system, nor even our output.

16.8   RECALL

We should next say a few further words about *recall*. We have seen that to *recognise* something is "to know what to do about it", but to *recall* something involves a variation on this same theme.

If C_1 has an input of a linguistic kind, then it may be a statement of the form mentioned earlier, e.g. "do you recall (remember) your cousin's name?" and this is the same as "do you recall how to play game X?" The process involved for C_1 is to search store to elicit (or not) either the cousin's name or the rules (or tactics) of X.

This means that recall is, as we have already suggested, a type of data retrieval. This links up directly with pattern recognition, since the ability to recognise data and its context in store and thus in experience (or vice versa) is precisely what data retrieval is about.

We shall say no more about recall at this stage, but the reader will appreciate that the universal computing system C_1, which has to provide our artificially intelligent system, must be capable of both data retrieval and data processing, and that they both involve the problem of pattern recognition. The previous two chapters have also emphasised the need for C_1 to be able to use language and carry out the operations necessary to logical inference making. All these features represent something like minimal requirements for a universal system such as C_1 purports to be.

16.9   RECENT ADVANCES

Pattern recognition permeates all aspects of cybernetics and new developments are taking place all the time. This perhaps more than any one other topic breeds new papers in new journals at a prodigous rate. We shall simply mention some selected recent papers briefly.

One novel paper by Kinoshita, Aida and Movi (1971) deals with pattern recognition by an artificial tactile sense such as occurs in the human hand. The artificial "hand" traverses the surface of a solid object, and detects the points of contact with the surface of the object and by exploration is capable of recognising such objects as cylinders and rectangular blocks. The authors also think of their recognition system as supplementing the visual sense — whether artificial or real — and this is a reminder of attitudes brought by philosphers to perceptual problems, where comparisons between visual and tactile senses are often referred to.

Another recent novel approach to pattern recognition is due to Radchenko (1971), who does not make his recognition depend upon the use of sampling spaces. He uses what he calls a "text" (made up of binary pulses) to represent the input. The recognition process involves transformations of the input texts into outputs, while at the same time a process of abstraction takes place. The output is to be interpreted as a set of classes to which the input texts belong.

This is an example in some ways similar to that of Simon and Roche (1971) in that it emphasises the statistical approach to pattern recognition, as indeed does the approach *via* perceptrons.

Let us finally say a few words on recent experiments with perceptrons. Simple perceptrons have been criticised, for example by Bongard, because the units in the sensory layer are shuffled arbitrarily (like dominoes before the game starts) in their connections to the association layer where discrimination is attempted. This means, among other things, that the perceptron is incapable of recognising a pattern if it is displaced even a small amount from the position it occupied when the perceptron learned it.

A variant of the perceptron has been investigated by Race (1972) under the title "SOPHIE — an outline specification for a device to recognise patterns under displacement". In SOPHIE the signals are not transmitted through a network of "wires" but through "wave-guides" which distribute any signal from each sensory unit to every unit in the association layer, without loss, but with a phase shift which depends on the separation in two dimensions of the pair of units concerned. When SOPHIE learns a pattern, an arrangement of interference fringes is set up. If the pattern re-appears, even if displaced up, down, left or right, the appropriate response unit will still be triggered. This has been demonstrated by digital computer simulation.

SOPHIE is thus a cross between a perceptron and an optical device like a hologram. It lays no claim to being a model of the way the brain works — for example, SOPHIE's "axons" have to transmit signals in either direction, and there is no evidence this happens in the brain. It is interesting to note, however, that the miniature "sweep's brush" radiation guides needed to make the radiation conform to the special rules of SOPHIE bear some resemblance to those in the neural nets of the retina, and that two dimensional expanding wave-fronts occur in these nets (as studied by Von Seelen).

The criticism of perceptrons mentioned above might be paraphrased as saying that they are *too* adaptable: They would have the same performance in any conceivable logical or physical world, from Flatland to Alpha Centauri. This reduces their efficiency in our world, in which there are many invariances a pattern recognition device should take advantage of. Indeed many serial pattern recognition schemes, using the algorithmic power of the digital computer, do take advantage of such invariances and even find them out for themselves by heuristic methods. In this way they compensate for the intrinsic slowness of serial processing. SOPHIE is an attempt to incorporate one invariance in an intrinsically fast *parallel* processor: one which is useful not only in identifying displaced visual patterns, but also-in principle — for manipulating symbols.

We should also mention here some of the most important contributions made to pattern recognition by Shimura (1971, 1973) which take a mathematically precise view of the sort of models required to carry through the suitable modelling process.

This brings us to the end of our brief survey of the vast problem of pattern recognition which spreads from visual models to conceptual models *via* statistical and deterministic modelling procedures.

16.10   SUMMARY

Pattern recognition is a basic problem of intelligence. It occurs at the visual level, or at the level of the other sensory processes, and involves the recognition of patterns of stimuli.

Internal to the organism is the problem of "conceptual" recognition and this the human being is also manifestly capable of performing. He is capable of seeing similarities among differences and differences among similarities.

This chapter has provided a number of examples of pattern recognition systems and dwelt at some length on the internal organisation of store for such pattern recognition purposes.

CHAPTER 17

Statistical and probabilistic methods

Argument

This chapter deals briefly with what is essentially a vast and complicated subject. Statistical and probabilistic methods run through the whole of cybernetics and much mention has already been made of such matters.

This chapter is mainly concerned with decision taking procedures under conditions of uncertainty and what is (or can be), in effect, the analysis of risk.

17.1 INTRODUCTION

Probability theory and statistical methods are quite basic to all of science and certainly to cybernetics in particular.

We have no intention of providing here an introductory text on probability or statistics since this can be obtained from any of a number of standard text books (Fisher, 1938; Weatherburn, 1946; Reichmann, 1962). We shall, however, give some background ideas to help the reader with our brief text that follows.

Let p be the probability favourable to the occurrence of some extent A, say the probability of a coin coming down heads in one toss. Then let q be the opposite probability, i.e. that the coin will not come down heads, which is of course tails in a two-valued case such as the toss of a coin.

We say $p_A = m/n$, where n is the total number of trials and m is the number of times A has occurred and where p_A is "the probability of A occurring".

In mathematics, we can rigorously define a probability so that for indefinitely large n the individual independent possibilities tend to certain limits. In the case of tossing a "proper" (unbiassed) coin, by definition each side is equally likely to appear uppermost on each toss if the limits are $p_A = 1/2$ and $q_A = 1/2$

$$p = m/n \tag{1}$$

and since $p + q = 1$

$$q = 1 - p = 1 - m/n = \frac{n - m}{n} \tag{2}$$

We extend this argument to a series of tosses (trials) so that the probability of, say, ten heads occurring on the run, i.e. *hhhhhhhhhh* is given by ($\frac{1}{2}$ x $\frac{1}{2}$ x $\frac{1}{2}$ x $\frac{1}{2}$ x $\frac{1}{2}$ x $\frac{1}{2}$ x $\frac{1}{2}$ x $\frac{1}{2}$ x $\frac{1}{2}$ x $\frac{1}{2}$) = 1/1,024. This illustrates the use of the *multiplication theorem*, where independent probabilities p_1, p_2, ..., p_n are multiplied together to find the total probability of a certain event. q here, say, is the event not occurring and $q = 1,023/1,024$ since $p + q = 1$ which is an instance of the *addition theorem*, which adds the probabilities of the total number of mutually exclusive alternatives that apply in the definition of any event.

We can from these simple beginnings quickly arrive at a very powerful tool for the description of events which may require the use of combinations and permutations and other more powerful mathematical techniques.

The link between probability and statistics is one that has caused a great deal of discussion and given rise to much polemic. We can think of the connection in one sense as the connection between a "mathematical" or "proper" coin, as mentioned above, and an actual tossing, among other things; one is an idealised model to which the other approximates.

We can develop probability distributions.

$$p_i x_i$$

for events x_1, x_2, ..., x_n and associated probabilities p_1, p_2, ..., p_n. Analogously we can develop frequency distributions

$$f_i x_i,$$

where the frequency f_i is the observed occurrences of the events x_i. From these beginnings we can derive the notion of a "normal distribution" and this coupled with such formalities as Schebychef and Bernoulli's theorems provide a sort of link between the (analytic) theory and the (empirical) model.

We are not here concerned with the precise relations which exist between statistics and probability theory any more than we are concerned with the foundations of probability; these are both vexed questions which have been discussed extensively expecially in the fields of philosophy of science (e.g. Russell, 1948; Feigel and Brodbeck, 1953) and in any case this is not our central theme.

17.2   THE CALCULUS OF PROBABILITY

Let us write p/h for the phrase "the probability of p given h". The following axiom set is then sufficient to provide a calculus.

1) Given p and h, p/h is uniquely defined.
2) p/h lies in the closed internal $(0,1)$ for all real numbers, i.e. $0 \leqslant p/h \leqslant 1$.
3) If $h \to p$, then $p/h = 1$, where $\to$ means "(logically) implies" and where 1 means "certainty".
4) If $h \to p$, then $p/h = 0$, where 0 means "impossibility".
5) $p \cdot q/h = p/h \times q/p.h = q/h \times p/q.h$
6) $p \vee q/h = p/h + q/h - p.q/h.$

We should note that p/h is a relationship between p and h, where p and h can be thought of as two propositions; we could write this Pph in Polish notation.

From axiom 5, we can derive the principle of inverse probability which is:

$$p/q.h = \frac{p/h \times q/p \cdot h}{q/h} \qquad (3)$$

(3) follows directly from axiom 5 by simply dividing each side of the second part of the formula by q/h.

Axiom 5, sometimes called the conjunctive axiom can be very simply exemplified. What is the chance of drawing two spades in succession without replacement from an ordinary pack of cards? p is the statement "the first card is a spade", q is the statement "the second card is a spade" and h is the fact that there are 13 spades in a set of 52 cards.

$$p/h = \tfrac{1}{4}$$

$q/p.h = 12/51,$
therefore $p.q/h = \tfrac{1}{4} \times {}^{12}/_{51} = {}^{3}/_{51}$.

Axiom 6, the disjunctive axiom, can be similarly exemplified.
So in the above example, the chance that at least one card is a spade is given by

$$\tfrac{1}{4} + \tfrac{3}{4} - \tfrac{1}{4} \cdot {}^{12}/_{51} = {}^{48}/_{51}.$$

Inverse probability is interpreted in terms of the above example as giving the probability p in the event that q is known to occur. So for the example of choosing two successive spades from a pack of cards, we get

$$p/q.h = \frac{\tfrac{1}{4} \times {}^{12}/_{51}}{\tfrac{3}{4}} = {}^{4}/_{51}.$$

We can interpret inverse probability in more general terms: so we say that if p is a theory and q is some statement relevant to p, thus we can think of p as being changed by q (either confirmation of infirmation). The special case where $p \rightarrow q$ and therefore where $q/p.h = 1$ reduces (3) to

$$p/q.h = \frac{p/h}{q/h}. \qquad (4)$$

The next step is to derive Baye's Rule since this is the basis of so many decision processes, some of which we shall be discussing briefly. Baye's Rule is usually written

$$p_r/q.h = \frac{q/(p_r.h).p_r/h}{\overset{n}{\underset{1}{\pi}} q(p_r.h).p_r/h}, \qquad (5)$$

where $p_1, p_2, ..., p_n$ are n mutually exclusive possibilities one of which is known to be true. A convenient alternative rendering of (5) is

$$P(H/D) = \frac{P(D/H)P(H)}{P(D)} \tag{5A}$$

where $P(D/H)$ is the conditional probability of an event D given another event H, and where $P(H) \neq 0$.

In terms of our above example of drawing two spades in succession, for $H =$ "drawing one spade" and $D =$ "drawing a second spade", Bayes in (5A) gives:

$$P(H/D) = \frac{{}^{12}/_{51} \cdot {}^{1}/_{4}}{{}^{1}/_{4}} = {}^{12}/_{51} .$$

This gives the conditional probability of the second card being a spade granted the first card actually was a spade. We say $P(H/D)$ is an *a posteriori* probability while $P(H)$ is an *a priori* probability.

17.3   WARD EDWARDS' MODEL

Ward Edwards (1967) has designed a series of computer programs to test out the effectiveness of Bayes Rule in man—machine situations. He used a version of Bayes Rule that is a modification of (5) above. This version is called the odds—likelihood ratio form.

Given two hypotheses H_A and H_B and some datum D (comparable to h in the earlier part of the last section):

$$P(H_A/D) = \frac{P(D/H_A)\,P(H_A)}{P(D)} . \tag{6}$$

Similarly for H_B, Bayes odds—likelihood ratio form is:

$$P(H_B/D) = \frac{P(D/H_B)\,P(H_B)}{P(D)} . \tag{7}$$

Dividing (6) by (7) gives

$$\frac{P(H_A/D)}{P(H_B/D)} = \frac{P(D/H_A)\,P(H_A)}{P(D/H_B)\,P(H_B)} . \tag{8}$$

We will write (8) as

$$L_1 = L_0. \tag{9}$$

L_0 is the ratio of the *a priori* probabilities for H_A and H_B, and L_1 gives the likelihood ratio, and $P(D/H_A)$ and $P(D/H_B)$ are both *a posteriori* probabilities. Only the likelihood ratios are needed for the application of Bayes Rule (Edwards, Lindman and Savage, 1963).

Ward Edwards uses this Bayesian property of aggregating information to set up a probabilistic information processing system which he called PIP. PIP works on the assemption that "men can serve as transducers for $P(D/H)$"; this means that given a situation where information is to be processed and predictions or diagnoses made, then the predictions are evaluated.

Ward Edwards (1967) made up a 50 page summary of the "imaginary history of the world from 1964 to 1975". It was such that eight hypotheses were plausible as a result. They were of the form

"Russia and China are about to attack North America."

Then at a later date additional information was supplied by sensors to the computer as a result of which the eight hypotheses would be re-assessed. Several likelihood ratios were assessed for each datum, and training occurred with the processing of vast amounts of information over a lengthy period.

The most important result to come out of this experiment was that PIP achieved a greater degree of certainty from the data than did the equivalent human group who acted much like a group of military or political leaders might. The *ad hoc* human group was called POP, and two other variants were called PEP and PUP respectively.

The results indicate clearly enough the advantages of using Bayesian methods over mere human judgment.

We now look at Bayesian Models from a slightly different point of view. We can think of Bayesian Models as models of deliberation (Jeffrey, 1965).

17.4   DECISION PROCESSING

In this section we shall look at such methods as Bayes Rule (Jeffrey, 1965) in somewhat greater detail.

In the first instance we define a desirability matrix as describing the ideal combination of events. For example, if we wish to have fish with chips, this will have a greater rating than having fish with boiled or roast potatoes. The desirability gives the relative weighting of some quality with respect to some others. Thus we might write a desirability matrix for fish in column 1 with beef in column 2, with chips in row 1 and boiled in row 2 and roast in row 3. We shall assume that boiled and roast potatoes are equally acceptable to go with beef. We thus have:

$$\begin{pmatrix} 1 & 0 \\ 0 & \frac{1}{2} \\ 0 & \frac{1}{2} \end{pmatrix} \qquad (10)$$

In practice, of course, an empirical analysis of tastes in a community might throw up something totally different. A matrix such as the following seems quite likely:

$$\begin{pmatrix} .88 & .06 \\ .08 & .48 \\ .04 & .46 \end{pmatrix}. \tag{11}$$

Alternatively, and considering the idealised desirability matrix, we might have included negative numbers giving:

$$\begin{pmatrix} 1 & 1 \\ -1 & 1 \\ -1 & 1 \end{pmatrix} \tag{12}$$

where -1 means completely unacceptable.

Suppose now we think of the probability matrix as suggesting beef and fish as equally likely (we obviously do not control the choice). Then we have probability matrix

$$\begin{pmatrix} \frac{1}{2} & \frac{1}{2} \\ \frac{1}{2} & \frac{1}{2} \\ \frac{1}{2} & \frac{1}{2} \end{pmatrix} \tag{13}$$

Now we multiply equivalent entries in the probability matrix (we shall use $*$ to symbolise this unusual type of matrix multiplication) and one of the desirability matrices (we shall take the last of these).

$$\begin{pmatrix} 1 & -1 \\ -1 & 1 \\ -1 & 1 \end{pmatrix} * \begin{pmatrix} \frac{1}{2} & \frac{1}{2} \\ \frac{1}{2} & \frac{1}{2} \\ \frac{1}{2} & \frac{1}{2} \end{pmatrix}$$

$$= \begin{pmatrix} \frac{1}{2} & -\frac{1}{2} \\ -\frac{1}{2} & \frac{1}{2} \\ -\frac{1}{2} & \frac{1}{2} \end{pmatrix}$$

Adding the row gives

$$\begin{pmatrix} 0 \\ 0 \\ 0 \end{pmatrix}$$

Here no one choice of potatoes is better than any other in this case.

If we had a desirability matrix:

$$\begin{pmatrix} 0 & 1 \\ -1 & 1 \\ -1 & 0 \end{pmatrix} \tag{14}$$

then we should have had:

$$\begin{pmatrix} 0 & 1 \\ -1 & 1 \\ -1 & 0 \end{pmatrix} * \begin{pmatrix} \frac{1}{2} & \frac{1}{2} \\ \frac{1}{2} & \frac{1}{2} \\ \frac{1}{2} & \frac{1}{2} \end{pmatrix}$$

$$= \begin{pmatrix} 0 & \frac{1}{2} \\ -\frac{1}{2} & \frac{1}{2} \\ -\frac{1}{2} & 0 \end{pmatrix}$$

giving

$$\begin{pmatrix} \frac{1}{2} \\ 0 \\ -\frac{1}{2} \end{pmatrix}$$

So that now the choice of chip potatoes in row 1 becomes the best choice according to this type of Bayes application.

We can of course deal just as easily with events which are not equiprobable, and we can deal with desirabilities which are not completely specified. In any case, of course, as with all applications of probability theory, it seems that the greatest single difficulty lies in establishing the appropriate numerical probabilities.

The rationale of the technique is easy enough to understand since, to put the matter crudely, highly desirable and very likely events are the first choice. Then we weight desirability against probability of occurrence and leave out the undesirable and the unlikely.

If I wish to eat a good meal at a good restaurant I would choose a very good meal at a very convenient restaurant as opposed to a superb meal at a hopelessly inconvenient one.

We shall not discuss further the technical apparatus which occurs in the full range of possible applications. We can though make the point that such methods which are closely related to forms of probabilistic logic are open to all sorts of objections and difficulties (Hintikka and Suppes 1966).

Another type of decision processing sometimes called "Games against Nature", very similar to that discussed by Jeffrey (1965), is discussed by Thrall, Coombs and Davis (1954). They consider various strategies under various conditions of uncertainty, subjective estimates of probability and the like. Here we come close to psychological theories.

To illustrate the viewpoint by a simple sort of example, consider that the rows of the following matrix represent states of nature which are all equally likely. Consider next the choice of a column you would make, being ignorant of which is the relevant row. Here is the matrix

$$\begin{pmatrix} 0 & 2 & 1 \\ 3 & 2 & 1 \\ 0 & 0 & 1 \end{pmatrix} \quad (15)$$

If we use Laplace's strategy, we take the arithemetic mean of each column, and select the column with the highest mean; in this example, column 2 is thus selected.

If, however, we were playing the optimist's strategy we select the column with the maximum pay-off, and that gives column 1 as the solution. If you are a pessimist, you consider which column loses you least in the event of your being wrong, and the answer now is column 3.

The matrix above does not supply a means of losing, since all the pay-off elements are non-negative. By reducing each element of the matrix by 1, we do not alter the argument by making the decision taking more realistic.

Thus for the following matrix you may also actually pay money out as well as receive it:

$$\begin{pmatrix} -1 & 1 & 0 \\ 2 & 1 & 0 \\ -1 & -1 & 0 \end{pmatrix} \quad (16)$$

A further factor which affects the strategy followed is the size of the units. If the integers about refer to single pounds (sterling) then your maximum loss is £1. If they refer to thousands of pounds, then you could lose £1,000. As the size of the prize and the risk goes up, so the decision may change along a sort of continuum between extreme optimism and extreme pessimism.

Let us look at the matter again now explicitly as risk analysis leading up to what has sometimes been called venture analysis.

17.5   RISK ANALYSIS

We shall indicate in quite simple terms the nature of risk analysis, since the ideas have already been partially explained. In intuitive terms, we are concerned with the taking of a risk, such as a gamble on a horse. Clearly we may be prepared to risk a few shillings and not worry if we lose; equally clearly, if we are instructed to put several hundred pounds on a horse, we should worry considerably and lacking any other information, we might be tempted to back the favourite, because of the odds which would imply a minimum risk. If we were allowed to back more than one horse, we might put a substantial amount on three different ones in an attempt to minimise the risk entailed. We are supposing in this latter case that we are not so much concerned with winning — since we are being *forced* to place our bet — but are more concerned with avoiding losing, since we cannot really afford the money; the risk is really too great.

The above situation, which may occur in a whole variety of ways, is the key to such things as business investment, launching a new product and similar activities. Our aim is to show how, while making a decision to carry out a business undertaking, we can minimise our risk.

First look at a simple example in matrix form:

$$
\begin{array}{cc}
 & B_1 \qquad B_2 \\
\begin{array}{c} A_1 \\ A_2 \end{array}
\left[\begin{array}{cc} 0 & 100 \\ 1 & 1 \end{array} \right] .
\end{array}
\tag{17}
$$

Suppose we take a "utility pay off" view of these numbers, and suppose we say that the numbers represent £0, £1 and £100 respectively. Suppose you have to play for A and your choice is between A_1 and A_2, and you do not know whether B_1 or B_2 is correct, which would you choose?

We say that to maximise your utility you choose A_1 because then you can win £100 which is clearly the maximum possible pay-off. But if we think of this problem in terms of regret as in the last section i.e. the extent we shall regret the loss if we are wrong, the matrix becomes:

$$
\begin{array}{cc}
 & B_1 \qquad B_2 \\
\begin{array}{c} A_1 \\ A_2 \end{array}
\left[\begin{array}{cc} 1 & 0 \\ 0 & 99 \end{array} \right] ,
\end{array}
\tag{18}
$$

which is derived by subtracting each value from the maximum value in the same column, i.e.

$$
\begin{array}{cc}
 & B_1 \qquad\qquad B_2 \\
\begin{array}{c} A_1 \\ A_2 \end{array}
\left[\begin{array}{cc} 1-0 & 100-100 \\ 1-1 & 100-1 \end{array} \right]
\end{array}
\tag{19}
$$

which, of course, gives you the above values from (3), and still leads to the choice of A_1.

In general, of course, we can consider cases of varying probabilities, whereas those above were considered to be equiprobable.

This argument is identical with that of the last section viewed from a slightly different point of view. But if (15) were substituted for (20) the argument would be more or less the same. Many different strategies are possible, and we must make a comparison between three of them to show how this choice may occur.

$$
\begin{array}{c c c c}
 & B_1 & B_2 & B_3 \\
A_1 & 0 & 3 & 0 \\
A_2 & 2 & 2 & 0 \\
A_3 & 1 & 1 & 1
\end{array}
\tag{20}
$$

Suppose the columns B_1, B_2, B_3 are all equiprobable, which A would you choose where the pay-off is in £'s? Maximum utility suggests A_1, since £3 is the maximum pay-off, minimum regret is derived as before, giving the matrix (21):

$$
\begin{array}{c c c c}
 & B_1 & B_2 & B_3 \\
A_1 & 3 & 0 & 3 \\
A_2 & 0 & 0 & 2 \\
A_3 & 0 & 0 & 0
\end{array}
\tag{21}
$$

so you would clearly choose A_3 to minimise your regret. A third strategy might be to choose A_2 since this (sometimes called Laplace's Strategy) could be supported by the view that it gives the maximum average pay off. The average of the three rows of (20) being 1, $1\frac{1}{3}$ and 1 respectively.

There are other more complicated strategies but these are sufficient for our purpose. Now if we take matrix (20) and change the value of the pay off from £'s to millions of pounds much as we changed (15) to (16), would you still bet the same way?

You now stand to lose — or fail to win — up to £3 million. If you now translate (20) into a new matrix (22), which satisfies all the same conditions the point becomes even more obvious:

$$
\begin{array}{c c c c}
 & B_1 & B_2 & B_3 \\
A_1 & -1 & 2 & -1 \\
A_2 & 1 & 1 & -1 \\
A_3 & 0 & 0 & 0
\end{array}
\tag{22}
$$

The same strategies exist and the pay offs are relatively the same, but now you may have to risk losing £1 million. This will almost certainly have the effect of moving your choice from A_1 as first choice, overlooking A_2, and moving to A_3, where you cannot lose anything. The fact that you cannot win anything is no longer the most important factor.

To summarise the situation, we shall say that it is fairly obvious that the choice of strategies to be used is a function of the size of the risk, and we must use this technique as a result of some quantification of the data where possible, whenever we are asked to take any decision which entails risk.

With the minimax approach to risk in mind, let us look at a technique which has been derived from such beginnings.

Links / Weps

17.6   VENTURE ANALYSIS

We now turn to venture analysis; given that we need to do something such as market a new product, we are faced by market uncertainties. We are unsure of the rate of market penetration and yet need to build a factory of some size. If we choose a fairly arbitrary measure such as the "net cash position", which is defined as the cumulative net earnings *plus* depreciation reserve *less* the permanent investment and working capital, we may choose to maximise this. Rather than predict market penetration, it is often easier to minimise regret (Stage 1).

For a particular factory size say of £5 million, £10 million and £15 million respectively, we could forecast in terms of, say, rates of market penetration:
great, medium and small.

So if our pay off is in terms of "net cash" at some later date (this is a function of budgetting), then we can construct a utility matrix as follows:

Factory size	Forecast "net cash" at time t		
£5 million	(60	40	20)
£10 million	(70	50	10)
£15 million	(90	42	18)

which gives a regret matrix:

$$\begin{pmatrix} 30 & 10 & 0 \\ 20 & 0 & 10 \\ 0 & 8 & 2 \end{pmatrix}$$

so the minimum regret, given by the lowest maximum value of a row, is given by the last row whose maximum value is 8. We therefore can say that our factory choice (on *this* basis) must be the largest one.

Fixing the price of the commodity now takes us into the second game-theoretic phase, and we repeat the procedure and find a solution to the game in the light of the customer's and competitor's likely action. The difficulty with all these methods is to select the best budgets and various estimates in the first instance. Success depends on seeing which are the most relevant features and optimising them in the manner suggested.

For the last phase we can think of the firm's price for the product as against the customer's price for the product. He is now considering what price of product maximises his market penetration.

Suppose we consider profits to the firm as a pay off defined in £'s as:

$$\text{Profits pay off} = \frac{\text{Firm's profits}}{\text{Customer's profits}}$$

Now make up the matrix:

$$
\begin{array}{ccc}
 & & \\
225 & {}^{14}/_{62} & {}^{26}/_{50} & {}^{38}/_{38} \\
200 & {}^{28}/_{96} & {}^{50}/_{74} & {}^{72}/_{52} \\
175 & {}^{43}/_{113} & {}^{76}/_{80} & {}^{109}/_{47} \\
150 & {}^{58}/_{119} & {}^{101}/_{71} & {}^{143}/_{29} \\
125 & {}^{73}/_{100} & {}^{126}/_{47} & {}^{178}/_{-5} \\
 & 50 & 75 & 100
\end{array}
\tag{23}
$$

Customer's price for product (rows)

Firm's price for raw material

Although $^{178}/_{-5}$ gives maximum pay off it is gained at the expense of financial loss to the customer, so that if we choose the marked diagonal we in fact find that this provides the minimax solution; and since 76/80 is the ratio which maximises the profit to the firm, we choose this as our solution to the game, the graph then tells us (by tracking back along the ordinates and abscissae) what the firm's and customer's price must be. The firm's price is 75, which could be some such measure as £75 per unit (such as a lb or cwt).

We are presupposing in this example some part of the principle involved in the theory of n-person games, so we shall now give some idea of what such a principle entails.

17.7   THEORY OF GAMES

No account of cybernetics would be complete without some mention of the theory of games. This approach to game playing situations (Von Neumann and Morgenstern, 1944; Luce and Raiffa, 1958) is concerned primarily with one-off games, or games where a decision is made and the consequences of the decision are not obviously sequential.

It is, when viewed as a problem of linear programming – equivalent to game theoretic situations – a process of seeking maxima and minima where the differential calculus cannot be used.

We want in this book to avoid describing the technical terms associated with these special branches of mathematics and concentrate, as we have done so far, on simple examples, showing their significance in the general information processing situation.

In general terms, we talk of n-person games where n people are involved, so contract bridge is a 4-person game and patience is a 1-person game. We say such games are *zero sum* if when viewed as a gamble what one person wins another loses and there is no residue. We need strategies and solutions. If we were considering contract bridge we should also need to talk of *coalitions*, but we shall restrict our discussion to games without coalitions.

Consider a simple example of a 2-person zero sum game, with a simple pay off matrix. The numbers in the matrix are, as usual, the pay offs to the recipients, A by rows and B by columns.

Let us again consider a simple pay off matrix:

$$
\begin{array}{c} & \begin{array}{cccc} B_1 & B_2 & B_3 & B_4 \end{array} \\ \begin{array}{c} A_1 \\ A_2 \\ A_3 \\ A_4 \\ A_5 \end{array} & \left(\begin{array}{cccc} 18 & 3 & 0 & 2 \\ 0 & 3 & 8 & 20 \\ 5 & 4 & 5 & 5 \\ 16 & 4 & 2 & 25 \\ 9 & 3 & 0 & 20 \end{array} \right) \end{array} .
$$

This time, we do not have a "game against nature" but a game between two intelligent people (the theory itself deals with any number of intelligent people i.e. n-person games).

If A_2 is chosen by the A-player and the B-player chooses B_3, then the B-player pays £8 to the A-player. Let us look at the matter from A's point of view. If A knew what B would choose the problem would be simple, but this is not the case, so A must assume that each will think of the other's best choice in the light of each other's maximum ability.

A's choice is governed by:

If B chooses:	B_1	B_2	B_3	B_4	
A must choose:	A_1	(A_3 or A_4)	A_2	A_4	(25)
A's pay off is:	18	4	8	25	

B's choice is governed by:

If A chooses:	A_1	A_2	A_3	A_4	A_5	
B must choose:	B_3	B_1	B_2	B_3	B_3	(26)
A's pay off is:	0	0	4	2	0	

Now A sees from this that he can be sure of the following:

A chooses:	A_1	A_2	A_3	A_4	A_5	
He is *sure* of:	0	0	4	2	0	(27)

So A_3 is the maximum pay off that can be guaranteed A for B:

B chooses:	B_1	B_2	B_3	B_4	
He is *sure* of:	-18	-4	-8	-25	(28)

So it is clear that provided both are optimal players, A must choose A_3 and B must choose B_2 and (A_3, B_2) is the so-called "solution of the game" The solution is, of course, a combination of the optima for both players in a 2-person game.

If there is any reason on either side to believe that their opponent's play is less than optimal — and this might be gauged over a series of games — then the solution might be improved. However, marketing tends to be a "one-off" type of activity and although some experience is possible, it must by the nature of things be very limited. In general, we assume what is called a "minimax" or "maximin" strategy, whichever way you look at it.

17.8   DYNAMIC PROGRAMMING

Finally we have what is something, a generalisation of certain of these methods in what has been called dynamic programming (Bellman 1957, Bellman and Dreyfus 1962).

Dynamic programming constitutes a specific set of techniques for sequential decision processing. In particular cases this process of finding optima in discrete cases degenerates into the various cases of Markov processes and linear programmes.

We shall not attempt to discuss these matters here, but merely note the existence of methods for sequential processing, special cases of which link with the probabilistic techniques of stochastic processes described in Chapter 9.

It should be added that the work described in this chapter is of the utmost importance, and is still somewhat disjointed. There is tremendous scope for developing new techniques and combinations of existing ones. These techniques can be used by a human or a computer, but more important than this they can be used to provide much of the core of a model designed to simulate or synthesise human-like intelligence.

17.9   RECENT ADVANCES

Unlike most of the other chapters of this book, this chapter has been primarily concerned with methods that have been developed over a period of time and there have been relatively few recent applications to cybernetics as such. Bell

(1973) and Baldwin (1973) have written interesting summary papers of recent developments and these summaries themselves contain further references.

Two further books on the subject in the more traditional view have been produced by White (1969) and Chance (1969). There is a further reference (Lerner, 1972) which readers should note.

CHAPTER 18

The next stages in cybernetics

Argument

Cybernetics is the science of control and communication, as well as being the science of artificial intelligence.

In the future, we may expect progress on all fronts, but especially in the programming of computers to make human-like decisions, and especially in the devlopment of organic systems that behave like digital computers. †

In particular, we may expect efforts to put together into increasingly large "chunks" the methods such as are involved in pattern recognition, natural language and heuristic programming and the like, to provide more integrated, and more autonomous, artificially intelligent systems.

The effect of all these developments on our social world will be great, but such a subject goes well beyond the confines of this book.

We have tried in this book to describe some of the ways in which cybernetics has developed over the last twenty-five years or so. Indeed the full life span of "cybernetics", in the strictest sense of the first use of the title, covers only some thirty years, but of course in a broader sense cybernetics and the ideas subsumed thereunder goes back hundreds of years. What is new is the development of a rich methodology, and some considerable evidence to support the underlying beliefs of cybernetics.

All the various approaches to cybernetics described in this book are still very much matters of current research (Collins and Michie, 1967; Dale and Michie, 1968; Meltzer and Michie, 1969; Michie, 1968). Thus we can say that self-adapting systems and their development, and their application in various fields of endeavour, are still very much matters being currently persued. In fact, these models are used both in the field of *artificial intelligence* and the field of application to business and governmental activities, and in both the field of human simulation and machine synthesis.

Hardware models of a kind which are intended to be indicative of organismic behaviour are being pursued still, but perhaps at a slower rate than before. It has been realised that "moving models" that can actually run mazes or perform other simple learning activities, while useful and suggestive, are not perhaps a very important end in themselves, if only because of their inevitable simplicity. It is indeed true to say that cybernetics at present depends more on mathematical, statistical and logical developments, (as well as developments in

---

†The series on "Machine Intelligence" published by Edinburgh University Press and the recent work of T. Winograd should certainly be looked at by the student interested in carrying on research in this field.

the field of computer programming) than it does on special purpose hardware models.

Finite and infinite (non-finite) automata are very much the domain of the mathematician and to some extent the domain of the cybernetician. A certain number of interesting mathematical problems arise which are closely connected with the philosophical foundations of mathematics and which are usefully couched in terms of automata theory. But increasingly, partly because of the development of algorithmic and heuristic programming, automata offer fields of effective theoretical development which are of the utmost cybernetic importance; they place limits on what is in fact possible.

The study of neural nets in particular has been a source of a considerable amount of development in the recent past. There was a time, when McCulloch and Pitts (1943) first developed neural nets, that it was felt that this would be a really important development in cybernetics. Since then it has lapsed to some extent, but recently again under the impetus of Blum (1962), Verbeck (1962), Lofgren (1962) and Cowan (1962), Memes (1969). Fonseca (1970), Lerner (1972) among others, interest has become renewed. Neural nets can be represented on computers more often than not in matrix form and they allow us to examine the anatomical structural capacity of systems, which one does not normally incorporate in one's automata, but this is a matter we have already discussed in some detail.

Automata themselves are usually designed to concentrate on the functional aspects of organismic behaviour, and it is only when we come to neural net automata that we come to grips with the actual structural or anatomical developments. The extent to which neural nets are likely to develop in the future, as opposed to the likely development of the general field of finite automata, depends more than any other single factor on the need we may have to understand the structural capacities of the system. One might guess that neural nets will be increasingly important in the field of human simulation, whereas the tape-type finite automata will continue to be more important in the field of artificial intelligence.

The impact of digital computers and its overlap with cybernetics is a field in itself. The range of their application to scientific, industrial and commercial problems alone ensure the enormous development of computer technology in the next decade. Indeed it is not perhaps too much to guess that computers may become the biggest single industrial development in the next half century.

Of all developments in the field of computers, which seem most likely to take place, those which create artificial intelligence, the making of human decisions, and human problem solving, as well as the simulation of human behaviour, are certainly among the most promising and the most exciting. This is indeed the very heart of Cybernetics. The reason, and we should underline the point, that computers are so essential to the development of cybernetics is not at all dependent on the logic of the situation, but on the speed and accuracy of the computer itself. All that cybernetics has done could as a matter of principle have been done independently of the computer. But it is no longer a matter of principle as soon as we move into practice, and it is here that the computer has become vital. Computers allow us to compute and carry out problem solving activities at a speed and in a domain which could never be achieved by any other means. This is why we can attempt to simulate the full range of human behaviour at its peak intellect, and this because of the very complexity of the problem relative to the life span of human beings would be impractical without the development of digital computers. Here, if anywhere, is the spearhead of the future cybernetic attack.

It is important to be clear that computer science and cybernetics are by no means the same subject. From one point of view they bear the same relationship to each other as any other science does to computer science in that the computer is a computational or modelling tool for the science. There is though a slightly closer relationship involved here because of the modelling itself, since in a sense the computer organisation especially involved in adaptive heuristic programming is a natural subject for cybernetic study.

On the other hand, cyberneticians are interested in the synthesis and simulation of intelligent behaviour of a human-like kind, and suitable methods for its description. Computer scientists are concerned primarily with the mechanics of systems analysis, program design, the writing of compiler languages and the like – very different fields of endeavour, even if of mututal interest.

We have discussed information theory in some detail. It has already been used in a variety of different ways as an alternative descriptive langauge for much of that part of science that is concerned with communication and control. This work in information theory is closely integrated with work on neural nets and finite automata, and therefore it is difficult to assess exactly how much this aspect of information theory as a descriptive language will thrive. Information theory, as we have seen, is itself a branch of probability theory and closely associated with statistics. One of the questions that arises here, as in all science, is the need to be able to translate from one type of description or representation into another. It is useful to depict some situations by information-theoretic descriptions and others by game-theoretic descriptions. To translate from one to the other can often be invaluable in simplifying a problem.

All of these fields of mathematics clearly play a vitally important part in our present scientific research, and we may expect to see this work carried much further in the future. However, rather as in the case of neural nets, information theory may perhaps be said to be not expanding as quickly as the equivalent development in computers, heuristic programming and the general development of automata theory. It is in the practical application of computer programming technique that most progress is being made.

We have already mentioned decision taking by artificially intelligent means, and the vital link that this has with the developments of artificial and symbolic languages. This is a field of development in its own right, and links with heuristic methods and natural languages and their development in computer terms, perhaps evolving a search for a universal language. On the other hand computer languages such as Algol, Cobol, Fortran, PL1, Language H and even the compiler-compilers all play an important role in cybernetic development. These are all compiler (or compiler-compiler) type computer languages, and only a part of a variety of such computer languages, which are likely to play an increasingly important part in the future as long as we use computers as our thinking aids. We may expect tremendous developments here with respect to list-processing and other languages particularly convenient for cybernetic modelling.

Programmed learning can be regarded as a part of automation. Indeed it is expected that the future development in computer based programmed instruction (C.A.I. or "Computer Assisted Instruction" as it is sometimes called) is likely to be revolutionary. However, even taking individual teaching machines, whether of the branching or linear variety, then we may expect to see the particular application of cybernetic ideas develop considerably. In the end, perhaps it is true to say that it is the simple ideas with the widest range of application which are most important to civilisation. If this is so, there can be no more simple exemplification of this than in the field of programmed instruction.

Most arguments about the troubles and the development of human beings whether in nations or in the world community as a whole bring us back to the education of the people. Education of even the most advanced countries of the world tends to be lagging sadly behind the need of the times. It is often asserted that our technological abilities and our scientific development have wholly outstripped our social development, and no doubt this is largely true.

We have often failed to realise practical application to scientific ideas, and we have the problem of dealing with our leisure time in a world which, in the future, is going to be largely automated. By "future" we may mean 50, or we may mean 500 years ahead, but what matters is that it is definitely coming in the future, and in the "not-so-far distant" future. Teaching machines should, therefore, be heavily emphasised as one of the simpler and more vital aspects of cybernetic applications, and therefore by our own definition an aspect of automation which will certainly prove essential to the whole of civilised society.

Particular fields of activity which have gathered momentum in recent years are those of natural language programming and logic theorem proving.

The work on natural language emanates in part from the idea of a conversation and of question-answering. Programs are being produced with ever more sophisticated syntactical analysis and the ability to formulate questions as well as to answer them. We are getting nearer all the time to the simulation of human conversation, which we know to be vital if we are to successfully simulate human intelligence. The bulk of a human being's knowledge comes from knowledge by description — whether being told by other people or whether read in a book. Without language, human intelligence could never have reached anything like its present standards, since each generation would have to rediscover knowledge and it could not be accumulated from generation to generation.

The ability to draw inferences is equally vital an ingredient of human intelligence and theorem-proving, apart from its use in mathematics and other axiomatic systems, provides an inference-making mechanism for the artificially intelligent system.

Two factors which will sometime require much more detailed analysis are the social features of human life and the emotional features. We, as human beings, are essentially social — language would hardly have arisen had we lived in total isolation from each other — and some of the characteristics must be reproduced in a study of societies of automata.

The emotions interact with the rational features of human behaviour providing additional stimuli and responses. The emotions no doubt are closely bound up with motivation and serve a clear biological purpose as an alarm system. All of these features could doubtless be reproduced in a computer, or better by the manufacture of a system of a colloidal kind which might then *be* an emotional system rather than a simulation or representation of one. Insofar as our efforts are directed at the simulation of human behaviour, the simulation of the emotions is clearly quite vital.

One word next about the word "cybernetics". In America it is now slightly frowned upon, and although the word is currently more acceptable in the United Kingdom, it is still suspect in some quarters and it has, in any case, taken many years to get even a semblance of acceptability for it. The problem stems from the arbitrary divisions we have in our sciences, and the very slow conservative attitude of scientists towards the development of scientific ideas and classifications, to say nothing of the application of those scientific ideas to practical problems. It is a curiosity of our educational system, apparently, that those people who have most ideas scientifically speaking, are least able to see the full value of those ideas in practical development and human evolution.

This book will be concluded by saying that cybernetics is a new science, and it has many aspects. This includes computers, automata theory, information theory and other techniques and methods which are all used in some measure to either simulate or synthesise human-like behaviour. It includes much of mathematics, but by no means all of it. It includes meta-mathematics and logic. Logic supplies a link with language and philosophy, and both of these with the behavioural and social sciences.

The field of applications is enormous and the need for cybernetics in the planning of the future of our society (George, 1968) is undoubted.

References

Adey, W.R. (1961) *Brain Mechanisms and Learning*. F. Delafresnaye (Ed.). Blackwells, Oxford.

Aleksander, I. and M.C. Fairhurst (1972) An automaton with brain-like properties. *Kybernetes*, 1, 11–18.

Apter, M.J. (1966) *Cybernetics and Development*. Pergamon Press.

Arbib, M.A. (1965) *Brains, Machines and Mathematics*. McGraw-Hill.

Arbib, M.A. (1969) *Theory of Abstract Automata*. Prentice Hall.

Arbib, M.A. (1971) Transformations and somatotopy in perceiving systems. *Second International Joint Conference on Artificial Intelligence*. 140–147.

Ashby, W.R. (1952) *Design for a Brain*. Chapman and Hall.

Ashby, W.R. (1956) *An Introduction to Cybernetics*. Chapman and Hall.

Baldwin, J. (to be published) Dynamic Programming. In *An Introduction to Management Cybernetics*. F.H. George (Ed.).

Banerji, R.B. (1960) An information processing program for object recognition. *General Systems*, 5, 117.

Banerji, R.B. (1962) A language for the description of concepts. *General Systems Yearbook*, 5.

Banerji, R.B. (1964) A language for the description of concepts. *General Systems*, 9, 135.

Banerji, R.B. (1969) *Theory of Problem Solving*. Elsevier.

Banerji, R.B. (1971) A language for pattern recognition. Pattern Recognition Society.

Baran, P. and G. Estrin (1960) An adaptive character reader. *IRE, WESCON*, Los Angeles.

Barnett, S. and C. Storey (1970) *Matrix Methods in Stability Theory*. Nelson.

Beer, S. (1972) *Brain of the Firm*. Macmillan.

Bell, R. (to be published) An approach to Theory of Games. In *An Introduction to Management Cybernetics*. F.H. George (Ed.).

Bellman, R.E. (1957) *Dynamic Programming*. Princeton University Press.

Bellman, R.E. and S.E. Dreyfus (1962) *Applied Dynamic Programming*. Princeton University Press.

Bexton, W.H., W. Heron and T.H. Scott (1954) Effects of decreased variation in the sensory environment. *Canad. J. Psychol.* 8, 70–76.

Black, M. (1966) Notes on the "paradoxes of confirmation". In *Aspects of Inductive Logic*. J. Hintikka and P. Suppes (Eds.) North Holland.

Bledsoe, W.W. and I. Browning (1959) Paper recognition and reading by machine. *Proc. Eastern Joint. Comp. Conf.* 16, 225–232.

Bledsoe, W.W. and I. Browning (1961) Recognition of sloppy hand-printed characters. *Proc. West. Joint Comp. Conf.*

Blum, M. (1962) Properties of a neuron with many inputs. In *Principles of Self-Organization*. H. von Foerster and G.W. Zopf (Eds.). Pergamon Press.

Bobrow, D.G. (1963) *Syntactic Analysis of English by Computer – A Survey*. Proc. FJCC. Spartan Press. Baltimore, Md.

Bobrow, D.G. (1966) METEOR: a LISP interpreter for string manipulation. *The Programming Language LISP: Its Operation and Applications*. M.I.T. Press.

Borko, H. (1968) *Automated Language Processing*. Wiley.

Braitenberg, V. (1967) On the use of theories, models and cybernetical toys in brain research. *Brain Research*, 6, 2, 201–215.

Brillouin, L. (1956) *Science and Information Theory*. Academic Press.

Brillouin, L. (1964) *Scientific Uncertainty and Information*. Academic Press.

Brooker, R.A., Morris and Rohl. (1963) See Napper, R.B.E. (1964b).

Buchanan, B., G. Sutherland and E.A. Feigenbaum (1969) Heuristic dendral: a program for generating explanatory hypotheses in organic chemistry. In *Machine Intelligence*, Vol. 4. B. Meltzer and D. Michie (Eds.). Edinburgh University Press.

Buchwald, N.A. and C.D. Hull (1967) Some problems associated with interpretation of physiological and behavioural responses to stimulation of caudate and thalamic nuclei. *Brain Research*, 6, 1, 1–11.

Burstall, R.M. (1966) A heuristic method for a job scheduling problem. Experimental Programming Unit, Edinburgh.

Bush, R.R. and F. Mosteller (1955) *Stochastic Models for Learning*. Wiley.

Cannon, W.B. (1929) *Bodily Changes in Pain, Hunger, Fear and Rage*. Appleton-Century.

Carnap, R. (1937) Testability and meaning. *Phil. Sci.* 3, 419–71; 4, 1–40.

Carnap, R. (1943) *Formalization of Logic*. Harvard University Press. Cambridge, Mass.

Carnap, R. (1947) *Meaning and Necessity*. Chicago University Press.

Carnap, R. (1952) Empiricism, semantics and ontology. In *Semantics and the Philosophy of Language*. L. Linsky (Ed.). University of Illinois Press.

Carnap, R. (1958) *An Introduction to Symbolic Logic and its Applications*. Dover Publications, N.Y.

Carnap, R. and Y. Bar Hillel (1952) An outline of a theory of semantic information. Technical Report 247. M.I.T. Research Laboratory of Electronics.

Chance, W.A. (1969) *Statistical Methods for Decision Making*. Irwin.

Chapman, B.L.M. (1959) A self organizing classifying system. *Cybernetica*, 2, 3, 152–61.

Chomsky, N. (1957) *Syntactic Structures*. Mouton, The Hague.

Chomsky, N. and M.A. Schutzenberger (1963) The algebraic theory of context-free languages. *Computer Programming and Formal Systems*. North Holland Publishing. pp. 118–161.

Church, A. (1936) An unsolvable problem of elementary number theory. *Amer. J. Math.* 58, 345–363.

Church, A. (1941) *The Calculi of Lambda-Conversion*. Princeton University Press.

Clarkson, G.P.E. (1963) A model of the trust investment process. In *Computers and Thought*. E.A. Feigenbaum and J. Feldman (Eds.). McGraw-Hill.

Cohen, M.R. and E. Nagel (1934) *Introduction to Logic and Scientific Method*. Kegan Paul.

Cohen, E. (1962) A recognition algorithm for a grammar model. *Rep. 7885. Nat. Bur. Stand.* Washington, D.C.

Collins, N.L. and D. Michie (1967) *Machine Intelligence*, Vol. 1. Oliver and Boyd.

Coombs, A.W.M. (1969) On the construction of an efficient feature space for optical character recognition. In *Machine Intelligence* Vol. 4. B. Meltzer and D. Michie, (Eds.). Edinburgh University.

Cornish, E.R. and P.C. Wason (1970) The recall of affirmative and negative sentences in an incidental learning task. *Q. J. Exp. Psychol.*, 22, 109–114.

Cowan, J. (1962) Many-valued logics and reliable automata. In *Principles of Self-Organization*. H. von Foerster and G. W. Zopf (Eds.). Pergamon Press.

Crowder, N.A. (1959) Automatic tutoring by means of intrinsic programming. In *Automatic Teaching: the State of the Art*. E.H. Galanter (Ed.). Wiley.

Culbertson, J.T. (1948) A mechanism for optic nerve conduction and form perception. *Bull. Math. Biophysiol.* 10, 31–40.

Culbertson, J.T. (1950) *Consciousness and Behaviour*. Brown, Dubuque, Iowa.

Culbertson, J.T. (1952) Hypothetical robots. Rand Project P-296.

Culbertson, J.T. (1956) Some uneconomical robots. In *Automata Studies*. C. E. Shannon and J. McCarthy (Eds.). Princeton University Press.

Curry, H.B. (1942) The combinatory foundation of mathematical logic. *J. Symb. Log.* 1, 49–64, (see also 8, p. iv).

Curry, H.B. (1949) A simplification of the theory of combinators. *Synthese*, 7, 6A, 391–399.

Da Fonseca, J. (1966) *Neuronal Models*. Lisbon. Centro de Estudos egas Moniz.

Dale, E. and D. Michie (1968) *Machine Intelligence*, Vol. 2. Oliver and Boyd.

Darlington, J.L. (1969) Theorem proving and information retrieval. In *Machine Intelligence*, Vol. 4. B. Meltzer and D. Michie (Eds.).

Davis, M. (1958) *Computability and Unsolvability*. McGraw-Hill.

Davis, M. (1965) *The Undecidable*. Raven Press.

De No and R. Lorente (1938a) Synaptic stimulation of motoneurons as a local process. *J. Neurophysiol.*, 1, 195–206.

De No and R. Lorente (1938b) Analysis of the activity of a chain of internuncial neurons. *J. Neurophysiol.*, 1, 207–44.

De No and R. Lorente (1947) *A Study of Nerve Physiology*. Vols. 1 and 2. In studies from the Rockefeller Institute for Medical Research. Vols. 131 and 132.

Deutsch, J.A. (1954) A machine with insight. *Quart. J. Exp. Psychol.* 6, 6–11.

Dodwell, P.C. (1957) Shape recognition in rats. *Brit. J. Psychol.* 43, 221.

Doran, J.E. (1969) Planning and generalization in an automaton/environment system. In *Machine Intelligence*, Vol. 4. B. Meltzer and D. Michie (Eds.). Edinburgh University Press.

Dotey, R.W. (1965) Conditioned reflexes elicited by electrical stimulation of the brain in macaques. *J. Neurophysiol.* 28, 623–40.

Doyle, W. (1960) Recognition of sloppy, hard-printed characters. *Proc. West. Joint Comp. Conf.* 17, 133–142.

Dunham, B. and J.H. North (with R.M. Friedberg) (1959) A learning machine: Part I. *IBM Jl. Res. Dev.* 2, 2–13.

Edwards, W. (1967) A taxonomy of decision-making functions, with an application to simulation of a decision-making system. NATO Publication.

Edwards, W., H. Lindman and L.J. Savage (1963) Bayesian statistical inference for psychological research. *Psychol. Rev.*, 70, 193–242.

Evans, J. St. B.T. (1972) Interpretation and 'matching bias' in a reasoning task. *Q. J. Exp. Psychol.*, 24, 193–199.

Feigenbaum, E.A. and J. Feldman (1968) *Computers and Thought*. McGraw-Hill.

Fisher, R.A. (1958) *The Genetical Theory of Natural Selection*. Dover. New York.

Freud, S. (1938) *The Basic Writings of Sigmund Freud*. Random House.

Fu, K. (1968) *Sequential Methods in Pattern Recognition and Machine Learning*. Macmillan.

Gelb, J.P. (1971) Experiments with a natural language problem solving system. In *Second International Joint Conference on Artificial Intelligence*.

Gelerntner, H. (1963) Realization of a geometry-theorem proving machine. In *Computers and Thought*. E.A. Geigenbaum and J. Feldman (Eds.). McGraw-Hill.

Gentzen, G. (1938) Neue Fassung der Widerspruchs-freiheitsbewerses fur die reine Zahlentheorie *Forschunger zur logic und zur Gurundlegung der exakten wissenschaflen*.

George, F.H. (1956) Logical networks and behaviour. *Bull. Math. Biophys.*, 18, 337–48.

George, F.H. (1956) Pragmatics. *J. Phil. Phen. Res.* 17, 226–235.

George, F.H. (1957) Logical networks and probability. *Bull. Math. Biophys.*, 19, 187–199.

George, F.H. (1959) *Automation, cybernetics and Society*. Leonard Hill.

George, F.H. (1961) *The Brain as a Computer*. Pergamon Press.

George, F.H. (1962) Minds, Machines and Gödel: Another reply to Mr. Lucas. *Philos.*, 37, 62–63.

George, F.H. (1965) *Cybernetics and Biology*. Oliver and Boyd.

George, F.H. (1966) Hypothesis confirmation on a digital computer. Paper read at Conference of Bionics. Dayton, Ohio. 739–748.

George, F.H. (1967) Learning, language and Computers. In *Automaton Theory and Learning Systems*. D.J. Steward (Ed.). Academic Press.

George, F.H. (1967) Computer applications in decision taking and process control. In *Long Range Planning*. pp. 393–408. Gordon and Breach.

George, F.H. (1970) *Models of Thinking*. Allen and Unwin.

George, F.H. (1970) *Cybernetics and Automata Theory*. Brunel Monograph on Cybernetics.

George, F.H. (1972) Mechanism, interrogation and incompleteness. *Kybernetes*. 1, 109–114.

George, F.H. (1972) Heuristic Generation. *J. Inst. Comp. Sci.* 3, 3, 55–68.

George, F.H. (1972) The foundations of cybernetics. *The Sixth International Congress on Cybernetics*. Namur.

George, F.H. (Ed.) (to be published) *A Handbook of Management Cybernetics*.

George, F.H. (to be published) *Pragmatics, Language and Automata*.

George, F.H. and J.H. Handlon (1955) Towards a general theory of behaviour. *Methodos*, 1, 25–44.

George, F.H. and J.H. Handlon (1957) A language for perceptual analysis. *Psychol. Rev.*, 64, 14–25.

Glushkov, V.M. (1969) Contemporary cybernetics. In *Survey of Cybernetics*. J. Rose (Ed.). Iliffe Press.

Gödel, K. (1931) Über formal unentscheidbare Sätze der Principia Mathematica und Verwandter Systeme I. *Monatschefle fur Mathematik und Physik*, 38, 173–198.

Goldsmith, W. (1972) Words and models. *Kybernetes*, 1, 4, 243–249.

Green, L.E.S., E.C. Berkeley and C. Gotlieb (1959) Conversation with a computer. *Computers and Automation*, 8, 10, 9–11.

Grimsdale, R.L., F.H. Sumner, C.J. Tunis and T. Kilburn (1900) A system for the automatic recognition of patterns. In *Pattern Recognition*. L. Uhr (Ed.). Wiley.

Grodins, F.S. (1965) *Control Theory and Biological Systems*. Columbia University Press.

Hayek, S.A. (1952) *The Sensory Order*. University of Chicago.

Hays, D.G. (1962) Automatic language data processing. In *Computer Applications in the Behavioral Sciences*. H. Borko (Ed.). Prentice Hall.

Hays, D.G. (1964) Dependency theory, a formalism and some observations. *Language*, 40, 4.

Hebb, D.O. (1949) *The Organization of Behavior*. Wiley.

Hempel, C.G. (1945) Studies in logic of confirmation. *Mind*, 54.

Hilgard, E.R. and D.G. Marquis (1940) *Conditioning and Learning*. Appleton-Century-Crofts.

Hill, A.V. (1926) *Proc. Roy. Soc. B.*, 100, 87. Acedemic Press.

Hill, A.V. (1938) *Proc. Roy. Soc. B.*, 117, 136. Acedemic Press.

Hill, A.V. (1970) *First and Last Experiments in Muscle Mechanics*. Cambridge University Press.

Hintikka, J. and J. Pietarinen (1966) Semantic information and inductive logic. In *Aspects of Inductive Logic*. J. Hintikka and P. Suppes (Eds.). North Holland.

Hiz, H. (1959) Steps towards grammatical recognition. *Int. Conf. Standards on Common Language for Machine Searching and Translation*. Cleveland.

Hodes, L. (1971) Solving problems by formula manipulation in logic and linear inequalities. *Second International Joint Conference on Artificial Intelligence*. 553–559.

Jeffrey, R.C. (1965) *The Logic of Decision*. McGraw-Hill.

Kaplan, R.M. (1971) Augmented transition networks as psychological models of sentence comprehension. In *Second International Joint Conference on Artificial Intelligence*. 429–443.

Kaplan, A. and J. Schott (1951) A calculus for empirical classes. *Methodos*, 3, 165–190.

Kappers, C.U.A., G.C. Huber and E.C. Crosby (1936) *The Comparative Anatomy of the Nervous System of Vertebrates, including Man*. Macmillan.

Kemeny, J.G. and J.L. Snell (1960) *Finite Markov Chains*. Van Nostrand.

Kinoshita, G., S. Aida and M. Mori (1972) Pattern recognition by an artificial tactile sense.

Kirsch, R.A. (1964) Computer interpretation of English text and picture patterns. *IEEE-EC*.

Kleene, S.C. (1951) Representation of events in nerve nets. *Rands Research Memorandum. R.M.* 704.

Kleene, S.C. (1952) *Introduction to Metamathematics*. Van Nostrand.

Kling, R.E. (1971) A paradigm for reasoning by analogy. In *Second International Joint Conference on Artificial Intelligence*. 568–585.

Klir, J. and M. Valach (1965) *Cybernetic Modelling*. Iliffe.

Koenig, E.C. and J.V. Schultz (1972) Analysis of a general logical discourse for man–machine interaction – Part I. *Kybernetes*, 1, 231–241.

Kohler, W. (1925) *The Mentality of Apes*. Kegan Paul.

Konorski, J. (1948) *Conditioned Reflexes and Neuron Organization*. Cambridge University Press.

Korzybski, A. (1933) *Science and Sanity*. Science Press.

Landahl, H.D. and R. Runge (1946) Outline of a matrix calculus for neural nets. *Bull. Math. Biophys.* 8, 75–81.

Lee, C.Y. (1961) Categorizing automata by W–machine programs. *J. Ass. Comput. Mach.* 8, 384–399.

Lee, R.C.T. (1971) Fuzzy logic and the resolution principle. In *Second International Joint Conference on Artificial Intelligence*. 560–567.

Lerner, Y.A. (1972) *Fundamentals of Cybernetics*. Chapman and Hall.

Lindsay, R.K. (1963) Inferential memory as the basis of machines which understand natural language. In *Computers and Thought*. A. Feigenbaum and J. Feldman (Eds.). McGraw-Hill.

Loehlin, J.C. (1963) A computer program that simulates personality. In *Computer Simulation of Personality*. S.S. Tomkins and S. Messich (Eds.). John Wiley.

Lofgren, L. (1962) Kinematic and tessallation models of self-repair. In *Biological Prototype and Synthetic Systems*. E.E. Bernard and M.R. Cane (Eds.). Plenum Press.

Lucas, J.R. (1970) *The Freedom of the Will*. Clarendon Press, Oxford.

Luce, R.D. and H. Raiffa (1957) *Games and Decisions*. Wiley.

Mackay, D.M. (1950) Quantal aspects of scientific information. *Philos. Mag.* 41, 289.

Mackay, D.M. (1951) Mindlike behaviour in artefacts. *Brit. J. Phil. Sci.* 2, 105–121.

Mackay, D.M. (1956) The epistemological problem for automata. In *Automata Studies* C.E. Shannon and J. McCarthy (Eds.). Princeton University Press.

Mackay, D.M. and W.A. Ainsworth (1964) Electrolytic growth processes with applications to self-adjusting automata. In *Neuere Ergebuisse der Kybernetik* K. Steinbuch and S.W. Wagner (Eds.). R. Oldenbourg.

Manescu, M. (1970) Some thoughts on the application of cybernetics in planned economy management. In *Progress in Cybernetics*. J. Rose (Ed.). Gordon and Breach.

McCarthy, J. (1961) A basic for a mathematical theory of computation. *Proc. West. Joint Comp. Conf.*

McCulloch, W.S. and W. Pitts (1943) A logical calculus of the ideas immanent in nervous activity. *Bull. Math. Biophys.* 5, 115–133.

McNaughton, R. (1961) The theory of automata, a survey. *Advances in Computers.* 2, 379–421. Acedemic Press.

Meltzer, B. and D. Michie (1969) *Machine Intelligence, 4*. Edinburgh University Press.

Meltzer, B. (1974) The programming of deduction and induction. In *The Robots are Coming*, F.H. George and J.D. Humphries (Eds.) NCC Publication.

Mesarovic, M.D. (1972) Conceptual basis for a mathematical theory of general systems. *Kybernetes*, 1, 35–40.

Mesarovic, M.D. and Y. Takahara (1975) *Mathematical Theory of General Systems*. In Press

Michie, D., J.G. Fleming and J.V. Oldfield (1968) A comparison of heuristic, interactive and unaided emthods of solving a shortest route problem. In *Machine Intelligence*, Vol. 3. D. Michie (Ed.). Edinburgh University Press.

Milner, P.M. (1957) The cell assembly: Mark II. *Psychol. Rev.* 64, 242–252.

Minsky, M. (1963) Steps towards artificial intelligence. In *Computers and Thought.* E.A. Feigenbaum and J. Feldman (Eds.). McGraw-Hill.

Minsky, M. (1967) *Computation: Finite and Infinite Machines.* Prentice Hall.

Minsky, M. and O. Selfridge (1961) Learning in random nets. In *Information Theory.* C. Cherry (Ed.). Butterworths.

Moore, E.F. (1956) Gedanken-experiments on sequential machines. In *Automata Studies.* C.E. Shannon and J. McCarthy (Eds.). Princeton University Press.

Moore, E.F. (1964) *Sequential Machines: Selected Papers.* Addison-Wesley.

Morofsky, E.L. and A.K.C. Wong (1971) Computer perception of complex patterns. *Second International Joint Conference on Artificial Intelligence.* 248–257.

Morris, C.W. (1946) *Signs, Language and Behavior.* Prentice Hall.

Munson, J.H. (1971) Robot planning, execution and monitoring in an uncertain environment. In *Second International Joint Conference on Artificial Intelligence.* 338–349.

Myhill, J. (1960) Linear bounded automata. *WADD Technical Note* 6–165. Wright-Patterson AFB, Ohio.

Napper, R.B.E. (1964a) *A System of Programming in Natural English.* Ph.D. Thesis, Manchester.

Napper, R.B.E. (1964b) A third-order compiler: a context for free man-machine communication. *Conference on Computers.* Edinburgh.

Napper, R.B.E. (1966) A system for defining language and writing programs in "Natural English". *Formal Language Description Languages for Computer Programming.* Steel (Ed.). North Holland.

Napper, R.B.E. (1967) The Third-Order Compiler: a context for free man-machine communication. *Machine Intelligence I.* D. Michie (Ed.). Oliver and Boyd.

Nemes, T.N. (1969) *Cybernetic Machines.* Iliffe Press.

Newell, A. (1961) *Information Processing Language V Manual.* Prentice Hall.

Newell, A., J.C. Shaw and H.A. Simon (1963) Empirical explorations with the logic theory machine: a case study in heuristics. In *Computers and Thought.* E.A. Feigenbaum and J. Feldman (Eds.). McGraw-Hill.

Oettinger, A.E. (1952) Programming a digital computer to learn. *Phil. Mag.* 1, 43, 1243–63.

Ogden, C.K. and I.A. Richards (1949) *The Meaning of Meaning.* Harcourt Brace (1938). Second Edition: Kegan Paul.

Osgood, C.E. and A.W. Heyer (1952) A new interpretation of figural after-effects. *Psychol. Rev.,* 59, 98–118.

Pask, A.G.S. (1959) Physical analogues to the growth of a concept. In *Mechanization of Thought Processes.* NPL Symposium.

Pask, A.G.S. (1961) *An Approach to Cybernetics.* Hutchinson.

Paul, R. (1972) Trajectory control of a computer arm. *Second International Joint Conference on Artificial Intelligence.* 385–390.

Pennacchi, R. (1972) Principles of an abstract theory of systems. *Int. J. Systems Sci.* 3, 1, 1–11.

Penfield, W. and T. Rasmussen (1950) *The Cerebral Cortex of Man.* Macmillan.

Pitts, W. and W.S. McCulloch (1943) How we know universals. The perception of auditory and visual forms. *Bull. Math. Biophys.* 9, 127.

Porter, A. (1969) *Cybernetics Simplified.* English Universities Press.

Porter, B. (1972) Probability of stability of a class of linear dynamical systems. *Int. J. Systems Sci.,* 3, 113–116.

Post, E.L. (1943) Formal reductions of the general combinatorial decision problem. *Am. J. Math.,* 65, 197–268.

Quillian, M.R. (1968) Semantic Memory. In *Semantic Information Processing.* M. Minsky

(Ed.). MIT Press.

Rabin, M.O. and D. Scott (1959) Finite automata and their decision problems. *IBM J. of Res. and Dev.* **3**, 2, 114–125.

Race, J.P.A. (1972) SOPHIE: a perceptual recognition system. A paper presented at the *International Conference of Cybernetics.* Oxford.

Radchenko, A.N. (1971) Pattern recognition by quasi-linguistic translation into artificial noise-resistant language. In *Second International Joint Conference on Artificial Intelligence.* 402–410.

Ramani, S. (1971) A language based problem-solver. In *Second International Joint Conference on Artificial Intelligence.* 463–473.

Rankin, B.K. (1961) A programmable grammar for a fragment of English for use on information retrieval system. *Rep. 7352. Nat. Bur. Stand.* Washington, D.C.

Raphael, B. (1964) SIR: a computer program for Semantic Information Retrieval. Ph.D. thesis. MIT. Camb. Mass.

Rapoport, A. (1955) Application of information networks to a theory of vision. *Bull. Math. Biophys.* **17**, 15–33.

Rashevsky, A. (1938) *Mathematical Biophysics.* University of Chicago Press.

Reichman, W.T. (1962) *Use and Abuse of Statistics.* Methuen.

Roberts, L.G. (1966) Pattern recognition with an adaptive network. In *Pattern Recognition.* L. Uhr (Ed.). Wiley.

Rochester, N., J.H. Holland, L.H. Haibt and W.L. Duda (1956) Test on a cell assembly theory of the action of the brain using a large digital computer. *IRE Transactions on Information Theory.* pp. 82–93.

Rogers, H. (1966) *Theory of Recursive Functions and Effective Computability.* McGraw-Hill.

Rosenblatt, F. (1958) In *Mechanization of Thought Processes.* NPL Symposium.

Rosenblatt, F. (1960a) Perception simulation experiments. *Proc. IRE.* **48**, 301–309.

Rosenblatt, F. (1960b) Perceptual generalization over transformation groups. In *Self-Organizing Systems* Yovits and Cameron (Eds.). Pergamon Press.

Rosenblatt, F. (1960c) Table of Q-functions for two perception models. *Cornell Aeronautical Laboratory* Report No. V G - 11 96-G-6.

Rosenblatt, F. (1962) *Principles of Neurodynamics.* Spartan Books.

Rosenbleuth, A., N. Wiener and J. Bigelow (1943) Behavior, purpose and teleology. *Philos. Sci.* **10**, 18–24.

Russell, B. (1948) *Human Knowledge: its Scope and Limits.* Allen and Unwin.

Sammet, J.E. (1971) Challenge to artificial intelligence: programming problems to be solved. *Second International Joint Conference on Artificial Intelligence.* 59–65.

Samuel, A.L. (1963) Some studies in machine learning, using the game checkers. In *Computers and Thought.* E.A. Feigenbaum and J. Feldman (Eds.). McGraw-Hill.

Samuel, A.L. (1969) Some studies in machine learning using the game of checkers. II. *IBM J. of Res. & Dev.* **6**, 601.

Sarkar, P.A. (1967) *Natural Language Programming.* Ph.D. Thesis. Bristol.

Schade, J.P. and D.H. Ford (1965) *Basic Neurology.* Elsevier.

Selfridge, O. (1959) Pandemonium: a paradigm for learning. In *Mechanisation of Thought Processes.* NPL Symposium.

Sellars, W. (1947) Pure pragmatics and epistemology. *Phil. Sci.* **14**.

Shannon, L.E. (1951) Presentation of a maze-solving machine. In *Cybernetics.* H. von Foerster (Ed.). Transactions of the eighth conference of the Josiah Macy Jr. Foundation. pp. 173–180.

Shannon, C.E. and W. Weaver (1949) *The Mathematical Theory of Communication.* Univ. of Illinois Press.

Sharlock, D.P., W.D. Neff and N.L. Strominger (1965) Discrimination of tone during and after bilateral ablation of auditory cortical areas. *J. Neurophysiol.* **28**, 673.

Shepherdson, J.C. (1959) The reduction of two-way automata to one-way automata. *IBM J. of Res. and Dev.* **3**, 2, 198–200.

Shepherdson, J.C. and H.E. Sturgis (1963) The computability of recursive functions. *J. Ass. Comput. Mach.* **10**, 217–255.

Sherrington, C.S. (1906) *Integrative Action of the Nervous System.* Constable.

Sillars, W. (1963) An algorithm for representing English sentences in a formal language. *Rep. 7884. Nat. Bur. Stand.* Washington.

Simmons, R.F., S. Klein and K. McConlogue (1964) Indexing and dependency logic for answering English questions. *American Documentation,* **15**, 3, 196–204.

Simmons, R.F. (1965) Answering English questions by computer – a survey. *A.C.M.I. of Computing.*

Simmons, R.F. and B.C. Bruce (1971) Some relations between predicate calculus and semantic net representations of discourse. *Second International Joint Conference on Artificial Intelligence.* 524–529.

Simon, J.C. and C. Roche (1971) Application of questionnaire theory to pattern recognition. *Second International Joint Conference on Artificial Intelligence.* 524–401.

Skinner, B.F. (1958) Teaching machines. *Science,* **128**, 969–977.

Spencer, D.C. (1970) The design of cybernetic control systems for manufacturing and distribution. In *Progress of Cybernetics.* J. Rose (Ed.). Gordon and Breach.

Spinelli, D.N. and K.H. Pribram (1970) Neural correlation of stimulus response and reinforcement. *Brain Research,* **17**, 3, 377–385.

Stellar, E. (1960) *Handbook of Physiology.* Section 1. Neurophysiology III. H.N. Field, H.W. Magoun and V.E. Hall (Eds.). Washington, D.C.

Stewart, D.J. (1959) *Automata and Behaviour.* Ph.D. Thesis. University of Bristol.

Suppes, P. (1966) See articles in *Aspects of Inductive Logic.* J. Hintikka and P. Suppes (Eds.). North Holland Publishing.

Sutherland, N.S. (1959) Stimulus analyzing mechanisms. In *Mechanization of Thought Processes.* NPL Symposium.

Tonge, F.M. (1963) Summary of a heuristic line balancing procedure. In *Computers and Thought.* E.A. Feigenbaum and J. Feldman (Eds.). McGraw-Hill.

Thrall, R.M., C.H. Coombs and R.L. Davis (1954) *Decision Processes.* Wiley.

Turing, A.M. (1936) On computable numbers, with an application to the Entscheidungs-problem. *Proc. London Math. Soc.* **2**, 42, 230–265.

Turing, A.M. (1950) Computing machinery and intelligence. *Mind,* **59**, 433–460.

Uhr, L. (Ed.) (1966) The transmission of information and the effect of local feedback in theoretical and neural networks. *Brain Research.* **2**, 1, 21–50.

Uhr, L. and Vossler (1963) A pattern recognition program that generates, evaluates and adjusts its own operators. In *Pattern Recognition.* L. Uhr (Ed.). Wiley.

Unger (1959) Pattern recognition and detection. *Proc. IRE,* **47**, 1737–1752.

Uttley, A.M. (1954) The classification of signals in the nervous system. *Electroenceph. Clin. Neurophysiol.* **6**, 479.

Uttley, A.M. (1955a) The conditional probability of signals in the nervous system. *RRE Mem. No. 1109.*

Uttley, A.M. (1955b) The probability of neural connexions. *Proc. Roy. Soc. B.* **144**, 229.

Varshavsky, V.I. (1969) The organization of interaction in collectives of automata. In *Machine Intelligence,* Vol. 4. B. Meltzer and D. Michie (Eds.). University of Edinburgh Press.

Verbeek, L. (1962) On error minimizing neural nets. In *Principles of Self-Organization.* H. von Foerster and G.W. Zopf (Eds.). Pergamon.

Von Bertalantly, L. (1950) The theory of open systems in physics. *Science,* **111**.

Von Bertalantly, L. (1952) *Problems of Life – An Evolution of Modern Biological Thought* Wiley.

Von Neumann, J. (1952) *Probabilistic Logics.* California Institute of Technology.

Von Neumann, J. (1966) *Theory of Self-reproducing Automata.* A.W. Burks (Ed.). Illinois.

Von Neumann, J. and O. Morgenstern (1944) *Theory of Games and Economic Behavior.* Princeton University Press.

Von Wright, G.H. (1966) The paradoxes of confirmation. In *Aspects of Inductive Logic.* J. Hintikka and P. Suppes (Eds.). North Holland Publishing.

Walter, W.G. (1953) *The Living Brain.* Duckworth.

Wang, H. (1957) A variant to Turing's theory of computing machines. *J. Assoc. Comp. Mach.* **2**, 63.

Wang, H. (1960) Toward mechanical mathematics. *IBM J. of Res. & Dev.* **4**,1.

Wason, P.C. (1965) The contexts of plausible denial. *J. Verb. Learn. Behav.* **4**, 7–11.

Watson, J.B. (1919) *Psychology from the Standpoint of the Behaviorist.* Lippincolt.

Weatherburn, C.E. (1946) *Mathematical Statistics.* Cambridge University Press.

White, D.J. (1969) *Decision Theory.* Allen and Unwin.

Wiener, N. (1948) *Cybernetics.* The Technology Press of MIT and John Wiley.

Wiener, N. (1961) *Cybernetics,* 2nd Edition. The Technology Press of MIT and John Wiley.

Wilson, J.A. (1966) *Information, Entropy and the Development of Structure in Behaviour.* Ph.D. Thesis. University of Bristol.

Woodger, J.H. (1937) *The Axiomatic Method in Biology.* Cambridge University Press.

Woodger, J.H. (1939) The Technique of Theory Construction. *Encyclopoedia of Unified Sciences.* **2**, 5. Chicago.

Woodger, J.H. (1951) Science without properties. *Brit. J. Phil. Sci.* **2**, 193–216.

Woodger, J.H. (1952) *Biology and Language.* Cambridge University Press.

Yamada, H. (1962) Real-time computation and recursive functions not real-time computable. *IRE Trans. on Electronic Computers.* EC-LL, 753–760.

Zannetos, S. and J.W. Wilcox (1970) The management process, management information and control systems, and cybernetics. In *Progress of Cybernetics.* J. Rose (Ed.). Gordon and Breach.

Subject index

Author index